THE(Y)OLOGY

Before you start to read this book, take this moment to think about making a donation to punctum books, an independent non-profit press,

@ https://punctumbooks.com/support/

If you're reading the e-book, you can click on the image below to go directly to our donations site. Any amount, no matter the size, is appreciated and will help us to keep our ship of fools afloat. Contributions from dedicated readers will also help us to keep our commons open and to cultivate new work that can't find a welcoming port elsewhere. Our adventure is not possible without your support.

Vive la Open Access.

Fig. 1. Detail from Hieronymus Bosch, *Ship of Fools* (1490–1500)

THE(Y)OLOGY: MYTHOPOETICS FOR QUEER/TRANS LIBERATION. Copyright © 2023 by Max Yeshaye Brumberg-Kraus. This work carries a Creative Commons BY-NC-SA 4.0 International license, which means that you are free to copy and redistribute the material in any medium or format, and you may also remix, transform, and build upon the material, as long as you clearly attribute the work to the authors (but not in a way that suggests the authors or punctum books endorses you and your work), you do not use this work for commercial gain in any form whatsoever, and that for any remixing and transformation, you distribute your rebuild under the same license. http://creativecommons.org/licenses/by-nc-sa/4.0/

First published in 2023 by punctum books, Earth, Milky Way.
https://punctumbooks.com

ISBN-13: 978-1-68571-086-6 (print)
ISBN-13: 978-1-68571-087-3 (ePDF)

DOI: 10.53288/0385.1.00

LCCN: 2023937499
Library of Congress Cataloging Data is available from the Library of Congress

Book design: Hatim Eujayl and Vincent W.J. van Gerven Oei
Cover design: Detail from Anselm Feuerbach, *Symposium* (1869). Staatliche Kunsthalle Karlsruhe.

spontaneous acts of scholarly combustion

HIC SVNT MONSTRA

The(y)ology

**Mythopoetics
for Queer/Trans
Liberation**

Max Yeshaye
Brumberg-Kraus

p.

Contents

Introduction · 19

Transcending the Real:
Mythopoetics and Liberation Theology · 33

Myth-on-Myth Action:
Denaturalizing Deities, Desires, and Dimorphism
in the Genesis Cosmogony · 67

Theyogony:
The Queer Cosmogonies of Erotic Worlding · 113

Theo-Transvestitism, or, on the Origin of Gods:
A Drag Theopoetic · 185

Bibliography · 245

Acknowledgments

Throughout *The(y)ology* is a consistent advocacy of "the many": many genders, many sexualities, many embodiments, many disciplines, many faces of the divine, and their expression in the poetics of queer mythmakers. This manifesto is also many in its origins, a chimeric baby born to a superfecundation of polyamory, if you consider with me that artistic collaborations, rehearsals, conversations, critiques, book readings, meals together, holiday festivities, community organizing, religious rites, and theological intercourse are manifestations of love.

The(y)ology began as my Master's thesis at United Theological Seminary of the Twin Cities, so my first thank you goes to my readers, Dr. Demian Wheeler and Dr. Jennifer Awes Freeman. Demian takes his students' writings as seriously as the books and treatises he assigns in class, questioning, drawing connections, delighting in (and challenging) each of our arguments. More so, for every paper handed in, including every chapter of this book, Demian finishes his detailed comments with a love letter to the scholarship because he believes everyone has something to offer in the long conversation of theology. As for Jennifer, there is much to say, but if I said it all, she would deflect the praise with a crass joke and a bit of snark. From being her student in numerous classes and attending her lectures, to being a guest lecturer in her courses, or our collaborating on performances and visual art, running events, and hosting weekly Arts Lunches, there is not one moment of my time at United that was not bettered by

Jennifer's warmth, humor, feedback, and intellect. She sets the example for what it means to be an artist and an academic, to truly practice interdisciplinarity, and truly to attend to the historical even in the most constructive of theological projects.

The United Seminary community as a whole welcomed me, a Jewish, pagan, nonbinary drag artist, into their arms as a student and employee and claimed, before I ever did, that I and all those who have been excluded or marginalized have something important to say about God, about justice, about the world. I am particularly thankful to Dr. Ayo Yetunde, for modeling pastoral care with creativity and zest for life and her consistent support of my poetry and writing; Rev. Dr. John Lee, for our many experimental, liturgical collaborations and conversations on nondualism; to Dr. Sara Wilhelm Garbers, who demonstrates how to hold complexity and conflict, hurt and forgiveness, through an acute feminist ethics; to Dr. Carolyn Pressler, whose feminist, queer, and womanist-influenced approach to the Hebrew Bible has opened up hermeneutic worlds that I could see myself and my loved ones in; to Dr. Jann Cather Weaver, whose revelations on the wealth of theological work done in art, pop culture, and film are undeniable; and to Rev. Dr. Cindi Beth Johnson, who encouraged me to enroll at United, to study Theology and the Arts, and continued to be a mentor and friend amidst institutional challenges and my own individual struggles as an artist. I must also give special thanks to fellow students Mary Beth Sonderegger and Sarah Berge. Mary Beth read through early drafts of my chapters and provided invaluable commentary. Equally important were our many coffees and lunches, teeming with discourse on feminism, ecology, pantheism, and a healthy dose of gossip. Sarah Berge, my seminary BFF, my particular and utterly unique friend, keeps me in the task of thinking through the strange, the difficult, the scary toward the profound. She is surely a modern-day mystic.

I thank my reader from punctum books, Dr. Zairong Xiang, for their feedback on the manuscript, having pushed me to take greater care with my sources and footnotes. I am especially grateful for their pushing back against some of my claims about

Genesis 1. I am grateful to Vincent W.J. van Gerven Oei, Eileen A. Fradenburg Joy, Lily Brewer, and Hatim Eujayl at punctum for the diligent care they took with my work and the community they foster through monthly conversations with punctum's authors.

Much of the thought on ancient Greek sources comes from my high school and my undergraduate degree in Classics at Beloit College, especially from being the student of Dr. Lisl Walsh and Dr. Kosta Hadavas. Lisl's research on Roman tragedy and Ovidian poetry introduced me to reception theory. With her, I learned to consider space, time, and embodiment in ancient texts. Being Kosta's teaching assistant for Ancient Tragedy informed my evaluations of Euripides' *Bacchae* and the role of Dionysian religion more broadly. However, it was at my entirely unique high school, School One in Providence, Rhode Island, where I first learned to enjoy learning. As a senior, I co-directed *The Bacchae* with theater teacher and now longtime friend, Casey-Seymour-Kim, without whose mentorship I suspect I would not be the performer, or playwright, I am today. I thank Cary Hoenig, for introducing me to gnosticism and the pre-Socratic philosophers; and I am grateful to the late Hedy Dowd, who fostered the myth-inspired poetry of a depressed, closeted teenager when they needed it most.

There are many individuals and affiliate communities who helped me develop drag theopoetics and explore queer and feminist eco-theologies: the Queertopia United theory reading group; the Reimagining Community in the Twin Cities; the Upper Midwest American Academy of Religion's Sex and Gender and Theology and the Arts Panels in 2019 and 2021; the curious and impeccably sharp Nova Fritz, and the Pandemic Reading Group she initiated; Callid Keefe-Perry, Tamisha Tyler, and Tuhina Rasche of Arts | Religion | Culture (ARC), and for bringing me into the 2019 ARC's Emerging Leaders Cohort and the 2019 Theopoetics Conference in Oakland, California where I first explored the concept of drag theopoetics in a public forum; David Harris for inviting me to participate in a salon about my drag and theological work in conversation with Dr. Noam Sienna through Rimon (The Minnesota Jewish Arts Federation); Rabbi Jonathan Schorsch and the Green Sabbath Project; and the 2021–22 Shmita Hives.

The performances discussed in this book occurred in queer and experimental venues in Minnesota and Wisconsin: Pangea World Theater, Patrick's Cabaret, 20% Theatre Company, the Art Heads Emporium, Intermedia Arts. In 2019–20, I began working with Rebecca Noon and Daisuke Kawachi and the Guthrie Theatre as well as the SITI Company to create community engagement opportunities around their 2020 production of *The Bacchae,* including the creation of a community bacchanalia hosted at United Seminary. While the bacchanalia had to be canceled due to the pandemic, our exploration of Orphic ritual and poetry and their relevance for today's audiences have shaped the trajectory of this book, particularly in the fourth chapter.

I give thanks to my ancestors who speak to me through ancient texts and seasonal rites, the mystics and gnostics, the heretics and traditionalists, radical feminists, gay pornographers, radical faeries, transgender performers, lesbian poets, gender-fucked punks, sexual revolutionaries, drag rebels, ecosexuals, queer pornographers, flower children, spiritual libertines, and the many people who died around my birth at the height of the AIDS Crisis: this book, my generation, and I have been midwifed into queer possibility through the labor of your fleshy, imperfectly beautiful bodies, your depths of pain, your rapturous pleasure.

I thank my mother Maia, my sister Zoya, and my brother-in-law Louis. Their refusal to withstand bullshit might make conversation at the dinner table occasionally feel like a battlefield but nonetheless has made me a truer, more thoughtful, and more ethical person. You are all lovers of arts, artists in your own right, and you beautify the world as much as you enrich my life. I thank my father Rabbi Dr. Jonathan Brumberg-Kraus, for his continued editorial feedback on my book. In the midst of writing *The(y)ology,* he and I have not only leaned into the parent–child bond, but have developed a collegial report that has proven invaluable to both our scholarly evolutions. I read his work, he reads mine, and our joined imaginations are greater than the sum of their parts.

And lastly, I must thank my queer chosen family. The House of Larva Drag Co-operative is the community within which I began to seriously and vulnerably reckon with gender, body image, sexual desire, trauma, healing, empire, violence, and communal responsibility. Pita Angeles/Enphanga Sphynx, and McKay Bram/Pouchet Pouchet: there is nothing so sublime as to see them perform, to create by their side, to be entangled in the messy creativity that they each personify with alternate grace and grossness. And I thank the artists and fans who have often conspired in many a performance: Michael Thomforde, Alice Gehrke, Sarah Berge, Danny Solis, Peter Foster, Stephani Pescitelli. I thank my friends scottie hall, Levi Moos, Nova Fritz, Ray Hommeyer, Deb Jance, Laura Jones, Claire Klein, Lux Knudson, and Diana Siegel for celebrating holidays together, and for the innumerable influences our conversations have had on *The(y)-ology*. I bow to the nonhuman members of my family: cat, Miss Kitka, and snake, Pier Paolo Pastalini, for being more adorable than you are distracting. I boop their respective noses in gratitude. And most significantly, I thank Allison Jones, who provided meticulous aid in grammar and spelling, patience with me in the most stressful periods of writing, and a conversation partner who helped me clarify many of my thoughts as I stumbled through them. I am most grateful for the quality of life I live by Allison's side. Throughout the last eight years, she has challenged me to be more vulnerable, attentive, and curious not only as an artist and scholar, but as a friend on this planet. To paraphrase the Waterboys, when I've only seen the crescent, Allison has shown me the whole of the moon. I know of no greater gift than that.

In memory of Jean Daniel Cadinot,

modern Empedocles

whose efforts continue to inspire

the inheritors of his heart.

Introduction

Say it. Say it.
The universe is made of stories,
not of atoms.

— Muriel Rukeyser, "The Speed of Darkness"[1]

I am a theologian because I am a performer, a writer, a poet. I am a theologian because I am an artist. Through my art I have the sometimes pleasure, sometimes unwelcome happenstance of speaking with, to, or about God. Or gods, as is more often the case. Do not let the last sentence (fragment) fool you. I am Jewish. But I am also an inheritor of Greek and Roman witness to gods, of hermeticism and gnostic texts, of various pantheisms and animisms. In fact, the very home and community-centered, land-based, and seasonally conscious — let alone mystically influenced — Judaism I was raised in and continue to practice in its own right treads awfully close to the wisdom I have learned from these other traditions. Perhaps I cannot separate being a theologian from being an artist because in Judaism, as far as I am concerned, it is in the performance of liturgy and ritual,

---

1 Muriel Rukeyser, "The Speed of Darkness," in *Out of Silence: Selected Poems*, ed. Kate Daniels (Evanston: Northwestern University Press, 2000), ix, ll. 56–58.

the theater of the festival, and the gnosis of the story where our sophisticated thinker–doers speak about, to, or with God. Keeping this in mind, when I speak about queer and trans theologies, it is also because I am a nonbinary, genderfucked artist.

As I write the introduction to this book, I am preparing for my act in 20% Theatre Company's *Controlled Burn: Queer Performance for a World on Fire*. It is the second year that my performance art group, the House of Larva Drag Co-Operative, will perform in this Twin Cities theater event. House of Larva was founded by Guadalupe Angeles and me at Beloit College in 2014. From 2015 to 2016 we hosted a number of hour-long midnight drag shows, usually featuring guest artists accompanying our acts. We transformed the student black box, Bunge Theatre, into a hive of chalk drawings and mood lighting where countless drunk twenty-somethings sat, stood, and danced in a circle around me and Angeles, as we whacked each other with bicycle chains, lip synced to Jayne County, or bathed in sour milk. Combining high camp, punk, body horror, and melodrama, we were, to quote Angeles, "not RuPaul's Drag Race, bitch!"

After graduating from Beloit College, Angeles moved to Chicago, and I moved to the Twin Cities. Soon after in 2017, dancer and choreographer McKay Bram joined the collective, becoming not only one of my closest friends but a cherished collaborator. I as Çicada L'Amour and Bram as drag king Pouchet Pouchet have performed across the Midwest and New England, with Angeles rejoining when possible or co-creating with us through digital means. We have mostly performed short acts as part of the Twin Cities queer experimental theater scene, although we also devised and performed full length narrative shows like *Lowlands* (2018) and *Viral Liaisons* (2019). My experience with House of Larva has not only helped me develop as a performing artist, but also explore my own gender and sexuality. Being in collaborative, experimental work helps me articulate what it means to be gay, genderfucked, and nonbinary. It is the laboratory in which I first encountered my queer/trans becoming.

According to 20%'s website, *Controlled Burn* is "a space for queer rage, revolution, and reclamation, aimed at regeneration," getting its name from "the practice of burning a prairie to promote new growth."[2] Rather than taking the form of a conference or a rally, *Controlled Burn* deploys theater, poetry, video, music, and performance art *by* queers of varying identities *for* queers of varying identities. *Controlled Burn* is an annual ritual that refuses a stark separation between the imagination and material action. *Controlled Burn* is a site to produce queer mythopoeia.

In a 1989 article, media theorist Patrick D. Murphy discusses the poetry of Ursula Le Guin, Denise Levertov, Adrienne Rich, Muriel Rukeyser, and Ann Stanford as examples of a feminist (re)mythopoeia, that is re-"mythmaking." Murphy writes:

> The remythopoeia involves the use of both low and high fantasy situations[,] [that] is to say, settings located in the recognizable world but complicated by fantastic aspects — whether of the uncanny, hesitational or marvelous […] or, settings that create an alternative, secondary world either of the poet's invention or already provided by literature. Such fantastic situations allow either a contrast or provide free space for the presentation of a feminist critique or perspective of the "real" world established by patriarchally imposed cultural consensus. They also enable the insinuation of an alternative mythopoeic heritage to compete with the culturally received one in the reader's mind and to provide a foundation for other poet's work.[3]

Feminist mythopoeia, according to Murphy, critiques the patriarchal world order — an unjustly established "real" — through the proliferation of fantasy worlds, that is, worlds on a continuum of imaginary distance from their proximity to the current reality. The creation of a myth is not creation out of nothing but a practice of reinterpreting inherited mythologies by changing

---

[2] "Controlled Burn: February 2020," *20% Theatre Company*, n.d., http://www.tctwentypercent.org/current-season/controlled-burn-20/.

[3] Patrick D. Murphy, "The High and Low Fantasies of Feminist (Re)Mythopoeia," *Mythlore: A Journal of J.R.R. Tolkien, C.S. Lewis, Charles Williams, and Mythopoetic Literature* 16, no. 2 (1989): 24.

dominant stories or invoking their silenced perspectives or by uplifting the myths of those women suppressed by patriarchal religion, history, and literature. Feminist mythopoeia involves deep, creative reflection on the past, and the feminist mythopoet is highly aware of historical myths, the normative and subcultural readings of myth, and the normative and subcultural retellings of those myths. All mythopoeia engages mythic traditions to help authors realize something about themselves, their consciousness, their morals. But feminist mythopoeia is concerned with how myth "contributes to the struggle against gender oppression."[4] Murphy identifies it as "reader-response-based judgement that defines the poem according to its affect in the world rather than defining its cultural role according to author intentionality or self-consciousness."[5] In imagining and imaging new worlds, feminist mythopoeia spurs change in the current world.

Not only concerned with queer rage but how queer rage might lead to revolution, the work of *Controlled Burn* is mythopeia similar to feminist mythopoeia. Only it centers queer and trans mythopoeia without ignoring the intersectionality of race, class, ethnicity, and ability in its resuscitation of suppressed mythologies.

In the weeks leading up to the performance, many of the artists agree to be interviewed, and these interviews are a great source for understanding some of the intentions behind the contributors' works. One artist, Jaffa Aharonov, discusses their act as "a sci-fi multimedia performance about trans persistence, rage, and resilience that's an exercise in imagining a utopian future rather than a dystopian one," adding "(It's hard…)."[6] Here we clearly see the invocation of another world, immediately through "sci-fi" as well as in the words "imagining" and "utopian." If, for trans people, the current world order is a dystopia,

---

4   Ibid.
5   Ibid.
6   "Jaffa Aharanov | Controlled Burn Featured Artist," *20% Theatre Company*, February 14, 2019, http://www.tctwentypercent.org/jaffa-aharonov/.

then it is the utopian imagination which is most different from this order and perhaps most clear in its denouncement of the current state of affairs. At the same time, Aharonov expresses that "it's hard" to engage utopian imagination. Utopia is so far off for some, that it is difficult, potentially even painful, to strain ourselves and glimpse beyond the cis-heteropatriarchal horizon.

Drag performer Oblivia Nukem Jun likes "breaking stereotypes and challenging norms. And looking evil and beautiful while doing so."[7] Jun performs to combat "the lack of non-stereotypical Asian representation," explaining, "even though my drag is inspired by heavy metal and fashion, a lot of my references are of Asian culture, whether it be '90s *wuxia* movies or ghost stories that my parents told me from when they were growing up in Thailand and Laos."[8] Jun embodies myths that are ignored or deemed unimportant in the "Western" mythopoetic canon, while simultaneously confronting the stereotypes of what an Asian drag performer should be. In resisting a white American idea of drag and refusing an Asian stereotype of drag while invoking Thai and Laotian mythologies, Jun provokes us not only to see gender, race, ethnicity, and drag differently, but also to imagine how we might embody our identities and our crafts without succumbing to rigid categorizations.

Denouncing the oppressive "reality" that is our world as well as the resistance of increasingly rigid identities are both key to Teighlor McGee's creation:

> I classify my piece as speculative poetry/theater — it is a performance of four separate monologues that together craft a story that discusses race, gender, disability, and familial ties and the ways in which these ideas intersect with identity politics and transcend the confinements of time.[9]

---

[7] "Oblivia Nukem Jun | Controlled Burn Featured Artist," *20% Theatre Company,* February 13, 2019, http://www.tctwentypercent.org/oblivia-nukem-jun/.

[8] Ibid.

[9] "Teighlor McGee | Controlled Burn Featured Artist," *20% Theatre Company,* February 13, 2019, http://www.tctwentypercent.org/teighlor-mcgee/.

Questions of identity are related to questions of time and of how we experience the moment the world is in. Indeed, exploration of identity is tied to exploration through time, and both are complicated. McGee's act includes moments that are in "the past and the present" and "dystopian elements."[10] The narrator is thoroughly implicated in this temporal confusion: "Are they a time traveler? Are they intended to be the same person in each of the time measures? Are they human or a spirit guide?"[11] The narrator evades singularity. They are many things, although what those things are is never exact. McGee's piece brings "to life the experience of living with multiple intersecting identities in a way that does not stick to one specific genre or style."[12] McGee's mythopoetic form, a hybrid of past and future, articulates the hybridity of a life with intersecting identities, in a way that transforms how the audience engages the performer. We are asked to doubt or rethink one answer to what the narrator is, to when the art takes place, to whom the performer is, and in turn, who we might be. Let us look at an act more closely.

House of Larva first performed in *Controlled Burn* in 2019 with a piece called "Bitchfaggot General." A dark satirical act, it spoofs revenge fantasies, courtroom dramas, the television show *Law & Order*, the 1968 folk horror film *Witchfinder General*, and, most centrally, the 2018 Supreme Court hearing of Justice Brett Kavanaugh.

The act begins with a voiceover in the style of the *Law & Order: Special Victims Unit* opening:

> In the criminal justice system, hetero-ass fuckboi offenses are considered especially heinous. In the empire of the bitchfaggots, the dedicated officer who investigates these vicious acts of breedery is known as the Bitchfaggot General. These are their stories.

---

10 Ibid.
11 Ibid.
12 Ibid.

My character, Çicada L'Amour, is the current Bitchfaggot General, a prestigious role in the mythical empire of the bitchfaggots. I begin the act in love with Kavanaugh and holding a sign with "Women for Kavanaugh" on one side and "Breeders for Brett" on the other. Audio clips from the coverage of the hearing begin to play. Pouchet enters in Kavanaugh drag. In the audio clips, numerous voices from the media describe the calls for Kavanaugh to be held accountable for his actions against Christine Blasey Ford as a witch hunt. Quotes from Kavanaugh, defending himself, talking about his school chums, and generally being a smarmy douchebag, are interspersed with Senator Lindsey Graham's fuming speech in defense of the soon-to-be admitted justice. As the recording progresses, Pouchet begins sweating and pulls out a beer from his pocket. Kavanaugh can be heard in the audio: "I drank beer with my friends. Almost everyone did. Sometimes I had too many beers. Sometimes others did. I liked beer. I still like beer."[13] Pouchet chugs it and pulls out another. Then another. Beer flows all over his clothes down to the stage floor.

By the time a third beer appears, the audio clips are drowned out by Avenged Sevenfold's cover of Pantera's "Walk." As Pouchet struts around the stage, lip synching and drinking a fourth, fifth, and sixth beer, I pull out a pair of angel wings and place them on Pouchet. I then place a golden wreath on his head, as the drag king stands on top of a chair, marches in place, and strikes a magnificent pose of unadulterated masculine rage. The song transitions to "I Don't Know How to Love Him," from *Jesus Christ Superstar*, to which I lip-sync. Indeed, my character, loving the conservative values, musky manliness, and aggression of Kavanaugh *doesn't* know how to love him. Shouldn't I care about his misdeeds, particularly to women? My dilemma is interrupted by a phone call from my boss, Commissioner

---

13 Stephanie K. Baer, "Here Are All the Times Brett Kavanaugh Said He Likes Beer at His Senate Hearing on Sexual Assault Allegations," *Buzzfeed News*, September 27, 2018, https://www.buzzfeednews.com/article/skbaer/brett-kavanaugh-likes-beer.

Benwa Breedwinner, who tells me that I have a new assignment as Bitchfaggot General to kill Pouchet Kavanaugh. I must put my (grotesque) feelings aside and take one for the team. I run offstage and prepare for the deed.

Meanwhile, the audio plays the announcement of Kavanaugh's admittance to the Supreme Court and is then drowned out with applause. Pouchet Kavanaugh descends from his statue pose and basks in the glory. I enter, as a trashy belly dancer, and lip sync to the Hebrew folk song "Dodi Li," lyrics originating in the Song of Songs. I seduce the drag king, push him onto a chair, massage him, jerk him off, lull him into a sense of security. Suddenly, I pull out a spoon and gouge out his eyes. The song changes, and I lip-sync to Nouvelle Vague's cover of Richard Hell's "Love Comes in Spurts." Matching the song, blood spurts from Pouchet's eyes as I dance around him. Then, after ripping into his back with the spoon, I hurl him to the ground and kick him. It is at this point in the act, that the audience has become most enlivened. Despite the comedy and horror of the staged moment, the audience embraces the revenge fantasy, the dream of the patriarchal villain getting his desserts. The political events parodied are still raw and personal to many in the audience. The audience indulges a righteous schadenfreude to see Kavanaugh's simulacrum beaten, abused, murdered—and with an upbeat soundtrack no less!

But then the fantasy ends. The stage lights grow cold and sober. Benwa Breedwinner's voice echoes in the chamber: deep, rough, threatening. Underneath the voice are soundbites from films about hunting witches. Breedwinner reveals that the whole act, up to this moment, had simply been a dream:

> Wake up, Çicada. You passed out. Had yourself a little fantasy. Seems you dreamed you were a Bitchfaggot General. Ha! Even if you defeated Kavanaugh, he's one model of a million. He is at the intersection of endless lines of equally wicked and therefore normal men, in every aspect of life, at every level. Each taking their turn to play God, taking, tak-

ing, taking. But as for you, faggot, you're nothing but a witch. And what do we do with witches? We make them bleed.

The speech, as well as a change of sobering lighting, reveal that this whole time my character had been detained for the crime of witchcraft. Imprisoned, I had fantasized about killing my tormentor, but as I wake up, I realize there is no empire of queers, of bitchfaggots successfully overthrowing the dominant machine of the breeders with Pouchet Kavanaugh, their rapist messiah. When Breedwinner finishes revealing the truth, Pouchet reenters, holding a large pin. He turns me around, my back facing the audience. He rips my shirt, and, in the tradition of the witch hunter, he searches for the Devil's mark by stabbing my back with the needle, over and over again. I scream. Blood drips to the ground. Music dissipates. I am still. The final sound is the crackling of flames.

The audience has become quiet too, at this point. The revenge fantasy, despite its violence, was welcome. The sobriety of continued violence at the hands of patriarchal agents is not, however familiar it may be. The sound of flames evokes the witch who flails on the pyre and the fate of the heretic who dares speak against *this* world's unholy order. But the sound of flames is not only the sound of death. The fire, the wood, and the body brutalized become ash, and out of the ash the body returns: grow again! That is the point of *Controlled Burn*! Inside the fantasy within the act is a rage of perpetuated, messy, perhaps-just-but-in-the-end-failed violence. Breedwinner's order is unmoved even if Çicada has killed Pouchet. An infinite line of the same sort of man waits in his shadow, eager to ascend. When Çicada wakes, the heat rescinds. The scene, the light, the voice, all cold. But after Çicada screams, the flames crackle. Yes, we snatched the "happy" resolution from our audience, and we rushed into the unbearable dystopia of the now with Kavanaugh and his ilk perpetuating Breedwinner's law. But we did not extinguish the fire. No. The flame demands, *this* world must burn.

There is no manual for our acts. If you do not accept how they end, do not accept them! Do not let them be the end. In fact, we want to know what seed is planted in your joy and laughter? What seed is planted in your discomfort, disappointment, and dread? Sifting through the ashes, what seeds do you find? If the fantasy gives you life, defend it from "the real," challenge "the real!" Breathe through the carcass of cynicism. Create.

This project is about the uses of mythopoeia for queer and trans liberation. What does theology have to do with this goal? Gustavo Gutiérrez writes, "theology does not initiate this future which exists in the present. It does not create the vital attitude of hope out of nothing. Its role is more modest. It interprets and explains these as the true underpinnings of history."[14] I align myself with this tradition of a "modest" theology. The theologian interprets and explains practice — practiced solidarity with the poor, with the violated, with the burdened. Theology interprets the moments when other worlds permeate a current one. Theology acts as "a criticism of society and the Church insofar as they are called and addressed by the Word of God [and] critical theory, worked out in the light of the Word accepted in faith and inspired by a practical purpose — and therefore indissolubly linked to historical praxis."[15] First comes "real charity, action, and commitment to the service of others," then "theology follows; it is the second step."[16]

What historical praxis and service looks like to others depends on culture and on community, and certain practices and embodiments are valued over others. What kind of service is the event of *Controlled Burn* in the eyes of some liberation theologies? Is this where God's world encounters ours? Queer theologian, Marcella Althaus-Reid, is critical of certain blind spots in traditional Latin American liberation theology:

> Latin American Political Theology has been ignorant of the non-heterosexual body and non-heterosexual loving pat-

---

14 Gustavo Gutiérrez, *A Theology of Liberation*, ed. and trans. Sister Caridad Inda and John Eagleson (Maryknoll: Orbis Books, 1973), 11.
15 Ibid., 9.
16 Ibid.

> terns of relationships which exist outside that theology of relationships from the centre which has become normative. If that theology has privileged in its discourse a grounding of its reflections on the perspective of the poor, the perspective has been a limited one, namely that of heterosexual bodies in (ideal heterosexual) relationships.[17]

Oppression measured on one axis obfuscates the impressions that other worlds leave on this one through our sexuality, gender, race, ethnicity, ability, and religion.

I look to Gutiérrez for the mission of theology: to be in community, to make, to embody, to be with, to act, *and then* reflect. But it is in Althaus-Reid's that I approach the core tenant through which I understand my project. The theologian reflects on experience, and sometimes the best or only medium to express experience is fiction.

> Permutations (reading in betweenness) use texts chosen from the experience of the reader. […] Queer texts, even if fictional, are able to convey images and experiences which we sometimes find ourselves unable to express. This is particularly true as we struggle for our sexual theological identity while using phallocratic language to speak of God and ourselves. At the end of our hermeneutical praxis we are trying to unveil or re-discover the face of the Queer God who manifests Godself in our life of sexual, emotional and political relationships. This is a God who depends on our experience of pleasure and despair in intimacy to manifest Godself, but who has been displaced, theologically speaking, by a God of grand heterosexual illusions, phantasmatic assumptions of the order of love and sexuality.[18]

Althaus-Reid's work is the uncovering of God's queer faces, and she does this by reading queer texts, particularly fictions, into

---

17 Marcella Althaus-Reid, *The Queer God* (London: Routledge, 2003), 114.
18 Ibid., 108.

scripture and theology. Uniquely, "literature needs to speak truth and lies at the same time."[19] It uses familiar language and symbols to express a world and relationships that do not exist, at least not yet. Althaus-Reid even draws a parallel between theology and fiction, where "theology's main function is to be fictitious. It aims to lie in the sense that its mission is to express the inexpressible, the utopia of the Kingdom, the intuitions manifested in vague suspicions and intuitions of different orders in sacred and human society."[20] Queer theology "rescues different forms of imagining love which exist amongst us and which may lead us to different and better understandings of God and life,"[21] and, I add, trans theologies rescue different forms of imagining body, gender, and self.

The current project is a project of permutations. Theological themes — religious myth, cosmology, scriptural hermeneutics, and embodiment — will be examined in light of transgender, nonbinary, and queer texts. Additionally, a significant portion of these chapters will emphasize literary criticism, including the reception theories of Hans Robert Jauss and Wolfgang Iser. In partnering with literary criticism and reception theory — how audiences receive and produce myth — we can expound on the mythopoetic symbology in Paul Tillich, Mary Daly, Gustavo Gutiérrez, and others. If, as Althaus-Reid argues, theology is fictitious, then trans and queer people invested in what is most important to us, should embrace a project that uses fiction to explore who we are, who or what divinity is, and what our world might be. This is to say, we should commit to a project not only of critiquing myth but of mythmaking: myth-writing, myth-singing, myth-acting, myth-sculpting, myth-painting, myth-dancing, and myth-being.

As for the name of this project, *The(y)ology,* I am celebrating the plurality of the multi-gendered body, of the interplay of different sexualities and genders to ascertain divinity but also

---

19 Ibid., 130.
20 Ibid.
21 Ibid.

the proliferation of many voices, traditions, and media needed to sustain a robust mythopoeia for queer and trans liberation. The "(y)" is a permutation into the letters comprising "theology" that both retains and transforms its meaning. It signals pluralism, which I believe is an underappreciated but necessary piece of liberation theology, as inherent but often obscured in a given theology. Of course, the "(y)" also transforms the word to reference the popular gender-neutral pronoun "they/them," my own preferred pronoun, pointing not only to this as a project of queer and trans theologies but one that takes special interest in theology for genderqueer, genderbent, nonbinary, and genderfluid persons.

Chapter 1 looks at the function of mythopoeia in liberation theologies by studying the relationship and controversies of mythopoetic practices in feminist theologies and trans and queer theologies, bringing into this mix comparisons between studies of fiction with studies of myth, and theological transcendence with queer utopianism. Chapter 2 begins an inquiry into queer cosmology by examining how cosmogonic myths are told in relation to systems of power and how, in turn, myths of the cosmos engage each other dialogically, deconstructing some myths of cosmic subjugation and producing other myths of cosmic freedom. Chapter 3 continues where 2 ends, offering a queer and trans cosmology I call "erotic worlding." I model erotic worlding off ancient Greek animisms and Anne Carson's poetic erotics, then I use it to imagine how such a cosmology might impact what we conceive our bodies to be as well as our environments, microcosmically and macrocosmically. Finally, chapter 4, "Drag Theopoetics," is hybrid in its form. Part fiction, part dialogue, part essay, it interweaves short, critical–theological reflections on the performances of selves in humans, gods, and everyone else, with an original mythopoetic story inspired by Euripides' *Bacchae,* countering Mary Daly's transphobic re-mythification of the same text.

As you read this book, I hope you delight in the feast of the many-faced gods, the many-gendered bodies, the many lovers, the many loves, and the many, many worlds. Notice how each of these manys is constituted by relationships. If there is anything I have learned from working with so many other queer and trans artists it is this: we form each other when we imagine together. So please create with me, play with me, or bypass me entirely so you might love the voices I cite, the voices I love, the other voices who live inside this book. And when you are done, and these words have settled in your stomach, run to the medium of your choice. Pick up a pen, some clay, extend your arm into a gesture, or simply open your mouth. Join the movement. Make a myth of your own.

1

Transcending the Real: Mythopoetics and Liberation Theology

Blessed are the legend-makers with their rhyme
of things not found within recorded time.
...
They have seen Death and ultimate defeat,
and yet they would not in despair retreat,
but oft to victory have tuned the lyre
and kindled hearts with legendary fire,
illuminating Now and dark Hath-been
with light of suns as yet by no man seen.
— J.R.R. Tolkien, "Mythopoeia"[1]

When it comes to critiquing patriarchal violence, restrictive gender roles, and sexual oppression, a theology of queer liberation shares commitments with and is indebted to the work of feminist liberation theology. The relationship between the two fields, however, has not been without conflict. A kind of lesbian-feminist separatism arising in the 1970s and '80s not only hier-

---

1 J.R.R. Tolkien, "Mythopoeia," in *Tree and Leaf* (London: HarperCollins, 2001), ll. 91–106.

archizes sexism over the interrelated but distinct oppressions of racism, heterosexism, and classism but awards a particular hostility toward transgender and transsexual people. For a contemporary example, one has only to look at recent protests in London Pride where a small group of lesbian activists interrupted the parade, claiming "transactivism [sic] erases lesbians" and that trans liberation is "anti-lesbianism."[2] While numerous trans women identify as lesbians and have been accepted by many cisgender lesbians and feminists, the hostility toward transgender people in some facets of feminist thought, including theology, is a serious problem for individuals and congregations committed to a diverse and heterogeneous vision of sexual and gender expression. Mary Daly, a key influence on feminist liberation theology, is thoroughly located in this anti-trans tradition. In *Gyn/Ecology,* Daly calls the phenomenon of the "transsexual operation" a form of rape as a patriarchal violation of female boundaries:

> The Frankenstein phenomenon is omnipresent not only in religious myth, but in its offspring, phallocratic technology. The insane desire for power, the madness of boundary violation, is the mark of necrophiliacs who sense the lack of soul/spirit/life-loving principle with themselves and therefore try to invade and kill off all spirit, substituting conglomerates of corpses. [...] Transsexualism is an example of male surgical siring which invades the female world with substitutes. Malemothered genetic engineering is an attempt to "create" without women. The projected manufacture by men of artificial wombs, of cyborgs which will be part flesh, part robot,

---

2 Josh Gabbatis, "London Pride: Anti-trans Activists Disrupt Parade by Lying Down in the Street to Protest 'Lesbian Erasure,'" *The Independent,* July 7, 2018, https://www.independent.co.uk/news/uk/home-news/anti-trans-protest-london-pride-parade-lgbt-gay-2018-march-lesbian-gay-rights-a8436506.html.

of clones — all are manifestations of phallocratic boundary violation.³

Daly even goes so far as to refer to transsexualism as the "Dionysian Final Solution."⁴ My point is not to argue that doctors, when Daly was writing, who were performing these early surgical procedures were not working within or from patriarchal, gender-essentialist, heterosexist, or misogynistic ideologies. Rather, what I find so violent in Daly's writing is the sheer nonhumanity granted to trans people. Whether as Frankenstein's monster or cyborg or nazi tool, Daly has described transgender people outside the confines of humanity. She does not cite trans women or their writing but rather her notoriously transphobic student Janice Raymond⁵ as an authority on the issue. She does not cite the experiences, feelings, and insights of trans women about their genders. Excluding trans epistemology and identity, Daly has no room for testimonies of gender and sexual morphology outside of sexual dimorphism.

In Daly's earlier *Beyond God the Father*, she brilliantly points out how the sexism of leading theologians might weigh heavily on their views not only of relationships between sexes but also their views of God. Implicating "liberal" theologians who nevertheless cite virulently sexist predecessors, Daly writes:

> Within the context of the prevailing social climate it has been possible for scholars to be aware of the most crudely dehumanizing texts concerning women in the writings of religious "authorities" and theologians — from Augustine to Aquinas, to Luther, to Knox, to Barth — and at the same time to treat their unverified opinions on far more imponderable matters with utmost reverence and respect. That is, the bla-

---

3 Mary Daly, *Gyn/Ecology: The Metaethics of Radical Feminism* (Boston: Beacon Press, 1990), 71.
4 Ibid., 67.
5 Ibid., 167, 287.

> tant misogynism of these men has not been the occasion of a serious credibility gap.[6]

Daly suggests that the sexism of these writers distorts, even taints, their whole theological work. If indeed humans are theomorphic, made "in [God's] image,"[7] then what we say or think about humans influences our perceptions of the divine. Viewed by the likes of Augustine or Karl Barth, women's entire witness to the divine is discredited and ignored. Feminist theologians might assert that no human is the same as God, but if women cannot talk about themselves as theomorphic and point to God with their experience, then the mystery and complexity of God is diminished. Feminist theologian Elizabeth Johnson writes that female images of God "not only [challenge] the literal mindedness [of] male images in inherited God-talk" and question their "dominance in discourse about holy mystery," but "insofar as 'the symbol gives rise to thought' such speech calls into question prevailing structures of patriarchy."[8] When theologians denigrate and dehumanize women and the efficacy of women's symbols for God, they are both minimizing the scope of the divine and legitimizing patriarchy. All this is to say, a restrictive and oppressive view of "the sexes" should challenge a theologian's credibility when it comes to god, cosmology, ritual, liturgy, and ethics. Running with Daly's critique, I add that restrictive and oppressive views of sexual and gender diversity, especially as relating to trans populations, challenges the credibility of a given theology, including Daly's gender-essentialist theology.

That said, a question of Daly's credibility does not, indeed must not, negate all of her thought or methodology. Combating the violence done to women through sexist and misogynistic

---

[6] Mary Daly, *Beyond God the Father: Toward a Philosophy of Women's Liberation* (Boston: Beacon Press, 1973), 22.

[7] Genesis 1:27 (NRSV).

[8] Elizabeth A. Johnson, *She Who Is: The Mystery of God in Feminist Theological Discourse* (New York: The Crossroad Publishing Company, 2017), 5–6.

theology, Daly consistently deploys myth and mythopoetics. Invoking Herbert Richardson's "Three Myths of Transcendence," Daly argues that necessary to the work of liberation is telling myths of "self-transformation and spiritual rebirth."[9] For Daly, in *Beyond God the Father*, reviving and composing myths of transformation can facilitate the real-world transformation of women and men into psychologically androgynous beings, fully restructuring the relationships between people, the divine, and the environment. Beyond God the Father could be subtitled "beyond hermeneutics" since Daly not only retells, reinterprets, and uncovers myth, but engages in mythopoeia. Daly writes *new* myths of transcendence in reframing Eve and the Fall, in naming a sublimated Goddess in the image of the Virgin Mary, in adopting for herself the personality of hag, witch, and muse in the "Original Reintroduction" and in reimagining the Antichrist as anti-patriarchal usher of the world into androgynous, relational, and creative being.

I need not agree on the particular vision of an androgynous transcendence to learn from Daly that resuscitation, application, and creation of myth is fundamental to a liberational project. Queer theologians like Marcella Althaus-Reid, Robert Shore-Goss, or Patrick S. Cheng (re)interpret mythology in their systems, particularly in imagining a queer God. Arguing for queer symbols of God is an important and noble task that should continue to be taken up. However, looking at the particular embodiment and performance of mythic, archetypal selves in Daly's writing begs the question, how can queer/trans theologians more robustly do mythic thought, performance, and creation in our praxes? For one, we can look to the rich cultural production from LGBTQIA+ artists and cultural figures through time who have not called themselves or generally been received as theologians. More than that, we must add to the work of interpreting specific religious myths examinations of the *function* of mythmaking in our theologies.

---

9   Daly, *Beyond God the Father*, 26.

In what follows, I ask: what does myth do? This is a complex question. There are endless systems and grammars of myth and explanations of what myth does across disciplines that I cannot address in this book. But what I offer to the question "what does myth do?" are *some* answers, not one definitive answer. My approach is to put Paul Tillich's analysis of myth in *The Dynamics of Faith* in conversation with reception theorists Hans Robert Jauss and Iser's analyses of fiction's dialogical role in history. Myth and mythopoeia, in light of fiction, both critique authoritative symbologies and put forth other symbols to open up horizons of personal, communal, and divine possibility.

Following this exploration of myth, I close in on a particular myth: the utopia. Utopianism, as conceptualized by theorist Ernst Bloch, plays a key role in Gutiérrez's liberational eschatology. Similarly, Muñoz follows a Blochian thread in his approach to queer utopia. Read together, the two Blochians yield rich insight into the role of utopian myth in a queer liberational project.

Finally, after examining utopianism in liberation theology *and* queer theory, I posit how, in response to Daly's "Frankenstein phenomenon," transgender scholar Susan Stryker's "My Words to Victor Frankenstein above the Village of Chamounix: Performing Transgender Rage," is an example of queer/trans mythopoeia and utopian art. Both Stryker's performance of the monster and her use of multiple genres in the essay are instructive to what mythmaking might look like in a theology of queer liberation. Mythmaking and utopian imagination are fundamental aspects of liberation theology, and thus queer/trans liberation theology must engage the work of robust mythopoeia.

Myth and the Horizons of Possibility

When I speak of queer/trans theology, I am talking about theology done for and by people whose sexualities and genders defy gender binarism or normative heterosexuality, including transgender, nonbinary, agender, gay, lesbian, and bisexual individuals. When I say "queer" specifically, I am referring to its more nebulous signification as boundary breaking, as liminality, as the strange, as verb, as deconstructive and post-structuralist approach to gender and sexual categorization. For instance, when I invoke Muñoz's queer utopian thought, the term "queer" will be used in light of these other definitions and disciplinary affiliations. However, when I speak of queer mythopoeia, I am mostly talking about LGBTQIA+ people constructing myths in our various idioms, including but not limited to the academic discipline of queer theory. Queer hermeneutics is the reading and interpreting of texts as LGBTQIA+ people in our idioms, academic or otherwise. Queer hermeneutics is the first step in developing a robust, queer mythopoeia.

Mythopoeia and any constructive endeavor begin with reception. How we share our interpretations, that is, the *forms* our interpretations take, determines in what ways they in turn can be received. Myths interpret other myths, but not every interpretation is a myth. Before exploring what myth offers to queer liberation theology, we must then clarify 1) what mythology *is,* and 2) what our reception of myth does in our communal lives.

Tillich's definition of myth is a good place to start. He writes that "myths are symbols of faith combined in stories about divine–human encounters."[10] This requires some explanation. Tillich describes six characteristics of symbols. Like signs, symbols "point beyond themselves to something else";[11] they participate in that which they signify; they open up levels of reality that we cannot otherwise access; they unlock parts of our soul in relation to reality; they arise from the collective and individual unconscious; and they grow and die.[12] Symbols are bound to religion since "whatever we say about that which concerns us ultimately, whether or not we call it God, has a symbolic meaning. It points beyond itself while participating in that to which it points," for "the language of faith is the language of symbols."[13]

---

10 Paul Tillich, *The Dynamics of Faith* (New York: HarperCollins, 1957), 56.
11 Ibid., 47.
12 Ibid., 47–49.
13 Ibid., 51.

All talk of the divine is symbolic. Of particular interest to liberation theology is the relationship between symbols and other realities. Tillich explains that "all arts create symbols for a level of reality which cannot be reached in any other way."[14] Through suppression, obfuscation, and other acts of epistemic violence, hegemonic power structures set boundaries to "the real." Symbols point beyond "the real" delineated not only by empiricism or reason but by racism, sexism, and classism. The empire employs symbols to say what community is, what the individual is, and what God is, but there are always other symbols pointing to other realities, to other possibilities.

Symbols do not hover in solitude. They are constituted by relationships, lives, and processes. Symbols exist in narratives, and these narratives are what we call myths. The form of a myth takes "material from our ordinary experience," and myth "puts the stories of the gods into the framework of time and space" and "divides the divine into several figures, removing ultimacy from each of them without removing their claim to ultimacy."[15] Myth is constituted by the realities of everyday lives and by the structures of our community. Another way of saying it is that the mythic is given shape by the nonmythic, where the models in which symbols act with and on each other are worldly models. I suggest that we can learn more about the relationship between the worldly and the mythic when we look at the similar relationship between the real and the fictive.

In *Question and Answer: Forms of Dialogic Understanding*, Hans Robert Jauss problematizes an assertion that fiction is somehow opposite to the real:

> However natural it may seem to us to define the fictive as the nonreal, to regard it as an autonomous construct, and conceive of it in contrast to the real world, this presumed ontological antithesis between fiction and reality is nonetheless a

---

14 Ibid., 48.
15 Ibid., 56–57.

far cry from the understanding of the world maintained in earlier epochs.[16]

Jauss argues that we cannot take it for granted that fiction and reality are opposites, substantiating his claim by surveying poetic thought from the classical to the medieval, enlightenment, romantic, and modern periods, and by engaging the work of Wolfgang Iser. In *The Fictive and the Imaginary,* Iser sets forth a literary anthropology that thinks through the relationship between the real, the fictive, and the imaginary. The imaginary is the visionary, the dreamed, the unconstrained possibility of what is not. The real is what is, what has been. Fiction is the intermediary. Therefore, fiction is not the same as the imaginary. Rather it reproduces and rearranges what *is* in ways that point to *what can be:* "fictionalizing outstrips the determinacy of the real" and "provides the imaginary with the determinacy that it would not otherwise possess."[17] In a fictional text, "reproduced reality is made to point to a 'reality' beyond itself, while the imaginary is lured into form."[18] Fiction is an intermediary, a source of movement and change between the world as is and worlds as they can be. As Jauss explains, "fiction is no more a reflection of the world than it is a representation of something entirely other than the world. It is rather the 'horizon of the world.'"[19]

Jauss uses language of horizons in his essay "Literary History as a Challenge to Literary Theory," where he develops his reception theory. Every text we, as readers, have come into contact with produces our horizon of expectations. When a reader engages a new text, it "evokes for the reader (listener) the horizon of expectations and rules familiar from earlier texts, which

---

[16] Hans Robert Jauss, *Question and Answer: Forms of Dialogic Understanding,* ed. and trans. Michael Hays (Minneapolis: University of Minnesota Press, 1989), 4.
[17] Wolfgang Iser, *The Fictive and the Imaginary: Charting Literary Anthropology* (Baltimore: John Hopkins University Press: 1993), 3.
[18] Ibid.
[19] Ibid.

are then varied, corrected, altered, or even just reproduced."[20] Past texts shape what we can recognize and inform the horizon of what we imagine. Our reception of text and the rules of specific genres inform the big events, like how we think of historical battles or movements, and small events, like at night when we reflect on our day. How and what we see and how we relay what we experience are shaped by the texts we have previously read.

Importantly, "works that evoke the reader's horizon of expectations, formed by a convention of genre, style, or form, only in order to destroy it step by step [...], by no means [serve] a critical purpose only, but can [...] once again produce poetic effects."[21] A text can work within our horizons of expectation just to refute them, whether to delight, or teach, or challenge! This break widens the scope of what we can imagine the next time we read and, more so, the next time we create. Criticism of a text or genre is not only done within the academic essay, but in every work that broadens, undermines, parodies, or reimagines the confines of its presumed genre and form. When we think of the relationship between fact and fiction, then, we can see just how fiction — especially the further it reaches beyond the perceivably, authoritatively determined real of our historical and present contexts — can affect our ability to imagine and create beyond those delineations.

Jauss addresses this dialogic quality in myth specifically in his later work on question and answer. Considering Genesis 3, Jauss writes:

> According to Karl Barth, Christian theology, which holds narrative to be *the first* dialogic experience of the divine, can interpret the question "Adam, where art thou?" in the sense of priority of God's answer (as revelation) in the face of all human questions.[22]

---

20 Hans Robert Jauss, "Literary History as a Challenge to Literary Theory," in *Toward an Aesthetic of Reception,* trans. Timothy Bahti (Minneapolis: University of Minnesota Press, 1982), 23.
21 Ibid., 24.
22 Jauss, *Question and Answer,* 53. Emphasis mine.

Presenting a singular myth as the original elevates it as *the* answer to all subsequent questions. It also suggests that, if the first myth is an answer to the human question, then the answer is also more important than the question. For someone like Barth, human questions may change but they always point back to the revelation. However, if we look at myth as always emerging through reception, then myth is "something whose meaning is constantly expanded through formal variation and contentual reinterpretations."[23] When we look at the ways myths are made and indeed make myths, we are partaking in a poetic process of question and answer:

> Drawn into the dialogic structure of poetic discourse, myth must open itself to inquiry, and reveal its history, that is, the progressive appropriation, from work to work, of the answer to some great question, one involving all mankind and the world, a question whose answer can acquire a different significance with each reformulation. […] *The poetic use of question and answer can* […] *accelerate "work on the deconstruction of the absolutism of reality."* […] *It can do so by contradicting the supposed finality of a myth, that is, by allowing a writer to impose a new ending in an "aesthetic demonstration of power."* […] *The inevitable result of such an event is that the author's solution challenges another, later author into trying out some other solution.*[24]

Through the lens of poetics, we can think dialogically about myth. Every poetic appropriation of a myth answers or questions a previous iteration of that myth. When we author our own myths, we are asking others to engage mythopoetically in a potentially liberational process, for in composing a myth, we are "demonstrating power." The power we enact is one that changes the conversation of past myths in our appropriations of them, expanding the future of myths and the realities to which they

---

23 Ibid.
24 Ibid., 57. Emphasis mine.

point. That is to say, myths change the world — the *real* world! Iser says as much, if we think of myths functioning like fiction, when he writes that fiction "leads the real to the imaginary and the imaginary to the real, and it thus conditions the extent to which a given world is to be transcended, a nongiven world to be conceived, and the reshuffled worlds are to be made accessible to the [believer's] experience."[25] Myths traverse the gap between what is already established and what is imaginary, laying the groundwork for us to transcend a regulated and static world order. Mythmaking is a powerplay.

In our current political climate with virulently anti-LGBTQIA+ legislators, with raging debates about conversion therapy, trans bathroom bills, hate crime legislation, the epidemic of homelessness among LGBTQIA+ youth, and the high murder rate of trans women of color, queer/trans assertions of power are vital. And what greater power is there than participation in naming, birthing, and transforming divinity? Tillich has shown that myth narrativizes the relationship between symbols of faith. Since symbols participate in what they symbolize, queer mythmaking — narrativizing symbols of the divine through queer aesthetic and communal modes — is necessary if we are to uncover, imagine, and make manifest queer divinity. Queer mythopoeia broadens the horizons of what is possible for God, for our world, and for all of us to be.

Transcendence and Utopia

Myth facilitates transcendence from a monolithic and determined "real" toward multiple possible "realities." When I use the word "transcendence," I am not referring to a transcendent God over and against the world, or something spiritual which transcends the material. Rather, I am talking about the transcendence of particular configurations, a transformation of "reality" as conditioned by oppressive powers into new possibilities for society, love, life, imagination, world, self, and god. I borrow

---

25 Iser, *The Fictive and the Imaginary*, 4.

"transcendence" from Daly when she writes about an androgynous future, a term she in turn borrows from Herbert Richardson's 1969 article "Three Myths of Transcendence." Richardson begins by discussing differences in religious symbology: "Discernible differences in piety, spirituality, and feelings of virtue provide a basis for discriminating among religions with regard to the experience of God."[26] Religions are not all the same, and thus our experiences of God, mediated through our various traditions, are not all the same. Myths are not all the same. We can differentiate between mythic structures and determine which ones best support the work of liberation. The myth of transcendence that Richardson advocates for, the third myth, is concerned with "integrity and transformation."[27] Citing Stanley Kubrick's *2001: A Space Odyssey* as an example, Richardson writes that the transcendence "correlated with the myth of integrity and transformation is that of self-transcendence, expanded consciousness, spiritual rebirth, and divinization."[28] The God correlating with this myth is one "who lives within us"[29] and whom we can bring out. Transcendence is in the evolution of the individual, not a return to the beyond or a victory into the beyond, but a transformation of the self into the beyond. However, this is not only an individualistic transcendence:

> To speak of the completeness and sufficiency of every man does not mean that men shall become more isolated and separated from one another. It means the possibility of a new kind of human community. If [...] I do not need another in order to complete my own identity, I can see the other for what he really is in himself rather than simply for what he is

---

26 Herbert W. Richardson, "Three Myths of Transcendence," in *Transcendence*, eds. Herbert Richardson and Donald Cutler (Boston: Beacon Press, 1969), 104.
27 Ibid., 110.
28 Ibid., 112.
29 Ibid.

with my own need. I can now love and affirm him as a unique friend.[30]

Richardson hopes for a transcendent community, a people without objectification, a land of mutual affirmations where each person is a subject. The myth of transformation and integrity is a myth of transcendent community. It is a utopian myth.

Utopia is a significant piece in Gustavo Gutiérrez's *A Theology of Liberation*. Gutiérrez's eschatology conceives of a utopianism in light of Marxist philosopher Ernst Bloch, writing, "the commitment to the creation of a just society and, ultimately, to a new humanity, presupposes confidence in the future."[31] Utopia, being the just society, is thus a society of the future and something for which we must hope. Hope is a profound part of Bloch's philosophy, as Gutiérrez shows: "For Bloch there are two kinds of affections: those of society (envy, avarice) and those of expectation (anguish, fear, hope). The latter anticipate the future. Of these hope is the most important as well as the most positive and most liberating."[32] He continues: "The human being hopes for and dreams of the future; but it is an active hope which subverts the existing order."[33] Hope, here, is active. It is material. It is informed by history. It is deeply political.

Utopia is a symbol. It is not yet but points beyond itself. It participates in its own efficacy. Utopian myths *do* something to reality: "For Bloch what is real is an open-ended process. On one occasion he asserted that the formula 'S is not yet P' summarizes his thought. Bloch brings us into the area of the possibilities of potential being."[34] Bloch's utopian thought, like Jauss's fiction, expands the horizon of the possible. Gutiérrez further cites the function of utopia through a distinction of functions first suggested by Paulo Freire:

---

30 Ibid.
31 Gustavo Gutiérrez, *A Theology of Liberation*, ed. and trans. Sister Caridad Inda and John Eagleson (Maryknoll: Orbis Books, 1973), 121.
32 Ibid., 123.
33 Ibid.
34 Ibid.

> Utopia necessarily means a denunciation of the existing order. Its deficiencies are to a large extent the reason for the emergence of a utopia. The repudiation of a dehumanizing situation is an unavoidable aspect of utopia. It is a matter of a complete rejection which attempts to strike at the roots of the evil. This is why utopia is revolutionary and not reformist. [...] But utopia is also an annunciation, an annunciation of what is not yet, but will be; it is the forecast of a different order of things, a new society. It is the field of creative imagination which proposes the alternative values to those rejected.[35]

The denunciation and annunciation functions of utopia echo the efforts of the Biblical prophets, denouncing Israel's sinful ways and announcing the Kingdom of God. It is clear why the Catholic Gutiérrez takes utopian thought so seriously: it is corroborated by important tenets of Christian mythology. For Gutiérrez, "the life and preaching of Jesus postulate the unceasing search for a new kind of humanity in a qualitatively different society."[36] When Jesus announces the Kingdom of God, he is signaling a new society. Importantly for Gutiérrez, "the Kingdom must not be confused with the establishment of a just society," though "this does not mean that it is indifferent to this society."[37] The Kingdom of God is that which is signified by the utopian myth. The utopian myth is our language for something which, for Gutiérrez, cannot be accomplished through human means. However, "the announcement of the Kingdom reveals to society itself the aspiration for a just society and leads it to discover unsuspected dimensions and unexplored paths."[38] The Kingdom of God is something divine, something other than human and other, even, than utopia. Yet, the "announcement" of the Kingdom, the language pointing to what will happen, the

---

35 Ibid., 136.
36 Ibid., 134.
37 Ibid., 135.
38 Ibid.

images of the future, and the myth of the eschaton have a material, social, and political function. We glimpse through the myth of the Kingdom of God that the world can be other than what it currently is, indeed it must be other. The myth is a symbol of our societal concern. It provokes our hope, which "opens us, in an attitude of spiritual childhood, to the gift of the future promised by God."[39] This hope "makes us radically free to commit ourselves to social praxis, motivated by a liberating utopia and with the means which the scientific analysis of reality provides for us."[40] Rather than lulling Christians into complacency, Gutiérrez's eschatology demands and inspires liberation.

Another Blochian, rather different from Gutiérrez, is queer theorist José Esteban Muñoz, though the latter author's utopian application can expand on the former's. In his 2009 book *Cruising Utopia*, Muñoz works with Bloch's writing to argue that utopia is queer and that the queer is utopia. This analysis begins with a denunciation of the queer as something which currently is:

> We cannot trust in the manifestations of what some people would call queerness in the present, especially as embodied in the pragmatic debates that dominate contemporary gay and lesbian politics. (Here, again, I most pointedly mean US queers clamoring for their right to participate in the suspect institution of marriage and, maybe worse, to serve in the military.) None of this is to say that there are not avatars of a queer futurity, both in the past and the present, especially in sites of cultural production. What I am suggesting is that we gain a greater conceptual and theoretical leverage if we see queerness as something that is not yet here.[41]

Muñoz's approach challenges my definition that queer theology is something that is done by LGBTQIA+ people. Perhaps I should

---
39 Ibid., 139.
40 Ibid.
41 José Esteban Muñoz, *Cruising Utopia: The Then and There of Queer Futurity* (New York: New York University Press, 2009), 20.

revise my definition to say that queer theology is a theology devised by the avatars of queer futurity. Or else I might say that queer theology is a theology of aspiration beyond the future "of reproductive majoritarian heterosexuality, the spectacle of the state refurbishing its ranks through overt and subsidized acts of reproduction."[42] Queerness is a potential. The leverage of queerness as a not yet is that it "must be called on, and insisted on."[43] Queerness requires doing, performing, acting. It requires movement toward.

Queerness is further like utopia because of its temporality. It refutes allegiance to a present that "is not enough," since the present "is impoverished and toxic for queers and other people who do not feel the privilege of majoritarian belonging, normative tastes, and 'rational' expectations."[44] The present that is not enough is straight time, "chrononormativity" as coined by queer theorist Elizabeth Freeman.[45] Queerness, like utopia, looks to the past and imagines the future to challenge the present. Queerness expands the horizon.

> To see queerness as horizon is to perceive it as a modality of ecstatic time in which the temporal stranglehold that I describe as straight time is interrupted or stepped out of. Ecstatic time is signaled at the moment one feels ecstasy, announced perhaps in a scream or grunt of pleasure, and more importantly during moments of contemplation when one looks back at a scene from one's past, present, or future.[46]

Queers are those who yearn for the queer, stepping out of the normative of sequential, chronological temporality presented by heteropatriarchy, which attempts to obscure, discredit, and destroy the utopianism of the queer. It is a two-way street,

---

42 Ibid., 22.
43 Ibid., 21.
44 Ibid.
45 Elizabeth Freeman, *Time Binds: Queer Temporalities, Queer Histories* (Durham: Duke University Press, 2010), 3.
46 Muñoz, *Cruising Utopia*, 32.

however, and if the queer is utopian, the utopian is also queer: "Fredric Jameson described the utopian as the oddball or the maniac. Indeed, to live inside straight time and ask for, desire, and imagine another time and place is to represent and perform a desire that is both utopian and queer."[47] By this thinking, Gutiérrez's eschatology is a queer eschatology. Gutiérrez denies the now as vigorously as does Muñoz.

In his book, Muñoz looks to queer art and queer embodiment as examples of the utopian reach into the past and present. He asks, "how do we enact utopia?"[48] I interpret this question as my own "how do we enact queer myths?" Reflecting on his youth in Los Angeles, Muñoz discusses the impact of the punk and queer aesthetic: "LA and its scene helped my proto-queer self, the queer child in me, imagine a stage, both temporal and physical, where I could be myself or, more nearly, imagine a self that was in process, a self that has always been in the process of becoming."[49] The fashion, music, and the photographic representations of the queer punk scene are symbols pointing to utopia. They are icons through which Muñoz glimpses queer potential. Queer punks perform utopian symbols. In relationship with each other, they are the making of myths.

One of the clearest religious implications of *Cruising Utopia* comes in its conclusion, with Muñoz's treatment of the song "Take Ecstasy with Me" by indie-pop band The Magnetic Fields and its queer lead singer–songwriter Stephin Merrett. Queerness demands "we must vacate the here and now for a then and there. Individual transports are insufficient. We need to engage in a collective temporal distortion. We need to step out of the rigid conceptualization that is a straight present."[50] For Muñoz, the speaker of "Take Ecstasy with Me" is asking the genderneutral addressee not only to take a drug, but to join the speaker in an outside of time: "Might it be a call for a certain

---

47 Ibid., 26.
48 Ibid., 97.
49 Ibid., 100.
50 Ibid., 185.

kind of transcendence?"⁵¹ Aware of the religious connotations of ecstasy, Muñoz connects the ecstasy of the pop song with that of Bernini's Saint Theresa whose ecstasy "represents a leaving of self for something larger in the form of divinity."⁵² The ecstasies of the saints inform the horizon in which Merritt composes and in which Muñoz listens to the song. "Take Ecstasy with Me" is not only an interpretation but a myth in dialogue with other myths. In Muñoz and Merritt's queer mythopoeia, a nothing-special drug of queer club culture becomes a conduit of divine rapture, a myth of transcendence.

If Gutiérrez shows that utopian imagination is key to any liberation theology, Muñoz demonstrates that myths and symbols of utopia hold special significance for queer liberation. Muñoz sees in queer stories, queer performances, and queer art a utopian imagination made flesh. The utopian myth is manifested when the oppressed engage it through embodied creativity.

Beyond Hermeneutics: Performing Queer and Trans Mythopoeia

Looking back at the relationship between feminist and queer theologies, Daly's *Gyn/Ecology* is, among other things, a call for mythopoetic praxis. In describing the subtitle, "Metaethics of Radical Feminism," Daly lays out her book as "concerned with the Background, most specifically of language and myth, which is disguised by the fathers' foreground fixations."⁵³ An exclusively hermeneutical approach to myth would share this concern, but Daly does not only interpret in an academic sense. She is also advocating for mythic thought and the performance of a mythic role, the hag, "for women who are on the journey of radical be-ing, the lives of the witches, of the Great Hags of our hidden history are deeply intertwined with our own process. As we write and live our own story, we are uncovering their history,

---

51   Ibid.
52   Ibid., 186.
53   Daly, *Gyn/Ecology*, 11.

creating Hag-ography and Hag-ology."[54] Hags are exemplars of power and wisdom that have been suppressed, violated, and distorted in patriarchal mythology. But for radical feminists, hags are symbols from a gynocentric prehistory that reach through time to sign a new future:

> The history of Hags and Crones is truly Prehistoric in relation to patriarchal history—being prior both in time and in appearance—haggard women should consider that our Crone-ology is indeed our chronology. In writing/recording/creating Crone-ography and in studying our own Prehistoric chronology, we are unmasking deceptive patriarchal history, rendering it obsolete. Women who refuse to be wooed by patriarchal scholarship can conjure the chronicles of the Great Crones, foresisters of our present and future Selves.[55]

Daly's Crone-ology denounces the now, a denunciation that Gutiérrez and Muñoz both articulate in their advocacy of utopianism. Indeed, Daly, like Muñoz, looks to myths of the past to imagine the future. Like Muñoz's artists, Daly performs the hag in her writing and advocates for other women to join her in such performance. In performing the myth of the hag, that is in practicing hag mythopoeia, not only will women be able to accomplish a feminist hermeneutic of patriarchal texts by using their cronish vision, but they will also participate in symbolizations that inspire other women to take up a mythopoetic mantel. Each hag with her hag eyes is staring down a patriarchal world, expanding the horizon of expectations, and announcing the radical feminist utopia. Becoming the hag is not to accept patriarchal myths of the hag. Rather, it "is a sense of power, not of the 'wholly other,' but of the Self's be-ing."[56] Daly's utopia appropriates Richardson's myth of transformation and integrity.

---

54   Ibid., 15.
55   Ibid., 16.
56   Ibid., 49.

Daly's myth points to a future of women's self-actualization and friendship.

The utopian vision of *Gyn/Ecology* is, however, a seriously flawed one. While the invocation of white European crones invites some women, it excludes many others. The only oppression that Daly denounces is that of patriarchal sexism, for in her analysis patriarchy is the fundamental evil. As Audre Lorde points out in her public letter to Daly, to intimate "that all women suffer the same oppression simply because we are women is to lose sight of the many varied tools of patriarchy. It is to ignore how those tools are used by women without awareness against each other."[57] Lorde is calling out the tool of racism in Daly's utopian myth. Daly's dismissal of the complexities of other forms of oppression — racism, classism, eurocentrism, ableism — and her non-inclusion of models for women of color dismisses Lorde's "heritage and the heritage of all other non-european women," denying "the real connections that exist between all of us."[58] Lorde enacts utopian denunciation, proclaiming: "Assimilation within a solely western european herstory is not acceptable."[59] Without acknowledging how racism affects Lorde and other women of color, Daly is not seeing a full enough picture of Black and Brown women's humanity. Pointing out an important repercussion of Daly's mythopoeia, Lorde addresses the other woman: "Since you have so completely unrecognized me, perhaps I have been in error concerning you and no longer recognize you."[60] The effect of Daly's writing on Lorde is the opposite of Richardson's mutual recognition of one another's subjecthood. If Daly's myth is utopia for some and dystopia for others, then it is a heterotopia. And for any queer liberationist, surely heterotopia is unacceptable.[61]

---

57 Audre Lorde, "An Open Letter to Mary Daly," in *Sister Outsider: Essays and Speeches* (Berkeley: Crossing Press, 1984), 67.
58 Ibid., 68.
59 Ibid., 69.
60 Ibid., 70.
61 When I say "heterotopia" I mean utopia for some and dystopia for others. Importantly, I am not using heterotopia in the same sense as Michel

Lorde's letter reveals Daly's universalization of her identity and failure to recognize the complexity of other people's reality. This nonrecognition compromises one's ability to see the other as a subject. It results in objectification. As her work ignores the myths and symbols of Black women, of women of color around the world, Daly's mythic interpretations in *Gyn/Ecology* also objectifies some women through a direct attack: I am speaking of her words for transgender people.

In hir 1992 *Transgender Liberation,* activist and author Leslie Feinberg writes that in

> recent years a community has begun to emerge that is sometimes referred to as the gender or transgender community. Within our community is a diverse group of people who define ourselves in many different ways. Transgendered people are demanding the right to choose our own self-definitions.[62]

Feinberg's experience as a labor activist translates to hir call for transnational solidarity in a fight of self-determination amongst a diverse group of people: "Feinberg called for a political alliance between all individuals who were marginalized or oppressed due to their difference from social norms of gendered embodiment, and who should therefore band together

---

Foucault when he writes of heterotopias as "real places — places that do exist and that are formed in the very founding of society — which are something like counter-sites, a kind of effectively enacted utopia in which the real sites, all the other real sites that can be found within the culture, are simultaneously represented, contested, and inverted. Places of this kind are outside of all places, even though it may be possible to indicate their location in reality." Michel Foucault, "Of Other Spaces: Utopias and Heterotopias," trans. Jay Miskowiec, *Diacritics* 16, no. 1 (Spring 1986): 3–4. Foucault's "heterotopia" is in fact a kind of liminal, contested territory that acts similarly to Iser's fictive discussed earlier in the chapter. Foucault's "heterotopia" is the hybrid space created when the utopia infringes on the real, physical locale and is, as such, a fertile ground for queer mythopoetics.

62 Leslie Feinberg, *Transgender Liberation: A Movement Whose Time Has Come* (New York: World View Forum, 1992), 6.

in a struggle for social, political, and economic justice."[63] Like "queer," "transgender" becomes a line of political solidarity, an identarian term, and the resistance to identarianism, and a theoretical perspective.

In her earlier works, transgender theorist Susan Stryker uses the term to cast a wide umbrella of

> all identities or practices that cross over, cut across, move between, or otherwise queer socially constructed sex/gender boundaries. The term includes, but is not limited to, transsexuality, heterosexual transvestism, gay drag, butch lesbianism, and such non-European identities as the Native American berdache or the Indian Hijra.[64]

Trans, as movement across, means that transgender people are those who move across gender boundaries. In Stryker's terminology, the various names and formations of anyone whose existence involves, is, or has been a movement across gender-sex boundaries is transgender. However, these early attempts at defining "transgender" by Feinberg and Stryker also risk a form of unintentional but deeply harmful epistemic colonialism. In 2016's *Asegi Stories,* Qwo-Li Driskill leverages a two-spirit critique of transgender studies, situating the field in a broader context of colonial gendering:

> Colonization has always used our genders and sexualities as a reason to attack, enslave, or "civilize" us. The word gender itself is from the Latin word genus, a species/sort/kind, and related to the word genre. "Gender" is a logic, and a structural system of oppression, whose sole purpose is to catego-

---

[63] Susan Stryker, "(De)Subjugated Knowledges: An Introduction to Transgender Studies," in *The Transgender Studies Reader,* eds. Susan Stryker and Stephen Whittle (New York: Routledge, 2006), 4.

[64] Susan Stryker, "My Words to Victor Frankenstein above the Village of Chamounix: Performing Transgender Rage," in *The Transgender Studies Reader,* eds. Susan Stryker and Stephen Whittle (New York and London: Routledge, 2006), 255.

rize people in order to deploy systemic power and control. It is a wholly colonial imposition.[65]

While in Daly's scheme, all forms of violence flood from the patriarchal, Driskill names gender oppression as the fruit of a poisonous tree, that is, Western imperialism and colonialism. Feinberg also names this relationship:

> Our focus has been on European history and consciously so. The blame for anti-transgender laws and attitudes rests squarely on the shoulders of the ruling classes on that continent. The seizures of lands and assets of the "accused" during the witch trials and Inquisition helped the ruling classes acquire the capital to expand their domination over Asia, Africa and the Americas. The European elite then tried to force their ideology on the peoples they colonized around the world.[66]

However, while Feinberg is particularly interested in groups of people around the world working in solidarity against gender as deployed by capitalist and imperialist powers, the term's evolution into transgender theory and studies, entangles transgender with epistemic violence of the Western academy: white-trans-theorist-subjects can study, allegorize, and admire colonized people and people of color as objects. Even more dangerous is transgender-as-identity, insofar as it is applied indiscriminately to people across cultures who do not fit into the Western gender binary. Such a maneuver overrides the complexity of world perspectives on gender, sex, and body with an anglophone and Eurocentric ideology: "Because transgender can be imagined to include all possible variations from an often unstated norm, it risks becoming yet another project of colonization — a kind of Cartesian grid imposed on the globe — for making sense of

---

65 Qwo-Li Driskill, *Asegi Stories: Cherokee Queer and Two-Spirit Memory* (Tucson: University of Arizona Press, 2016), 167.
66 Feinberg, *Transgender Liberation*, 16.

human diversity by measuring it within a Eurocentric frame of reference, against a Eurocentric standard."[67] When I claim an identity for someone else using my own lexicon, I risk annihilating their subjectivity in self-determination. When I do this as a white American of European descent to Indigenous people and to people of color, I perpetuate an imperial approach. To decolonize transgender studies means that "categories of gender-nonconforming practices or embodiments need to be understood in their geographic and cultural specificity and not simply as a local instance of a falsely universalized 'transgender.'"[68] White transgender people have no monopoly on understandings and critiques of gender systems.

A closed focus on an identarian "transgender" risks the recreation or perpetuation of a Eurocentric gender system, enmeshed with individualism and taxonomy. However, when we harken back to Feinberg's initial call for global solidarity, we can think of transgender as a meaningful sight for political, social, and creative cross affiliation. While transgender studies "can operate both as a practice of decolonization that opens new prospects for vitally necessary and radically democratic social change and as a vector for the perpetuation of colonialist practices," I agree with Stryker and Paisley Currah that "transgender can function as a rubric for bringing together, in mutually supportive and politically productive ways, gender-marginalized people in many parts of the world, who experience oppression because of their variance from socially privileged expressions of manhood or womanhood."[69] These alliances are important for political, social, and spiritual organization and collective liberation. Transgender is an assemblage of theories, experiences, bodies, and identities, even if it can also be used as a singular term misapplied through cultural colonialism to those who do

---

67 Susan Stryker and Paisley Currah, "Introduction," *TSQ: Transgender Studies Quarterly* 1, nos. 1–2 (May 2014): 8.
68 Aren Z. Aizura, Trystan Cotton, Carsten Balzer/Carla LaGata, Marcia Ochoa, and Salvador Vidal-Ortiz, "Introduction," *TSQ: Transgender Studies Quarterly* 1, no. 3 (August 2004): 314.
69 Stryker and Currah, "Introduction," 8.

not consent to a Western paradigm. Importantly, in the history of "transgender" in this country and beyond, transgender identities, theories, and cultural production is a direct response to having transgender voices silenced in medical and psychiatric literature on one hand and in certain feminist critiques on the other. Even with its epistemological pitfalls, transgender studies encompass "the possibility that transgender people (self-identified or designated as such by others) can be subjects of knowledge as well as objects of knowledge. That is, they can articulate critical knowledge from embodied positions that would otherwise be rendered pathological, marginal, invisible, or unintelligible within dominant and normative organizations of power/knowledge."[70] The subjectivity of transgender people within transgender poetics is a necessary corrective to Daly's deeply objectifying argument.

For Daly "the most basic and paradigmatic form of boundary violation is, of course, rape."[71] This leads to Daly approaching sex- and gender-crossing as a form of rape, a hermeneutic that she applies to the myths of Dionysus and Frankenstein. First, Dionysus is the "androgynous alternative to the stereotypically rigid Apollonian masculine model."[72] Dionysus was conceived between the divine Zeus and the human, Semele. However, Semele was killed by Zeus's lightning before Dionysus was born, and so Zeus sewed the fetus into his divine thigh, gestating Dionysus there until his birth. Daly sees this myth in relation to a male desire to kill off the mother: "Zeus dispenses with the woman and bears his own son."[73] I do not think Daly's interpretation here is problematic. Zeus, king of the Gods, Olympian father, *is* a patriarch, a notorious violator of women, and men and boys, throughout myth. Where I disagree strongly with Daly is in the following analyses of another myth of Dionysus where he is his own father. Daly writes, "the apparently contra-

---

70 Ibid., 9.
71 Daly, *Gyn/Ecology*, 69.
72 Ibid., 64.
73 Ibid., 65.

dictory aspects of Dionysus—his self-fathering and his femininity—coincide"[74] and that the "femininity of Dionysus should be seen also in connection with his glorification as boundary-violator, as the one who drives women mad."[75] Daly is asserting a definitive connection between Dionysus's androgyny, his miraculous birth, and the one who drives women to madness. I challenge that not one of these characteristics is necessarily contingent on any other. If the hypermasculine Apollo or Zeus are rapists and violate women's bodies, then I question that Dionysus's femininity is the cause of his own acts of boundary violation. Athena, born from Zeus's head, is another motherless divine birth, and yet to presume that she inevitably portrays a human dream to replace the woman entirely begs the question, then why is Athena female? Daly attributes to Dionysus "the ability to shatter cognitive boundaries in women, that is, the capacity to drive women mad—which he did whenever possible,"[76] while ignoring the ways women, slaves, and foreigners are empowered, if ambiguously, by Dionysus, as well as the men who Dionysus turns mad, the men Dionysus and his followers mutilate, Dionysus's most famous victim being the hypermasculine Pentheus in Euripides' *Bacchae*. For Daly, Dionysus represents a Final Solution, where because of Dionysus's appearance as woman-like, women have an "inability to distinguish the female Self and her process from the male-made masquerade."[77] What is at stake for women is the mutual recognition between women of a true womanhood.

Daly imagines drag performance, at least drag queens, as a real life descendent of the Dionysian myth: "The phenomenon of the drag queen dramatically demonstrates such boundary violation. Like whites playing 'black face,' he incorporates the oppressed role without being incorporated in it."[78] While refreshing that Daly admits that blackface is oppressive and therefore

---

74 Ibid., 66.
75 Ibid.
76 Ibid.
77 Ibid., 67.
78 Ibid.

racism is indeed a reality, her example is thoroughly flawed. It presumes that women can inevitably not tell when a drag queen is a drag queen, and the purpose of drag is indefinitely to trick. The parallel she draws between the ability of the white actor to take off the black and the drag queen's removal of her womanhood must be scrutinized.[79] If the analogy is indeed true, then why the history of state violence against drag queens, the police rape of drag queens, the historical stigmatization of drag performers in mainstream gay and lesbian cultures, and the necessity for drag queens to organize and demand rights during the Stonewall riots? While aspects of drag can propagate misogyny, a distinction must be made between what kinds of boundaries are violated and for whom. The danger of misogynistic drag is that it is prescriptive of how women should be. It violates the authenticity and complexity of women who are subjects. However, the crossing of a boundary applied from the outside onto the self, for instance the gay male drag queen's violation of the borders of manhood or masculinity, is a reclaiming of subjecthood under cis-heteropatriarchy.[80] Acknowledging that we are all colonized by ideologies is an acknowledgment that all our liberations require the breaking of certain boundaries within ourselves, but this does not mean that we are given free rein to violate other subjecthoods.

Following Daly's investigation of the Dionysian myth is her discussion of the Frankenstein phenomenon, wherein she relates the anti-mother myth of Dionysus's motherless birth with a necrophilic desire of men to replace mothers and women through unnatural, scientific means. Daly argues that justified murder through militarism and gender boundary violation are interconnected, claiming that Mary Shelley foresaw this

---

79 Additionally, in using blackface as an analogy to drag, Daly once again ignores the intersections of Black women, Black trans people, Black queer people, and Black drag. It is especially careless to ignore the distinct histories of predominantly Black and Latinx drag, for instance in ball culture, to make her point.

80 A more thorough conversation about drag will be taken up in the final chapter of this book, "Drag Theopoetics."

connection: "Mary Shelley displayed prophetic insight when she wrote *Frankenstein,* foretelling the technological fathers' fusion of male mother-miming and necrophilia in a boundary violation that ultimately points toward the total elimination of women."[81] As mentioned in the introduction of this essay, Daly argues that medical transition is men appropriating motherhood. The Frankenstein–Doctor–Patriarch desires to overcome nature. But in direct contradiction to Mary Shelley's novel, Daly does not give a voice to the monster created by this assault on nature. The transsexual of *Gyn/Ecology* is not a subject with desires, dreams, emotions but an object to prove a point about doctors' violation of womanhood. Daly's text begs the question, where is the monster's voice? Stryker's mythopoeia in "My Words to Victor Frankenstein above the Village of Chamounix" is a profound answer.

A commonality between Daly and Stryker is the reclamation of and identification with a mythological villain. As Daly performs the hag, Stryker performs the monster: "I want to lay claim to the dark power of my monstrous identity without using it as a weapon against others or being wounded by it myself. I will say this as bluntly as I know how: I am a transsexual and therefore I am a monster."[82] Stryker resonates with the monster myth yet also wants to make sure that the comparison is not harmful, so she reframes what it is to be monstrous: "'Monster' is derived from the Latin noun *monstrum*, 'divine-portent,' itself formed on the root of the verb *monere*, 'to warn': [...] Monsters, like angels, functioned as messengers and heralds of the extraordinary."[83] There is something of Muñoz's queer avatars in Stryker's monsters, people whose embodiments open up our access to other worlds.

Theologically rich, Frankenstein's monster is a created monster. Claiming monsterhood is a claim to creatureliness, that is,

---

81 Daly, *Gyn/Ecology*, 70.
82 Stryker, "My Words to Victor Frankenstein," 246.
83 Ibid., 247.

> words like "creature," "monster," and, "natural" need to be reclaimed by the transgendered. By embracing and accepting them, even piling one on top of another, we may dispel their ability to harm us. A creature, after all, in the dominant tradition of Western European culture, is nothing other than a created being, a made thing. The affront you humans take at being called a "creature" results from the threat the term poses to your status as "lords of creation," beings elevated above mere material existence. As in the case of being called it, being called a "creature" suggests the lack or loss of a superior personhood.[84]

If Augustine or Reinhold Niebuhr were alive to read this! Stryker as transsexual participates in a symbolism which points to the creatureliness of us all. Her ontology deconstructs the interlocutor who calls her "creature" or "unnatural." This is iconoclasm — destroying the idol of the self, the human presumption as ultimate creator.[85] As the monster, Stryker is a prophet in the face of essentialist presumptions. To the person offended by Stryker's body she can respond:

> It is a fabrication that cloaks the boundlessness of the privilege you seek to maintain for yourself at my expense. You are as constructed as me; the same anarchic Womb has birthed us both. I call upon you to investigate your nature as I have been compelled to confront mine. I challenge you to risk abjection and flourish as well as have I. Heed my words, and you may well discover the seams and sutures in yourself.[86]

The monster that Stryker reclaims not only speaks, but speaks potently beyond herself. Her myth has ramifications for the laws of gender and the laws of nature. Performing the myth of the

---

[84] Ibid., 246.

[85] A more thorough discussion of a queer/trans critique of the self will be taken up in the second and third chapters, "Myth on Myth Action" and "Theyogony," respectively.

[86] Stryker, "My Words to Victor Frankenstein," 247.

monster, Stryker launches an assault on one of the tools of patriarchy, that is, essentialist categorization and the presumption of natural genders. Embodying creatureliness, Stryker deploys a theodicy wherein the evil of patriarchal reality can be overcome.

The form of Stryker's text reflects its content of creaturely reclamation. The essay is an adaptation of a performance piece, and its sections span multiple genres. One section is a description of a monstrous costume. One section is a monologue, another a literary critique. There is a journal entry that includes a poem about rage. There is a theory of transsexual rage, and finally, the essay ends with a benediction. Stitched together in the fashion of the monster, the text moves beyond a hermeneutic. It moves into the dialogical poetics of a new myth which calls upon old myths:

> By speaking as a monster in my personal voice, by using the dark, watery images of Romanticism and lapsing occasionally into its brooding cadences and grandiose postures, I employ the same literary techniques Mary Shelley used to elicit sympathy for her scientist's creation.[87]

Stryker dares to think poetically. She refuses to speak in one idiom and denies a restrictive separation between artist and critic. As Muñoz observes: "Attempting to imagine a convergence between artistic production and critical praxis is, in and of itself, a utopian act in relation to the alienation that often separates theory from practice, a sort of cultural division of labor."[88] The utopian is called upon in the very artifact of Stryker's essay, an early and foundational text of trans theory. Stryker embodies the hybrid of artist and critic, a strategy that others have employed in the past and in this very day. Where have I seen this hybridity before? I have seen this hybridity in feminist theology: Biblical scholar Phyllis Trible as artist and critic in *Texts of Terror* when she includes her original prayers; Wilda Gafney employing Jew-

---

87 Ibid., 254.
88 Muñoz, *Cruising Utopia*, 101.

ish hermeneutics and mythopioea through a womanist commitment to interdisciplinarity, creativity, and embodied community in *Womanist Midrash;* the feminist liturgies and mythic imagination of the Reimagining Movement. I have seen the artist and critic tradition of queer theorists and artists like Vaginal Davis and her performance art or Nguyễn Tân Hoàng and his films. In theology, I think of queer/trans Latinx theologian and activist Robyn Henderson-Espinoza and their collaborations with poets and photographers. I think of my own work with the House of Larva Drag Co-Operative, and our queer gnostic performance art. Womanist and feminist theologians have been prosperous in the realm of mythopoeia, of speaking about the ultimate in new, other, and horizon-broadening ways. So too have queer and trans theorists responded to questions with mythopoetic answers and, in reverse, created myths to question the heteronormative and homonormative now. Stryker's essay is a foundational work in queer and trans mythopoeia, emerging through a complicated network of mythopoetic receptions. And it is a potent charge, particularly for us at the intersection of queer/trans embodiment and theological production, to engage full-heartedly this project of mythmaking.

Concluding her essay, Stryker leaves the reader through the ritualistic, churchly genre of the benediction:

> If this is your path, as it is mine, let me offer whatever solace you may find in this monstrous benediction: May you discover the enlivening power of darkness within yourself. May it nourish your rage. May your rage inform your actions, and your actions transform you as you struggle to transform your world.[89]

I take Stryker's benediction as Muñoz takes Merritt's "Take Ecstasy with Me": as an invitation. Tillich has shown that we talk about God through symbols, and symbols interact through myth. Myths are not only the subject of our theological work.

---

89 Stryker, "My Words to Victor Frankenstein," 254.

They are also the medium. Myths, like the fictive, function in particular ways, broadening our horizons of the possible. Mythmakers are emissaries of the future and transmutators of the past. But localized individual queer theologians practicing mythopoeia are not enough. In our day and age, queer theology is in its emergence. To my fellow queer theologians, let us not only practice interpretation but give to our world something to be interpreted. Let us illuminate the "Now and dark Hathbeen."[90] For our liberation, that is the global transcendence of a hegemonic, oppressive real, let us dive into the work of mythmaking.

---

90 Tolkien, "Mythopoeia," l. 105.

2

Myth-on-Myth Action: Denaturalizing Deities, Desires, and Dimorphism in the Genesis Cosmogony

How sly they are, our creators. They allow you to be almost human. Tease you with taste and touch. But deny you free will. It's sadistic in a way: you can taste the meal, but you cannot choose to make it.

— John Logan, *Alien Covenant* screenplay[1]

Behind God's eyes
There might
Be other lights

— Mina Loy, "Songs to Joannes"[2]

---

[1] John Logan, *"Alien Covenant:* Screenplay by John Logan." *AvP Galaxy,* November 20, 2015. This is not the final script that was ultimately used for Ridley Scott's *Alien Covenant* (2017).
[2] Mina Loy, "Songs to Joannes," in *The Lost Lunar Baedeker: Poems of Mina Loy,* ed. Roger Conover (New York: Farrar, Straus and Giroux, 1996), ll. 87–89.

I sit in my basement apartment on a gray couch. I wear a leopard-print caftan and black socks. There is detangler in my hair so that, by afternoon, my curls will fall and spring back with ease, and the extra humidity of the subterrane aids in this process. My facial hair is damp, conditioned, rinsed, and softening with beard butter. Like a benign, self-addressing Buffalo Bill, I put the lotion on my skin, its clean efflux muddied with the living room's stench of incense, ash, and coffee grounds. A panoply of processes adjusts my cells, makes them soft, moist, supple, utterly lubed up for the difficult work of producing the atmosphere of my body. Some of these processes are self-applied, many others are the product of the space I am in and the distances between and intermingling of various things. This is a picture of my being constituted by modifications and becomings and of a body emerging in relationship to the surrounding scene. Sing, Muse, of the birth of a queer mythopoet!

The invocation of Ovid's *Metamorphoses* is just as apropos: "My soul would sing of metamorphoses," "bodies becoming bodies,"[3] as this chapter and the following are concerned with the becoming of forms and shapes. Such is the work of cosmological thinking. Cosmology follows the first chapter, asking "what is the real," that is, the structure of the universe, and how does the individual, if such a thing exists, situate itself within the broader mechanism? How did, does, will the world or worlds come into being? Am I *a part* of my surroundings or *apart* from them? And, for our purposes, what mythopoetic treatments of the cosmos are most efficacious to the work of queer/trans liberation?

Cosmology can be a subdiscipline of astronomy, physics, philosophy, religion, metaphysics, or mythology. Under the umbrella of theology, cosmological thought combines and prioritizes its various manifestations from these disciplines to articulate the value, meaning, and purpose of the cosmos, with, until the last few centuries and especially the twentieth, a prior-

---

3   Ovid, *Metamorphoses*, trans. Allen Mandelbaum (Boston: Houghton Mifflin Harcourt, 2017), 1.

itization of the philosophical and mythological discourses over the scientific. As the progenitors of much Western philosophy, Plato and Aristotle differentiate between myth and philosophy and practice forms of demythologization, interpreting "scientific," ethical, political, or philosophical allegories from popular myth. For example, in Plato's *Phaedrus,* the aristocratic Phaedrus asks if Socrates believes the tale of Orithyia, who was raped and abducted by Boreas, the North Wind. Socrates responds:

> The wise are doubtful, and I should not be singular if, like them, I too doubted. I might have a rational explanation that Orithyia was playing with Pharmacia, when a northern gust carried her over the neighbouring rocks; and this being the manner of her death, she was said to have been carried away by Boreas.[4]

This exchange between student and teacher indicates that a philosopher should be skeptical about myth, or at least about myth as it is used in one way and interpret from it a rational or allegorical meaning. Of course, I am taking this quote out of context. *Phaedrus* also includes Socrates' encounter with his daemon and a discussion of madness as inspired by Apollo, Dionysus, the Muses, and Aphrodite, instances that a modern reader would surely recognize as mythic, and the dialogue is not uniformly myth-skeptical. Still, Greek philosophers and their inheritors, whether articulating through poems, dialogues, or analytical prose typically, though not categorically, differentiate their works from the folktales, epics, dramas, and hymns of myth. Indeed, the origins of Greek philosophy have been attributed to those who first put forth demythologized orderings of the world, that is, those who supposedly engaged cosmology from outside the realm of myth.

In his book on the pre-Socratics, Richard D. McKirahan writes: "Since antiquity the beginning of Greek philosophy has

---

[4] Plato, *Phaedrus,* trans. Benjamin Jowett (Boston: Action Press, 2010, 1892), 229c–229d.

been placed in Miletus in the early sixth century BCE. The first philosophers — Thales, Anaximander, and Anaximenes — the story goes, invented and made rapid developments in a new way of looking at and thinking about the world."[5] According to tradition, the Milesians, with their experiments and theories, are the founders of philosophy, and philosophy in turn begins first and foremost with questions about the world's formation and material. Philosophy *is* a subdiscipline of cosmology at this early stage. However, McKirahan problematizes Greek philosophy and cosmology's beginning with philosophers. His book suggests a turn to the mythographer.

McKirahan argues that the questions which set the initial perimeters of pre-Socratic inquiry are found in Hesiod's epics *Theogony* and *Works and Days*. Hesiod lived between 750 and 650 BCE, with Thales, the "first" Greek philosopher being born sometime around 624 BCE, potentially a generation or two after Hesiod. In *Theogony,* meaning "birth of the gods," Hesiod describes the origin of the gods, the organizing of the world, and the beginnings of humankind all through a mythic narrative. Just as the world comes not from nothing but from chaos in his poem, Hesiod is not inventing these myths *ex nihilo.* So why might *his* text be so foundational to cosmological thought as opposed to earlier myths? McKirahan points to "Hesiod's belief that the world is ordered in a way that humans can understand — in other words that it is a *kosmos* (world order, ordered world)," and it "can be correctly described and communicated to others in language."[6] Hesiod weaves established myths into an epic poem that emphasizes a cosmos.

By citing McKirahan's suggestion of Hesiod as progenitor of cosmological thinking, I am not so interested in the differences between mythological cosmologies and philosophical cosmologies, and to chronologize which comes first, as much as I am interested in their similarities and interrelations. Both disci-

---

5   Richard D. McKirahan, *Philosophy before Socrates: An Introduction with Texts and Commentary* (Indianapolis: Hackett Publishing, 2010), 7.
6   Ibid., 8.

plines argue that there is a cosmos or cosmoi and that we can and should articulate them. Hesiod's capital "T" *Theogony* is an example of a genre of myth: theogony and the closely related cosmogony. Indeed, philosophers throughout time have utilized the mythic sub-genres of cosmogony and theogony to illustrate their cosmologies. Plato is a master philosopher and mythographer, employing myth from the origins of love in the *Symposium* to the cave and the Myth of Er in the *Republic* to the demiurge of Plato's most explicitly cosmological work the *Timaeus*. In the *Timaeus,* the demiurge is an all-good creator god who shapes the chaos of unseparated elements (air, earth, fire, water) based on the true and eternal forms which the demiurge sees, and which Platonists will later interpret as existing in the demiurge's mind. Since the forms exist in the Eternal One, the world, as created in the image of the form, is singular. One eternal creator god accesses the Eternal "One" and in its image creates the one eternal world. Philosophy turns to myth, and myth informs philosophy.

Written down after *Theogony* but well before the *Timaeus,* Genesis 1 and 2 put forth cosmogonies that continue to influence not only how theology is done by Jews, Christians, and, through Quranic retelling, Muslims, but *anyone* engaging theology or myth or "the real" in a context, like the US, dominated by one of these religious traditions. In Genesis 1, an all-powerful God speaks the world into being in seven days, while separating dark from light, waters from sky, earth from sea, and decreeing which beings live in which domains. In the more intimate and localized creation of Genesis 2, God sculpts man and breathes life into his nostrils, a river bursts through the dust, God plants Eden and tasks Adam to look after it, God creates the animals to be companions for Adam, and, when that fails, God creates Eve out of Adam to be his partner in this new world.

While both creations in the Bible are cosmogonies, they are not theogonies in so far as God is simply presumed to exist as God's self. The stories *are* cosmological because they establish the structure of the cosmos as well as the relationships between God and world, God and animals and plants, God and humans,

humans and other animals and plants, and humans and world. Likewise, Plato's demiurge is not born, formed, or originated but is presumed to exist as in the Biblical tales. Of these three stories, Genesis 2 alone has a God who backtracks, sees, retreats, recreates, and evolves in relation to new contexts, providing much synchronicity to contemporary process theology. Indeed, one could argue that it lays the ground for God to have new ways of being, potential theogonies of God's existences in response to new contexts. However, God as it is written in the text of Genesis 2 does not have an origin.

Let us return now to my earlier question: what mythopoetic treatments of the cosmos (cosmogonies) are most efficacious to the work of queer/trans liberation? While Genesis is a complex text understood in different, even contradictory ways, there is nothing novel in pointing out that it has quite effectively been wielded to the detriment of queer and trans people. From "Adam and Eve not Adam and Steve" to smugly reasserting "male and female He created them" to the sanctification of marriage between men and women, the commandment to procreate, and the attribution of the Fall to Eve and her subsequent punishment of birth pangs, these texts have been used to enforce sexual and gendered rules and punish those who do not abide by them. The charge to Adam of dominion over the Earth, while inspiring many devout readers to protect the environment, for many others with power, money, and ammunition, it is used as justification to exploit the Amazon, dig for oil, sell and enslave people to till the land, expand empires by stealing land and murdering Indigenous populations. The order established in Biblical cosmogonies has been deployed to justify a cosmos where under God is (white, straight, cis) Man, and under him all other people, the animals, the plants, the Earth itself. A cosmology rises throughout history that has been forged by gender essentialism, empire, racism, and conquest which sets a singular God and theomorphic Man above and *against* the world. Such a cosmology benefits the few, and, needless to say, that one percent does not include queer/trans people. Rather, it justifies our oppression.

Christian feminist theologian Sallie McFague writes in *The Body of God* that theologians must work "toward a unified view of reality, one in which theology is done in the context of and contributes to the picture of reality current in our time. Such a unified view would give us a functional cosmology, one in which we could understand where we belong [...] in the scheme of things as currently interpreted."[7] Theologians must respond to our contexts and shape them through proffering cosmological models. Cosmologies are highly ethical in that specific relationships and orderings determine specific etiquette. How we, worlds and bodies both, come into being informs how we be with one another. Importantly, McFague uses the word "functional," which implies one cosmological model need not be exhaustive or complete to the exclusion of others. Rather, there is a range of models that speak to our contexts and formations, and as theologians invested in liberation, some cosmological models may function for our purposes better than others. If the "scheme of things as currently interpreted," a current reality, includes the cultural, political, and physical assault on queer/trans populations and the struggle for our liberation, then we need functional cosmological models that account for our culture, politics, and bodies.

From here and into the next chapter, I will delve into cosmological creativity, or cosmopoetics, for queer/trans folks. This chapter begins by defining a dialectic of mythopoetic production between allegorization and remythification. We will then see how this dialectic is at play throughout the cosmogony of Genesis and the mythopoetic response of gnostic retellings of creation from the ordered, symmetrical, and authorized Priestly narrative to the multitudinous and erring-God Yahwist remythification. I argue that these gnostic texts both remythify Genesis and act as a form of mythopoetic criticism in order to expose and undermine hegemonic cosmologies. Using the work of Celene Lillie and Jonathan Cahana-Blum, I suggest that gnostic

---

7   Sallie McFague, *The Body of God: An Ecological Theology* (Minneapolis: Fortress Press, 1993), 40–41.

mythopoeia deploys theogonies to critique the God of Genesis and His presumption of an eternal, autonomous, and singular self, the "naturalness" and necessity of His gendered order, and the function of eros and sexuality in maintaining His illusory and oppressive world.

The gnostic myths reveal a cosmology of divine and human presumptions of singularity and selfhood in and against multiplicity, preserved through a system of gender essentialism and reproductive sexuality at the expense of other erotics. All three aspects of this oppressive cosmological model can be and have been particularly devasting toward queer/trans people. I will respond to the gnostic critique by offering one model of queer cosmos, an erotic worlding, that answers each of the highlighted critiques: the one over the many, gender as a static and hierarchical order, and sex as a reproductive scheme.

Both chapters weave ancient and postmodern discourses on eros, body, sex, gender, and world to explore what a liberational queer/trans cosmology might look like. Aspiring toward the multiple in myth, in possibility, in identity, the chapters combined are not intended as the be-all end-all of queer/trans cosmologies. They are not about replacing one monolithic "reality" with a another monolithic "reality." Together, they are intended as *one* exercise in queer cosmogonic and theogonic mythopeia. My hope is that they are playful and exploratory, and some will want to sojourn with me in this wacky, sticky, and erotic cosmos for a lifetime, and others will take up their own queer cosmopoetic projects. Now, let us begin!

The Mythographer's Dialectic

The cosmopoet, like any mythographer, exists in the middle of certain dialectics. As discussed in the first chapter, one dialectic is between the text, the author, and, crucially, the reader. Jauss writes: "The critic who judges a new work, the writer who conceives of his work in light of positive or negative norms of an earlier work, and the literary historian who classifies a work in its tradition […] are first simply readers before their reflexive relationship to literature can become productive again."[8] To write is to write in response. This is as true of myth as it of every other medium or genre. Amid producing and propagating texts that pursue a horizon of *particular* ends, for instance the liberation of queer and trans people, it is prudent to analyze how we read texts so that we can attempt certain reading strategies over others. This brings us to a second dialectic of importance for the current project.

Working in part with Jauss's term *remythisation,* professor of medieval literature Jeff Rider proposes the dialectic of allegorization and remythification, that is, "two kinds of response to myth [...] whose interplay sustains a myth, keeping it alive through time."[9] The first of these interpretive modes, allegorization, involves two moments:

> The first moment is the perception of the explanatory or paradigmatic power of a narrative — a recognition of it as myth. This general perception is followed, in a second moment, by the discovery and elaboration of a particular meaning. We move from a feeling that "this seems to mean something" to an assertion that "this means that." What permits us to move from the first moment to the second is the discovery or choice of a context and a code which will enable us to produce a meaning.[10]

When we read or hear a myth, like Genesis 1 and 2, we might recognize its "explanatory or paradigmatic" force and deduce that this is a myth. The second moment is the application of various codes based on our various contexts to interpret the text. For the Biblical accounts, we might deploy a lens of ministerial service to our community of worship, and thus read in the

---

[8] Hans Robert Jauss, *Toward an Aesthetic of Reception,* trans. Timothy Bahti (Minneapolis: University of Minnesota Press, 1982), 19.

[9] Jeff Rider, "Receiving Orpheus in the Middle Ages: Allegorization, Remythification and Sir Orfeo," *Papers on Language and Literature* 24, no. 4 (1983): 343.

[10] Ibid.

text lessons of meaning that speak to our congregational needs. We might use historical critical analysis in an attempt to understand the texts' meaning for their earliest audience. We might approach the text through postmodern literary analysis, Latin American liberation theology, rabbinic or midrashic discourse, an allegiance to the social gospel, an allegiance to the prosperity gospel, white feminism, Black feminism, anti-feminism, or any other code with its historical, ideological, and geographical context. Allegorization is the application of one of these codes to a myth to determine its "meaning." An allegory is a given interpretation.

Within the process of allegorization is an assertion of one context over another, even that only certain contexts and their codes can elucidate a myth's "true" meaning that allegorization

> asserts, at least implicitly, the general merit of the chosen context and code and their power to produce meaning and organize a body of narratives. To claim that a poem receives its best meaning — or its true meaning — when it is read in a particular context is at some level an attempt to annex or capture that poem for that context. The more texts a given context is able to explain and organize — annex and capture — the more powerful, comprehensive and valid it proves itself to be. Differences of opinion between critics about the meaning of a particular narrative are thus the concrete and punctual manifestations, the flash points, of a larger, more general conflict between critics over the most appropriate basic contexts and codes for the allegorization of texts.[11]

When we receive and thus interpret myths, we engage in a contest of contexts. Those with the most power — state, religious, or epistemic — have a greater say as to which allegories are fair game and which are not. As the horizon of interpretation is limited by the dominant reader's specific contextual codes, the myth undergoes allegorization, until only one allegory is

---

11 Ibid., 344.

allowed any claim to a meaning of a text. Indeed, we can think of heresy as the act of interpreting an allegory outside the scope of a dominant interpretive lens. Ideologies foment and are reflexively constituted by allegorizations.

> The assertion of the general validity — or perhaps even the universal validity — of an interpretational code and context effectively elevates that code and context to the level of ideology. It asserts that our way of making sense out of the things is best because it best corresponds to the reality of the texts. The proof? Our way of making sense out of things explains and organizes more texts, and does so in a better way, than yours. What makes this claim ideological is its more or less understood but unexpressed consequent, and we therefore legitimately have, or ought to have, more authority and power than you. To say that a text means this or that, then, is also to argue for the value of one or another interpretational context and code, one or another way of determining meaning and thinking about the world.[12]

A dominant power determines what we can read in a text. In turn, we draw allegories from a text that reflect a *more* dominating experience of world. A reader comfortable within that hegemony can easily access the hegemonic allegory and extrapolate its relationship to the hegemonic world. Meanwhile, someone who does not fit within a dominating population will discern allegories that do not reflect the dominant world. As such, the former interpreter will be recognized as brilliant for expertly relaying a meaning from a myth which correlates to an understanding of the world that all are familiar with, for even those oppressed by such a world's order must be familiar with the dominant rules. Meanwhile, the disadvantaged interpreter's allegory will come off as "otherworldly" to hegemonic audience, and force others alienated by hegemony to out themselves as somehow "other" if they validate the disadvantaged allegory.

---

12 Ibid., 344–45.

Therefore, while the former interpreter appears wiser, truer, or smarter with his privileged allegory, gaining status and thus more power, the latter interpreter will be perceived as foolish, stupid, crazy, or even dangerous, losing status and power. The former's interpretation fits in the dominant cosmology, the latter's does not.

However, we have only covered part of the dialectic. Where there is allegorization that makes myths' meaning more rigid, there is remythification that destabilizes any one allegory. Rider defines remythification as consisting of "two moments":

> Its starting point is an existing allegorization and an imaginative perception or intuitive projection of all the potential meaning which that allegorization necessarily denies or ignores. It then proceeds to a reelaboration of the allegorized material which moves beyond the allegorization and renders it inadequate. This remythification does not seek to imbue the material with a particular new meaning — this would in effect be but one more allegorization — but to make it more meaningful. It starts from a feeling that "this means more than just that" and produces a new narrative that "just means."[13]

When receiving one telling of a myth, the reader might feel such an initial telling is rigid or lacking, that there is more to the story. That is the first moment. The second moment is when the reader retells the story with an intention toward multiple meanings. This multiplicity of meaning is sought out in opposition to a tradition's rigid allegorization. So, while any creator hopes to create meaningful work, that is, work with more than one meaning, there are specific intentions of remythification:

> To the degree that there is a difference, it lies in the deliberate working against an interpretive tradition which is involved in remythification. Any author may of course write against

---

13 Ibid., 347.

such a tradition, but the power of that tradition is present to the author of a remythification in a particularly urgent way.[14]

The (re)mythographer is familiar with hegemonic interpretive traditions and actively works to expand beyond them, to disturb their foundations, and to imbue their singular allegories with multiplicity. With the dialectic, Rider concludes that

> remythization and allegorization are forever involved in a tug-of-war which might be described in terms of a struggle between freedom and authority or played out between the notions of multivocal, equivocal, and univocal. *Remythization is always subversive.* If it is successful, it undoes existing allegorizations and restores to the myth its full aura of provocative meaningfulness. It removes the myth from the context in which and for which allegorization has captured it and denies that that context and its attendant code have any particular power or merit as semiotic systems. It undoes the work that has been done, destroys an existing order and contests the ability of any context or code to comprehend and control the meaningfulness of myth.[15]

Remythification and allegorization affect every myth. A mythographer may be pulled toward one over the other but engages in both processes. A once radical myth might, through transhistorical processes of allegorization, become rigid and authoritarian. Meanwhile, a myth that once served oppression could be exploded through remythification, not only in offering one liberating allegory, but in empowering a diversity of allegories so that multiple identities, meanings, and worlds are possible. We will now see how this dialectic is at play in the Genesis cosmogony.

---

14 Ibid.
15 Ibid., 348. Emphasis added.

Myths Destabilizing Myths: Dueling Geneses

The creation myths of Genesis 1 and 2 are fraught with allegorization and remythification. The very form of dueling and contradictory creation narratives placed back-to-back implies an appreciation, on behalf of the first redactors, for the multiplicity of meaning ascribed to remythification. On the other hand, by placing the two stories together, comparisons between the two can be highlighted, and with those certain allegories shine out and against other allegories that would be more apparent if the stories were kept separate. In the reception history of the Bible in the West, 1 and 2 are often retold as one, as consistent, as 1 seamlessly leading into 2 and 2 into the Fall in 3. Of the many allegorizations the text has been subjected to, one of the most rigid and authoritarian allegorizations concerns gender dimorphism and the heterosexual matrix. Queer Biblical scholarship on the Genesis creation narratives can highlight the processes of remythification and allegorization as they relate to dominant sexual and gendered contextual codes.

In his chapter in *Take Back the Word: A Queer Reading of the Bible,* Biblical scholar Ken Stone explores how "the structure and content of [the Genesis] accounts makes them especially attractive as rhetorical supports for the heterosexual contract."[16] Deploying Monique Wittig's "heterosexual presumption," Stone writes that different cultures "(including those that produced the Bible) have valorized the sexual relation between women and men, especially in terms of its reproductive potential, and have stigmatized to varying degrees other forms of sexual contact."[17] This valorization of opposite-sex relationships necessitates that there are two sexes and genders, which are essentially opposites of each other, and that those two sex or genders, for the sake of order, are also complementary. The challenge those of us who

---

16 Ken Stone, "The Garden of Eden and the Heterosexual Contract," in *Take Back the Word: A Queer Reading of the Bible,* eds. Robert Goss and Mona West (Cleveland: Pilgrim Press, 2000), 59.
17 Ibid., 58.

do not love according to the heterosexual contract or who do not fit into its essentialist gender binary is the text's naturalization of its ideology by attributing it to God. Queer and trans readers of the mythology might focus on homoerotic themes or explicit condemnations of sexual otherness, yet

> once the binary sexual division of humanity is attributed to God and located at the moment of the creation of humankind, endless arguments over the explicit biblical attitude toward homoeroticism can appear to be somewhat beside the point. The emphasis can now fall, not so much upon the occasional biblical condemnation of same-sex sexual activity, but rather upon the divine imperative to have sexual relations with the opposite sex. [...] What is important is that the Bible does promote, naturalize, and sanctify a particular "obligatory social relationship between 'man' and 'woman.'"[18]

The code of the heterosexual contract delineates which allegories can be read within the myths and that the myths are allegorized with sexual dimorphism in mind. But Stone highlights the contradictions and holes that arise from the inclusion of two different texts. While the Priestly text of Genesis 1 almost seamlessly supports the heterosexual contract, the Yahwist text of Genesis 2 is more ambiguous. Stone approaches the Yahwist text with "a reading that focuses upon the instability and incoherence of this textual foundation," adding: "While such a rereading can never turn Genesis into a queer manifesto, it may reveal potential openings for queer contestation of the heterosexual contract or, in any case, of biblical justifications given for that contract."[19]

Genesis 1 presents God "as the creator of an orderly cosmos."[20] Sexual dimorphism is part of that order: "The priestly creation account notes at the first appearance of humanity its two-

---

18 Ibid., 58–59.
19 Ibid., 59.
20 Ibid.

fold sexual division [...]. The binary sexual differentiation of humankind seems, therefore, to be part of God's orderly cosmos from the beginning."[21] If, at this point, the emergence of two sexes does not necessarily dictate heterosexual relationships, what immediately follows is God's commandment to "be fruitful and multiply, and fill the earth and subdue it; and have dominion over the fish of the sea and over the birds of the air and over every living thing that moves upon the earth."[22] I agree with Stone that while the "commandment is concerned with procreation and not with sexual ethics, [...] sexual intercourse between males and females is obviously presupposed."[23] I also add that the imperative of procreation does not only reproduce human generations but also the very order of the world. God commands humanity to be in a relationship of dominance to animals and plants.[24] Human procreation is therefore a part of cosmic perpetuation, for without the important cog of humans, themselves ordered by complementary sexual dimorphism, the machine of light and darkness, sky and water, land and sea, and especially plant and animal will be missing a key component: their herders, protectors, farmers, exploiters, and consumers.[25]

It is important to acknowledge that we cannot fully know the Priestly author's initial intent. But when we look at the readership, that is, the text's history of reception, it becomes apparent how easily Genesis 1 "lends itself to interpretations that valorize the relation between woman and man and make that relation key to the understanding of human ontology and vocation."[26] Stone points to two very different readers of Genesis 1 who nevertheless see the centrality of Creation's sexual dimorphism in human ontology. The first is Karl Barth, who "seizes upon the fact that human binary sexual division is juxtaposed in Genesis 1:27 with

---

21 Ibid.
22 Gen. 1:28 (NRSV).
23 Stone, "The Garden of Eden," 59–60.
24 Gen. 1:28 (NRSV).
25 For more on this, see Ken Stone, *Reading the Hebrew Bible with Animal Studies* (Stanford: Stanford University Press, 2017).
26 Ibid., 60.

an affirmation that human beings are created in the image of God. Thus, [...] Barth can imply a direct link between these two, arguably distinct, phenomena: sexual dimorphism and the image of God."[27] Barth looks to Genesis to justify conservative gender roles and to decry the "malady called homosexuality."[28] Coming at Genesis from a very different angle, is feminist biblical scholar Phyllis Trible who, by "taking her reader through a consideration of parallelism, tenor, and metaphor," concludes "from Genesis 1:27 that 'male and female' is the finger pointing to the image of God."[29] Trible appeals to the "male and female" toward the goal of "constructing non-patriarchal communities of faith, a goal that [Stone and I] share. Yet it has to be recognized that Trible's argument veers perilously close to the rhetoric of 'gender complementarity' that is so often used in support of heterosexist positions."[30] Allegorization from the Priestly mythographer as well as allegorization from the transhistorical readership of the mythic text, instill in the text's readers, even in readers with opposing ideological commitments, a profound allegory of sexual dimorphism and heterosexual complementarity.

Transitioning to his analysis of Genesis 2, Stone introduces the work of queer theorist and feminist philosopher Judith Butler:

> If Wittig's work encourages us to look with suspicion at biblical texts that undergird the heterosexual contract, Butler's work encourages us to focus upon instabilities and ambiguities in those texts, instabilities and ambiguities that might represent weak spots in the biblical foundation of the het-

---

27 Ibid., 61.
28 Karl Barth, *Church Dogmatics*, vol. 3, part 4: *The Doctrine of Creation*, eds. G.W. Bromiley and T.F. Torrance, trans. A.T. Mackay et al. (London: T&T Clark International, 1961), 166.
29 Stone, "The Garden of Eden," 61.
30 Ibid.

erosexual contract and, hence, openings for a queer contestation.[31]

Stone deploys Butler to show that even the dominating gender binary which forms us can be contested and that a close analysis of the Yahwist text points to this fragility.

The Yahwist account begins in Genesis 2:4b. God has created the earth and the sky but there are no animals or plants. Furthermore, there is no one to care for the land. After a river bursts through the land, "the Lord God formed *adam*[32] from the dust of the ground and breathed into his nostrils the breath of life; and *adam* became a living being."[33] Then God creates Eden:

> And the Lord God planted a garden in Eden, in the east; and there he put [*adam*] whom he had formed. Out of the ground the Lord God made to grow every tree that is pleasant to the sight and good for food, the tree of life also in the midst of the garden, and the tree of the knowledge of good and evil.[34]

---

31 Ibid., 62–63.
32 The New and Revised Standard Version translates the Hebrew *adam* into "man," and I have chosen to retain *adam*. Translation of *adam* into "the man" obscures the ambiguity of the Hebrew. The footnote in the NRSV names the wordplay: the Hebrew *adam* and *adamah* (arable land) signify "the relation of humankind to the soil from which it was formed" (13). *Adam* as opposed to "the man" also blurs whether adam is a name or if it is a class of creature. Additionally, *adam's* gender is contested. Trible translates *adam* as "earth creature" and that "this creature is not identified sexually" and that "grammatical gender (*adam* as a masculine word) is not sexual identification" (80). Stone notes how Trible's translation "coheres in certain respects with the interpretations of early Jewish readers" (65). "In the hour when the Holy One created the first human, He created him [as] an androgyne/androginos." Bereishit Rabbah 8:1, trans. Sefaria Community Translation, *Sefaria,* https://www.sefaria.org/Bereishit_Rabbah.8?lang=bi&with=all&lang2=en. I will discuss the potential androgyny further when my focus turns to gnostic appropriations of the Adamic myth.
33 Gen. 2:7 (NRSV).
34 Gen. 2:8–9 (NRSV).

God creates Eden and delegates His forming the world by putting *adam* "in the garden of Eden to till it and keep it."[35] This is not laborious and brutal work but something very different, since Eden, as Trible emphasizes, is "a place of delight," adding that "the Hebrew word *'eden'* recalls the sound of another Hebrew word meaning enjoyment."[36] In this pleasurescape, *adam* has all the plants to eat from, save only the tree of life and the tree of the knowledge of good and evil. But amidst this pleasure, something is lacking. *Adam* is lonely. Observing this, God says: "It is not good that *adam* should be alone; I will make him a helper as his partner."[37] God proceeds to make the animals out of the earth, and, for the second time, delegates some of His power to *adam*, by letting *adam* name the animals. Still, none of these animals are the right fit for *adam*. Finally, God

> caused a deep sleep to fall upon [*adam*], and he slept; then he took one of [*adam*'s] ribs and closed up its place with flesh. And the rib that the Lord God had taken from [*adam*] He made into a woman and brought her to [*adam*].[38]

Awaking to the companion, *adam* spurts out a poem with ecstatic joy:

> This at last is bone of my bones
> and flesh of my flesh;
> this one shall be called Woman,
> for out of Man[39] this one was taken.[40]

---

35 Gen. 2:15 (NRSV).
36 Phyllis Trible, "A Love Story Gone Awry," in *God and the Rhetoric of Sexuality* (Minneapolis: Fortress Press, 1978), 79–80.
37 Gen. 2:18 (NRSV).
38 Gen. 2:21–22 (NRSV).
39 Here is the first sexually specific term for him who was once *adam*: the Hebrew word *ish*. From here on, I will use Adam as the proper name for this newly created *ish* and continue to use *adam* when referring to the ambiguous creature of Gen. 2 who exists before the act of sexual differentiation.
40 Gen. 22:3 (NRSV).

Following the poem is an etiology — "Therefore a man leaves his father and his mother and clings to his wife, and they become one flesh"[41] — and a picture of Adam and Eve at the conclusion of this chapter, that "the man and his wife were both naked, and were not ashamed."[42] In contrast to the Priestly account:

> No procreative purpose characterizes this sexual union; children are not mentioned. [...] Beginning with the one flesh of the earth creature followed the creation of two sexual beings from it: woman and man. From one comes two; from wholeness comes differentiation. [...] [T]his differentiation returns to wholeness; from two come the one flesh of communion between male and female. Thus is Eros consummated.[43]

According to Trible, this story is about the origin of *eros*, or at least the origin of desire between two humans. Of course, these two humans are of "opposite" sexes. The heterosexual matrix determines the dimorphism of the players, but the ambiguity of the myth lies in an erotics that does not name or show any interest in reproduction. While the text can be "a sort of explanation for the origins of opposite-sex marriage, an attempt to explain and perhaps justify that institution by narrating the way in which it came into existence," there are "certain features of [it] that make its support for the heterosexual contract somewhat more problematic."[44]

Both the narrative of Genesis 2, which ends with love, and Genesis 3, when it all crumbles, can be read as expanding on the Priestly account:

> So God created humankind in his image,
> in the image of God he created them;
> male and female he created them.[45]

---

41 Gen. 2:24 (NRSV).
42 Gen. 2:25 (NRSV).
43 Trible, "A Love Story Gone Awry," 104.
44 Stone, "The Garden of Eden," 62.
45 Gen. 1:27 (NRSV).

The Priestly account does not describe the *how* of God's creation. It naturalizes the male and the female by refusing any prehistory to sexual dimorphism. The Yahwist account *does* imagine a before to the male and the female. It tells a story where the gender binary is not determined at every moment. A possibly androgynous *adam* is eventually split into Man and Woman, and while their genitals — we might presume, although the details elude the text — fit the heterosexual aesthetics' complementarity, the absence of a procreative impulse or commandment belies an obvious conclusion about their genders and sexuality. Sex is about *eros*; difference is about the pleasures of being two entities in friendship fluctuating into fleshy oneness and back again.

Reproduction, which helps substantiate the heterosexual contract, only appears in the Yawhist account as part of Adam and Eve's disobedience. Once Eve, egged on by the serpent, eats the fruit of the tree of knowledge and offers some to Adam, who likewise eats, then and only then are the details of sexual difference expanded on, hierarchized, and explicitly tied to reproduction. God curses Eve:

> I will greatly increase your pangs in childbearing;
> in pain you shall bring forth children,
> yet your desire shall be for your husband,
> and he shall rule over you.[46]

Reproduction is only mentioned as part of a woman's life as a curse. Reproduction will be painful. Eve's desire for her husband is another consequence, and, as Stone suggests, "a reader might very well conclude that heterosexual desire on the part of the woman is a consequence of — or even punishment for — the woman's misdeeds rather than an original component of her nature."[47] Finally, God will make man rule over woman, illustrating another disruption of the peace and pleasure found at

---

46 Gen. 3:16 (NRSV).
47 Stone, "The Garden of Eden," 63.

the end of Genesis 2, a movement from two parts becoming one flesh to two entities being thoroughly delineated as separate. The text is in tension with a heterosexual context, at least one that is presumed to necessarily have been here from the beginning.

Stone articulates the tension of the Yahwist story as relating to its etiological form, as "it is precisely the goal of this text [...] to buttress the heterosexual contract by sketching the etiology of 'humanity as male and female.'"[48] Stone continues:

> In order to do this, the Yahwist text — in distinction from the priestly account — attempts to speak about a moment prior to the establishment of binary sexual difference, but it does so from an ideological position [...] that both presupposes and promotes compulsory heterosexuality and patriarchy. It is this difficult project of trying to imagine a moment before the establishment of an institution — the heterosexual contract — which is nevertheless everywhere presupposed, that leads the Yahwist to formulate a text with interpretive problems that continue to vex readers to the present day.[49]

Part of the power of the Priestly text is that *there is no process of becoming gendered.* Gender is prediscursive. Here only God, the creator, speaks. Only God acts. The Yahwist story is still trying to explain why sex or gender and sexuality are the way they are, quite possibly to show that heterosexuality is the way it is and cannot be changed. However, this account has multiple agents who act and change their various courses. Nothing is predetermined here: not sex, not gender, not a cosmic order. Even if the Yahwist text so often is read as supporting the heterosexual contract, it is "riven with tensions and contradictions, problems of logic that cannot be completely resolved."[50]

Considering the redactors of the Pentateuch in light of the mythographer's dialectic, we might determine that the Yah-

---

48 Ibid., 66.
49 Ibid.
50 Ibid., 65.

wist account resists allegorization to a higher extent than the Priestly text. Its inconsistencies are inconsistencies of singular meaning.[51] By placing this myth right after the Priestly myth, the Biblical redactors engage in a process of remythification. Stone suggests "that an appropriate 'queer' response to this text is, not to resolve the tensions and contradictions, but rather to emphasize them."[52] I follow that this is also an appropriate stance for the mythographer. For any of us who seek to remythify a text so it both disrupts an oppressive meaning and allows for a multiplicity of meanings, we can look at the curation of these stories as one example.

At the same time, we must be honest in assessing the ebbs and flows of allegorization and remythification. There is significant political, religious, and social power behind the allegorization that gives dominance to the allegory of heterosexuality and sexual dimorphism. Still, we can follow Stone's train of thought:

> If we are able to contest what Butler calls "the regulatory fiction of heterosexual coherence" by showing that the rhetorical foundations of this fiction — including the supposed biblical foundations — are never quite so coherent as we have been led to believe, we may open up spaces for the production of alternative queer subjects of religious and theological discourse.[53]

---

[51] Admittedly, my presentation of Genesis 1 is quite reductive. Complications to my argument include that *elohim* is a plural noun and that the waters and chaos exist before God speaks. Agency and animacy are not necessarily as straightforward (or even just straight!) as I have presented. See Catherine Keller, *Face of the Deep: A Theology of Becoming* (London: Routledge, 2003); Ellen Bernstein, *Splendor of Creation: A Biblical Ecology* (Cleveland: Pilgrim Press, 2005); and Zairong Xiang, *Queer Ancient Ways: A Decolonial Exploration* (Earth: punctum books, 2018). The continued mythic resonance of Genesis 1 for ecologists, theorists, clergy, and artists of all sorts of backgrounds proves that no allegorization of the scripture, including the present interpretation, is total.

[52] Stone, "The Garden of Eden," 67.

[53] Ibid., 68.

As queer readers of myth, we must expose the holes in heterosexual coherence. We can open these incongruities through critical analysis, and we can do this task through remythification. In telling stories that respond to their narrative predecessors by resisting allegorization, we open the horizons of our fictions, and in turn, the horizons of our possibilities. Since white imperialist heteropatriarchy is an insidious and potent force, our art will constantly be under fire from allegorization, and our myths can be turned against us in the ways that they are interpreted and retold. Not only must we be prolific in our mythopoetic dialogues, we must refuse any attempt at a singular, dominant queer mythology.

Ken Stone opens small gaps within the texts of Genesis 1–3. He deploys a critical scholarship strategy of using the texts' own incoherences to attack their ideology. Each of the gaps he points to becomes a fruitful space for other allegories to be interpreted, other myths to be told. But what might these other myths be? What fills the gaps of the biblical narrative? Some of the most profound mythopoetic responses to Genesis can be found in heretical gnostic texts from the Nag Hammadi library. Indeed, what we have seen in the analysis of Genesis, is that the Yahwist account opens gaps in the heterosexual contract by showing that "male and female" has not always been the case but is in fact the result of a process, and in that space of becoming we can imagine and strive for becoming something else. The gnostic texts we will look at take this mythopoetic denaturalizing of sexuality and gender a step further by supplying not only an origin myth to humans and the world but to the worldmaker Himself.

Gnostic Remythification: In the Beginning, God

The gnostic canon is huge, wily, and debated. As part of a primarily theological and mythopoetic project, this section *will not* enter the discussion of classification and historical categories and heretical sects. That is a task better suited for scholars of the ancient Mediterranean, for philologists, and historians of Early Christianity. I will also not be discussing all or most of the so-called gnostic texts from the Nag Hammadi. There simply are too many. Rather, I will look at three texts,[54] *The Secret Book of John*, *The Nature of the Rulers*, and *On the Origin of the World*, as examples of gnostic mythopoeia, and explore how gnostic remythification exposes and disturbs the gendered, sexual, and cosmic allegories of the Genesis myth. In addition, I will incorporate recent scholarship by Cahana-Blum, who argues for gnosticism as a kind of ancient critical cultural theory, and Celene Lillie, who shows how the gnostic Genesis retellings critique an alliance between sexual violence and subjugation at the hands of the dominating culture that was the Roman Empire.

The title for Cahana-Blum's book *Wrestling with Archons* plays with a definition of cultural studies by one of the founders of the discipline, Stuart Hall. "Hall likens cultural studies to 'wrestling with angels,' […] stressing that this is a 'metaphor you can take as literally as you like,' and that 'metaphors are serious things. They affect one's practice.'"[55] Cahana-Blum suggests this is paralleled in the gnostic texts, which not only struggle with but are suspicious of angels — or in gnostic terminology, *archons* — both in very literal and metaphorical senses. Cahana-Blum writes:

> Who are these angels (or archons) we are struggling with? In a nutshell, it may refer to any cultural authority or concept that aims to explicate or […] naturalize a localized and specific situation as "true," "real," "universal," or "benign," whether as this situation actually is or as it should be. In other words, the struggle is against the concepts or narra-

---

[54] The texts I am working with belong to a subcategory of gnosticism called Sethianism, a body of work rooted in the Jewish tradition of Sophia or Wisdom that puts a particular emphasis on the creation stories and the saviors of humanity Seth (male) and Norea (female). For further reading, see John D. Turner, "The Sethian School of Gnostic Thought," in *The Nag Hammadi Scriptures*, ed. Marvin Meyer (New York: HarperOne, 2007), 784–89.

[55] Jonathan Cahana-Blum, *Wrestling with Archons: Gnosticism as a Critical Theory of Culture* (Lanham: Lexington Books, 2018), 50.

tives that appear invincible by masquerading as prediscursive: if something is "natural" it cannot be argued against but must serve as the very premise for argumentation. But this is exactly what critical theories of culture refuse to do.[56]

Gnostic texts poke holes in the narratives of our world, our gods, and ourselves that we presume are true. Gnostics critique the mytho-historical and theological premises of their inherited traditions. The strategy they employ is to "dismantle an overall system of mass deception by underscoring how and to whose benefit this system functions."[57] In other words, gnostic texts are in the business of pointing out that one, there is an emperor and, two, he is not wearing any clothes. And they do this "through the vehicle of myth."[58] Their myths begin where cultural criticism also first proceeds, with "the deconstruction of the most naturalized premises, including the premise of the very independent or prediscursive existence of 'nature,' and 'the natural.'"[59]

In the Elohist creation, God, without an origin and eternal, creates humans as male and female. There is no human before male or female, which is to say no process of humans becoming sexually dimorphic, and humans are ordained as such from the start and have never been otherwise. In contrast, when the Yahwist elaborates on "male and female he created them" through an etiological story, other possibilities of desire and embodiment can be glimpsed. Man and woman—the ways they are differentiated from each other in body, society, and desire—are discursive processes. Androgyny precedes dimorphism, *eros* exists beyond a reproductive commandment, and gender roles are the consequences of agents, actions, and events, implying that other agents, actions, and events may lead to different results. So, even if it does not undermine the authority of the heterosexual contract, the Yahwist account *does* undermine its

---

56 Ibid.
57 Ibid., 52.
58 Ibid., 2.
59 Ibid., 50.

presumed "naturalness." Gnostic retellings of Genesis similarly and more explicitly deconstruct these sexual and gendered presumptions. Even more distinctly from either the Elohist or the Yahwist, the gnostic texts also attack the "naturalness" of God. By providing complex theogonies wherein the creator God is himself a result of actions and events, the gnostic texts resist a prediscursive deity who creates the cosmos.

The Secret Book of John begins with the apostle John being told off by a Pharisee for having abandoned traditional teachings. Disturbed by this interaction, John asks his Savior several questions pertaining to human purpose, cosmology, and salvation, and the question of how the Savior was chosen. The heavens open to John, and light fills the scene. John describes the light:

> I saw within the light (someone standing) by me. As I was looking, it seemed to be an elderly person. Again it changed its appearance to a youth. Not that there were several figures before me. Rather, there was a figure with several forms within the light. These forms were visible through each other, and the figure had three forms.
>
> The figure said to me, "John, John, why are you doubting? Why are you afraid? Aren't you familiar with this figure? Then do not be fainthearted. I am with you always. I am (the Father), I am the Mother, I am the Child. I am the incorruptible and the undefiled one. (Now I have come) to teach you what is, what (was), and what is going to come."[60]

The Savior-being that appears to John is one figure and multiple figures, a being that is light and beings within light, an entity that contains multiple relationships and genders. Only such a being can speak truly on the nature of heaven, in this gnostic text, because, as we will see, its complex simultaneity of being

---

60 *The Secret Book of John,* trans. Marvin Meyer, in *The Nag Hammadi Scriptures,* ed. Marvin Meyer (New York: HarperOne, 2007), 108. Parentheses in original.

singular and many is representative of the heavenly realm. The light tells John about the One, who is "a sovereign that has nothing over it [who] is God and Parent, Father of the All, the invisible one that is over the All, that is incorruptible, that is pure light at which no eye can gaze."[61] At first this description implies an all-powerful, prediscursive deity in line with Genesis. All this talk of incorruptibility and sovereignty resonates with the demiurge of Plato's *Timaeus* who "was good, and [since] nothing good is ever characterized by mean-spiritedness over anything; being free of jealousy, he wanted everything to be as similar to himself as possible."[62] However, the similarities dissolve here. The text immediately says of the One "we should not think of it as a god or like a god," nor does the One need to create a world since "it has never lacked anything in order to be completed," for everything "exists within it."[63] The One is the All, or at least contains the All, and in no way requires a division of the One's self — does it have a self? — in order to create something to rule over. The text continues to apply a series of negations to describe the one: "illimitable," "unfathomable," "immeasurable," "invisible," "unutterable," and "unnamable."[64] Though called the One, it is referred to consistently in non-dualistic ways, and the One is not "just perfection, or blessedness, or divinity," but it is also those things. Furthermore: "The One is not corporeal and it is not incorporeal," and it "is not large and it is not small."[65] Nondualist, the One is not an incorporeal agent against corporeal matter but contains both and is neither, a radical distinction from a deity who is incorporeal and affects the corporeal. Finally, before transitioning to the mytho-historical origin of our world, the texts layer another complexity on top of what is already so complex, that is, the One is a realm:

---

61 Ibid.
62 Plato, *Timaeus*, in *Timaeus and Critias*, trans. Robin Waterfield (Oxford: Oxford University Press, 2008), 29e.
63 *The Secret Book of John*, 108.
64 Ibid., 108–9.
65 Ibid., 109.

> The One is a realm that gives a realm,
> Life that gives life.⁶⁶

The One has now been described in ambiguous terminology of the light, as the good, blessed, and divine through a series of negations, through nondualist comparisons, and now through the spatial descriptor of the realm. Indeed, the One is a body, not a body, and more than a body — a place, not a place, beyond all places. Additionally, the One can create and does give life, although this genesis is distinct from a genesis that is enacted on an "other" and an "elsewhere." The One gives other life and creates other realms, but these are not separate from the One. It is a kind of autogenesis. The eternity of the One, as we shall see, resists an eternity that implies stasis. That the One "gives" implies a certain movement. Even if it is complete, it is composed of various entities who, through their movements and relationships, constitute the One.

There is a multiplicity to the One, indeed the realm metaphor is employed to help us visualize the seeming paradox of the One's plurality. Within the realm of One are multiple agents who are the One and yet are named specifically. The first is the Father

> who beholds himself in the light surrounding him, which is the spring of living water and provides all the realms.⁶⁷ He

---

66 Ibid.
67 The image of the father looking in the pool is an allusion to Narcissus. As Ovid tells it:
> [Narcissus] is stricken by the sight
> he sees — the image in the pool. He dreams
> upon a love that's bodiless: now he
> believes that what is but a shade must be
> a body. And he gazes in dismay
> at his own self; […]
> in sum, he now is struck with wonder by
> what's wonderful in him. Unwittingly,
> he wants himself; he praises, but his praise
> is for himself; he is the seeker

reflects on his image everywhere, sees it in the spring of the Spirit,[68] and becomes enamored of his luminous water, (for his image is in) the spring of pure luminous water surrounding him.[69]

This brings us to another being within the One, Barbelo. The Father's thought becomes "a reality, and she who appeared in his presence […] is the first power who preceded everything and came forth from [the Father's] mind as the Forethought of All."[70] At this point we have three entities designated as existing within and helping to comprise the One, that is, the Father, the Spirit — the pool the Father gazes into — and Barbelo. Barbelo is similar to others since she "shines like the Father's light," and is made in "the image of the Perfect and Invisible Virgin Spirit."[71] And what is the image like? Barbelo is described as

the Mother-Father,
the first Human,
the holy Spirit,
the triple male,
the triple power,
the androgynous one with three names,
the aeon among the invisible beings,
the first to come forth.[72]

---

and the sought, the longed-for and the one who longs. (Ovid, *Metamorphoses*, III.94)

Ovid highlights the tragedy of Narcissus's self-love, which eventually keeps him stuck at the pool, wanting himself but unable to consummate his desire. Narcissus's autoerotics are reconfigured in *The Secret Book of John* as the Father's, but while the former's eros leads to an unquenchable desire, the latter's autosexuality leads to the emergence of a new entity: Barbelo, the Forethought.

68 This spirit is another entity within the realm that is the One.
69 *The Secret Book of John*, 110.
70 Ibid.
71 Ibid.
72 Ibid.

Barbelo reflects the nondualism of the light in two newly demarcated ways: she is mother, and she is father. She is human, and she is spirit. Barbelo is the "universal womb"[73] and is yet associated with maleness and the Father. And again, these characters act and create. Barbelo asks the Spirit for the entities Foreknowledge, Incorruptibility, Life Eternal, and Truth, and each time Spirit consents to produce the beings with her. Foreknowledge, Incorruptibility, Life Eternal, and Truth with their progenitor Barbelo are "the five aeons of the Father," that is, "the five androgynous aeons, which are the ten aeons."[74] An aeon is a personality, or an emination, of divinity. Each aeon is double sexed, both a singular and a double entity, and the five or ten aeons are also the Father. They make up the One and are *of* the One. The One is synonymous with another gnostic term, πλήρωμα (*plēroma*). In Greek, pleroma means "fullness" or "that which fills," though I prefer the latter definition because it includes a subject ("that") and a verb ("fills"), and as we have seen, there is activity in this "fullness." Scholar of gnosticism, Gerard van Groningen, explains that pleroma

> is the fullness, the totality, the completeness of all things. From it all good has come, to it all good will return and be taken up completely in it. That what has come from it are the aeons and the "spiritual" seed in some of humanity. Indirectly, all evil has come from it also.[75]

Pleroma, as divinity, is not the origin of good alone but of all things, including evil. This is a distinction between pleroma and a model where the divine is good and evil is either a separate entity or an absence of good. In this definition of pleroma, Van Groningen challenges an assumption that many might bring to gnosticism that it is rigidly dualistic. The careful reader notes

---
[73] Ibid.
[74] Ibid., 111.
[75] Gerard van Groningen, *First Century Gnosticism: Its Origins and Motifs* (Leiden: Brill, 1967), 177.

that if the pleroma is the good, and what eventually will follow is the evil, evil still follows from the good. As we will see, evil, or whatever you might call what follows in this gnostic myth, is not apart from the good but rather, indirectly, is *a part* of it.

The "the spiritual seed" can also imply a spirit and matter binary, but this too is complicated. Van Groningen cautions us from reading the "spiritual realms" of the aeons outside of a mythological context that "deals with the physical, the natural, the material in an abstract manner," where "gods and goddesses are thought of in terms of the physical, the material and natural," and as "natural forces, conceived of as actually physically present."[76] Thus, Van Groningen continues:

> Gnosticism cannot be said to place a sharp and distinct cleavage between the spiritual and the physical because it basically is oriented only to the physical, which is thought of in two basic and fundamental ways: the good, ethereal, not earthbound material and the evil, earthy, restricted and restricted material.[77]

There is some consistency between cautioning a dualistic reading of gnosticism and the nondualist descriptors of the One we have already seen. At the same time, in the myth there will be a binary between the material pleroma and the material world. However, as we continue to move through *The Secret Book of John,* we might read this dualism not as prescriptive but as descriptive, and that "the evil" that is about to enter the picture is not an entity representing one half of a good–evil binary, but the idea itself of dualism. For we are about to encounter an entity that obsessively separates one kind of matter from another, presumes his own singular authority, obscures the multiplicity of human beings, and enacts systems of control that are fueled by binary, dualistic thinking.

---

76 Ibid.
77 Ibid., 178.

Barbelo and the Father conceive a Child, whom the Spirit delights in and anoints. The Child is called "the divine Self-Generated" — after all, these various entities are also the One — and is "set over everything" to organize the various realms.[78] The text continues to describe four realms in the pleroma, each governed by an angel, and within each realm abide three aeons. In the fourth realm are the aeons Perfection, Peace, and Sophia; from aeons Foreknowledge and Perfect Mind, ordained by the Spirit and the Self-Generated, came the first perfect human Pigeradamas, or "old Adam." Pigeradamas has a son, Seth, who is sent to the second realm. Seth has children, who are sent to the third realm, and there are more beings, who are ignorant of the pleroma, who are sent to abide with the aeons Perfection, Peace, and Sophia in the fourth realm. These relationships and offspring, and their placement, represent a harmony that is about to be breached by a distorted act of creation.

Sophia desires "to bring forth something like herself,"[79] but she does so without the knowledge or consent of the other entities of the pleroma, including the consent of the Spirit and the consent of the Father. However, being a powerful aeon, she autosexually gives birth: "Something came out of her that was imperfect and different in appearance from her[,] misshapen[,] [with] the figure of a snake with the face of a lion."[80] Seeing the monster she has created, Sophia casts "it away from her, outside the realm so that none of the immortals would see it."[81] Sophia puts her child, named Yaldabaoth, in a throne in the middle of a cloud, and only the Spirit has any knowledge of this creature's whereabouts.

Yaldabaoth is the demiurge, the God who makes the world! What a journey it has been to get to Him. Here is a much more complex, or should I say convoluted, road than that of God's simply presumed existence in Genesis. This narrative so thor-

---

78 *The Secret Book of John*, 112.
79 Ibid., 114.
80 Ibid., 115.
81 Ibid.

oughly removes the creator God from something that is natural, that must be, or that always has been. That of course does not stop Yaldabaoth from acting like he simply is and has always been. He is ignorant of his origin, but because his mother is Sophia, he has an incredible amount of power. And what does he do with it? He masturbates. His masturbation results in offspring, the rulers of our world, and these rulers follow Yaldabaoth and create their followers, what the Bible calls angels and the gnostic texts rechristen as archons.[82] Yaldabaoth organizes the realms within his cloud and sets the rulers in each realm, from the seven Heavens to the Abyss. Pleased with himself, Yaldabaoth exclaims to his creation, "I am God and there is no other beside me."[83] The irony of it all is that his creation is a replica of the pleroma, where those other "gods" reside:

> Yaldabaoth organized everything after the pattern of the first aeons that had come into being, so that he might create everything in an incorruptible form. Not that he had seen the incorruptible ones. Rather, the power that is in him, that he had taken from his mother, produced in him the pattern for the world order.[84]

The instinct to order the world in such a way contends the full autonomy that Yaldabaoth assumes he has. Something other than himself exists within him: the fire or the light, that is the generative power, of his mother. On some level, he doubts his godhood. He remembers his mother. He responds to this memory not with humility but a savage double-down on his illusory

---

82 The Greek word *archōn* (ἄρχων) means "ruler," and was used by different city-states as titles for a variety of governmental positions: sometimes a king and other times more like a governor or magistrate. The gnostic appropriation of the word as an alternative to "angel," implies that the so-called angels of Biblical stories are more akin to human politicians than truly divine entities, and like earthly leaders, susceptible to corruption, greed, and incompetence.
83 *The Secret Book of John*, 116.
84 Ibid., 117.

autonomy. He tells the angels, and all of creation, "I am a jealous god and there is no other god beside me."[85] But this utterance betrays his shaky claim that "by announcing this, he suggested to the angels with him that there is another god. For if there were no other god, of whom should he be jealous?"[86] Yaldabaoth creates a legion of followers and claims that he alone is the most powerful and that he is god. Yet he has memories of his mother and of an order that he can only half-replicate. He fears the multiplicity within himself and that precedes him, setting the stage for a constant struggle of his illusory and authoritarian autonomy against the multiplicitous interrelationships that comprise the pleroma.

The much shorter text, *The Nature of the Rulers*, corroborates this picture of the demiurge, here called Samael, and his delusional state:

> The leader of the authorities is blind. (Because of his) power, ignorance, and arrogance, he said, with (power), "I am God, there is no other (but me)."
>
> When he said this, he sinned against (the realm of the All). This boast rose up to Incorruptibility, and a voice answered from Incorruptibility and said, "You are wrong, Samael" — which means "blind god."[87]

The demiurge's assertion of his own singular godhood is lambasted even further in this account than in *The Secret Book of John:* immediately, a voice from the pleroma undermines Samael's ludicrous claim. Similarly, when the demiurge makes the same proclamation in *On the Origin of the World*, he sins "against all the immortals who speak forth, and they watched

---

85 Ibid.
86 Ibid.
87 *The Nature of the Rulers*, trans. Marvin Meyer, in *The Nag Hammadi Scriptures*, ed. Marvin Meyer (New York: HarperOne, 2007), 191.

him carefully."[88] Here, a voice from the pleroma not only ridicules the demiurge but foretells his downfall, saying:

> An enlightened, immortal human exists before you and will appear within the forms you have shaped. The human will trample upon you as potter's clay is trampled, and you will descend with those who are yours to your mother the abyss. And when your work comes to an end, all the deficiency that appeared from truth will be dissolved. It will cease to be, and it will be like what never was.[89]

As we read from *The Secret Book of John*, before the demiurge, there was the Self-Generated ideal human. This being of incredible power can and will, in *On the Origin of the World*, undo the demiurge's creation, a distorted simulacrum of the realms. While we have already discussed the ways in which the demiurge's own power proves that he is not one, alone, and omnipotent, as his power is borrowed or stolen from his mother and the realms, now the pleroma presents the demiurge with the human being, both a part and an emissary of the complex and shifting entities of the One. The human, reflecting primordial multiplicity, generativity, and power, becomes a foil to the demiurge who worships the illusion of his own self. The former undermines the latter's claim and will be his undoing. The three gnostic myths describe a complicated process of the ideal human being projected into the demiurge's creation, and then somehow the projection is trapped in the demiurge's earthly matter, but putting each text's details to the side, what is clear is that the human being is a threat to the creator. Humans prove that their "god" is proud, ignorant, and, above all, a construct, a being created in a process, and whose power and life are contingent on certain processes continuing. The demiurge must perform schemes of greater and greater subtlety and manipulation to keep humans

---

88 *On the Origin of the World*, trans. Marvin Meyer, in *The Nag Hammadi Scriptures*, ed. Marvin Meyer (New York: HarperOne, 2007), 206.
89 Ibid.

docile and alienated from their true powers. At the heart of the oppressive structures that the demiurge institutes are strict gender roles and the subjugation of eros to a heterosexual reproductivity.

Gnostic Remythification: Male and Female He Created Them/Be Fruitful and Multiply

Similar to *On the Origin of the World,* a voice calls out to the demiurge and the archons in *The Secret Book of John:*

> Humanity exists
> and the child of humanity.[90]

This proclamation is accompanied by a projection of light with the human inside of it onto the water of the world's abyss. The light, that is the power of this entity, incites Yaldabaoth's greed. He says to his archons, "let's create a human being after the image of God and with a likeness to ourselves, so that this human image may give us light."[91] The demiurge wants to create a human so that the human can give him power. This is a foolish idea because the demiurge already has this power, from his mother, but he is ignorant of the pleroma and the other aeons. Thus, he sets up a plot to acquire what he already has, and in the process he loses his mother's spark. The archons work to create a human being based on the image they see in the light. Each archon is assigned to create a different body part, and the list is extensive and detailed. There is an archon for everything from "molars" to "the left underarm" to "the navel," "the liver," "the left buttock," "the right buttock," "testicles," and "toenails."[92] Like the aeons, this human is also androgynous, containing both "the

---

90 Ibid., 118.
91 Ibid., 119.
92 Ibid., 119–21.

penis"[93] and a "the womb."[94] The archons "worked together until, limb by limb, the psychical and material body was completed," but "for a long time their creation did not stir or move at all."[95]

It is at this point in the story that Yaldabaoth's mother, Sophia, repents. She prays "to the most merciful Mother-Father of the All,"[96] and the Mother-Father, the androgynous aeon of the pleroma, sends into Yaldabaoth's mind a suggestion to "breathe some of your spirit into the face of Adam, and the body will rise."[97] Yaldabaoth, believing this is great advice to animate the archons' creation, does this. However, the Mother-Father has deceived the foolish god. Yaldabaoth breathes "his spirit into Adam," but it is not his spirit, this "spirit is the power of his mother."[98] So, the generative power that Yaldabaoth has, that spark from his mother and from the realms, exits his body and goes into Adam. Desiring power, the demiurge loses power. Adam awakens, and he is enlightened. The archons realize Adam is powerful and throw him into the darkest depths of the demiurgic world. The Mother-Father responds to this by sending a divine helper down to Adam, enlightened Insight or "Eve," to help him rise from the descent into darkness, teaching him once again about his powers. Frustrated, the archons then create another, cruder body out of the elements and trap the primordial Adam in it. However, enlightened Insight is also inside the material Adam and continues to reveal to him the truth. The archons place the new, trapped, and mortal Adam in the Garden of Eden and put him under "a deep sleep," meaning "a loss of sense."[99] Insight continues to resist the demiurge by hiding inside of Adam's body. The demiurge tries to capture her and take her out but fails to apprehend her. When this fails, He removes part of Adam's power by creating a female from him, in

---

93 Ibid., 121.
94 Ibid., 122.
95 Ibid., 124.
96 Ibid.
97 Ibid.
98 Ibid.
99 Ibid., 126.

the likeness of Insight. Adam is now male and this new figure, a material Eve, is female, and both are under the demiurgic spell of delusion, a literal magic sleep where they dream their false reality.[100] But once again, Insight comes to the rescue, removing "the veil that covered his mind"[101] and Eve's as well. Seeing that Insight is with Eve as well, Yaldabaoth attempts to seize her through sexual defilement. With the help of aeons, Insight leaves Eve's body, but Yaldabaoth does rape Eve. She conceives two sons, Yahweh and Elohim.[102] The text presents this story as an etiology for reproductive sex:

> To this day sexual intercourse has persisted because of the first ruler. He planted sexual desire within the woman who belongs to Adam. Through intercourse the ruler produced duplicate bodies, and he blew some of his false spirit into them.[103]

Yaldabaoth puts his own deluded, false, and wicked spirit into the human line, literally turning the human body and its descendants into a battlefield for the fight between his rule and that of the aeons.

Again, the gnostic narrative complexifies and rethinks the Genesis creation narrative in a new, more suspicious, light. Adam begins as an androgynous being but through a series of cat-and-mouse chases between Adam, Insight, and the demiurge, Adam is eventually split into two sexes. The demiurge uses this split to his own gain, employing reproduction as one of the tools for the perpetuation of his power. In plot, it is not the most

---

[100] It is a similar illusory world to that depicted in the Wachowskis' film *The Matrix*: what we mostly experience as "reality" is a dream created by a demiurge (analogous to the film's robots) who fears what we might do if we were cognizant of the "actual" state of our world and its rulers.
[101] Ibid., 127.
[102] An example of gnostic mythographers throwing shade at their source material: the two most prominent names of God in the Bible are repurposed for the ungodlike, illegitimate children of the demiurge.
[103] *The Secret Book of John*, 128.

removed from the Yahwist account, since a woman is cut out of the man, but its allegory has changed significantly. By applying a different contextual code to an event described in an earlier myth, this remythfication presents a gnostic allegory where *"marital* sex [...] is bad *because* of procreation."[104] Cahana-Blum elaborates:

> The agent of sexing is evil, and the act of division [...] is made in order to oppress humans and hide from them the truth regarding their origin. [...] At least as far as the regulated opposite-sex act is concerned, it is far from exhibiting the wish to become androgyne; it is instead the very place where sexual division blossoms.[105]

This said, I find it difficult to fully understand, just from reading *The Secret Book of John*, exactly how this division of the androgynous into two sexes perpetuates the demiurge's rule. It is helpful then to turn to an even more explicit denunciation of the gender binary that we get in *On the Origin of the World*. Here, Eve is similarly a divine agent sent to help Adam. She coaxes him to life. When the archons see Eve speaking to Adam, they say to one another:

> Who is this enlightened woman? [...] Come, let's seize her and ejaculate our semen into her, so that she may be unclean and unable to ascend to her light, and her children will serve us. But let's not tell Adam, because he is not one of us. Instead, let's put him to sleep and suggest to him in his sleep that Eve came from his rib, so that the woman may serve and he may rule over her.[106]

This retelling is as straightforward as a gnostic remythfication can be, and the Yahwist account of Eve being made from Adam's

---

[104] Cahana-Blum, *Wrestling with Archons*, 45.
[105] Ibid., 87.
[106] *On the Origin of the World*, 214.

rib is simply a false memory, a dream. This myth describes the demiurge as planting a false narrative in Adam's mind that Eve is somehow derivative of Adam, and that that makes Adam her superior. Here is an etiology of both gender and gender oppression. Cahana-Blum reflects: "Everything in this text is articulated in such a way as to lead one to the conclusion that gender is no less than an overarching conspiracy that is meant to enslave humans and serves only the evil creator god and his collaborators."[107]

Consider the meaning when the demiurge and the rulers attack Eve. Eve realizes what the rulers are about to do, and her response is to laugh at them. She then "blinded their eyes and secretly left something that resembled her with Adam."[108] Eve then enters the Tree of Knowledge. Still, the story is horrific. The rulers come to and find the shadow woman that Eve has left behind, and they gang rape her and "ejaculated their semen upon her" and "defiled the seal of her voice."[109] Celene Lillie puts forth two these reasons behind the ruler's actions in *On the Origins of the World:*

> It seems their purpose in raping her is to defile her in order to accomplish two things. The first is to prevent her from ascending to her light, that is, the divine realm, and the second, to make those born to Eve subject to the rulers, authorities, and angels.[110]

The violence of the demiurge is not only cruelty and lust but involves a long-term plan. He and the other rulers hope to anchor the woman to their realms by filling her with material semen. Secondly, they intend to use procreation to their advantage, in a similar way as described in *The Secret Book of John*. At

---

107 Cahana-Blum, *Wrestling with Archons*, 87.
108 Ibid.
109 Ibid., 215.
110 Celene Lillie, *The Rape of Eve: The Transformation of Roman Ideology in Three Early Christian Retellings of Genesis* (Minneapolis: Fortress Press, 2017), 213.

the same time, the description of the rulers' actions can also be read as an example of what gendering does, particularly in the creation of toxic masculinity.

Lillie, in *The Rape of Eve*, argues that these three gnostic myths critique the ties between sexual violence and conquest in the Roman empire. The rulers then are mythopoetic treatments of Roman authorities and, by extension, Roman masculinities. She writes of *On the Origin of the World*: "Eve is literally violated by all of the levels of the world's 'government,' exposing not only the violences perpetrated by individuals, but the exploitations, subjugation, and violence of the entire system and structure created by the rulers."[111] The rulers represent a system of suppression and violence. And while the shadow Eve and Adam are clearly the victims of this exploitative system, *On the Origin of the World* includes in the rape narrative that "the authorities and their angels erred. They did not know they defiled their own body and likeness in all these ways."[112] This is a confusing point from the text. The rulers attempt to control and demean an entity of divine worth when they attempt to attack Eve. But the shadow Eve is not the divine helper they seek to vanquish but a material simulacrum. In mating with the simulacrum, the rulers further demonstrate their own alienation from true divine power. At the same time, they perpetuate the line of Eve, that is humans, and they lose the remnants of their own divine origins through this copulation. Humans, like Eve, now contain the holy spark which the rulers have lost. If humans have a spark of divinity within them, that spark can be reawakened as knowledge of reality, which challenges the demiurge's power:

> [T]he one thing that the rulers are able to grasp, the earthly Eve, makes all that they wish to grasp forever ungraspable. Their act of violence in grasping and possessing the earthly Eve, raping her to create bodies that they hope to subjugate, becomes their undoing. [These] bodies become containers of

---

111 Lillie, *Rape of Eve*, 218.
112 *On the Origin of the World*, 215.

the light, conduits of enlightenment, unmasking the rulers and allowing humanity to see them as they truly are.[113]

Lillie discerns that these texts

> seem to be saying something very specific about the intersubjective nature of violence — that it reverberates back upon the one perpetrating it. Because of the claims of divine rule — where Yaldabaoth claims to be god, where emperors claim to be gods, where their sovereignty is seen as divine favor — these texts say that this is not true, and that eventually their own actions will be their undoing.[114]

I am inspired by Lillie's reading to return to Cahana Blum's to suggest that one violence the rulers do unto themselves parallels the violence they inflict on the human being: gendering.

Cahana Blum writes, "the gnostic *pleroma* presents us with a series of non-demarcated androgynous beings."[115] While crude, the demiurge and his minions are replicants of the aeons, and likewise have multiple sex characteristics. But they delude themselves into having a singular gender just like they delude Adam into thinking he is singularly man and has power over Eve, singularly woman. Despite his biology, the demiurge "is consistently portrayed as male, is consistently referred to by masculine pronouns, and acts as male — indeed he sometimes seems to be a parody of masculinity in his relentless and unsuccessful attempt to sexually molest every female figure he encounters."[116] The demiurge is at points a brutish parody and a sobering reflection of men in power. Such power is the conclusion of a gender binary and the heterosexual matrix, which serve patriarchy.

In proclaiming "I am God alone," the demiurge dishonors his multiplicitous allegiances and origins, effectively mutilating

---

113 Lillie, *Rape of Eve*, 223.
114 Ibid., 277.
115 Cahana-Blum, *Wrestling with Archons*, 80.
116 Ibid., 84.

himself from the source of his power. In a similar vein, he rejects his androgyny for a heightened and toxic masculinity, acting as if he was always gendered as such. He then tricks Adam into acting similarly, although Eve is constantly spoiling his plans. The demiurge hopes Adam will treat Eve as a subordinate object, as he himself treats his own creations. He hopes that this system of gender will facilitate an eros in Adam that functions like his lust and serves the expansion of his control. This is not what happens.

Later, in *On the Origin of the World,* Adam and Eve eat the fruit from the Tree of Knowledge:

> When they became sober [from the demiurgic spell]
> They saw they were naked
> And they fell in love.[117]

This love is a return, once again, to the love that has constantly been a part of Adam and Eve's relationship, since before either was gendered. Indeed, it reflects the mutuality of giving and blessing and generating among the aeons that make up the pleroma. It is also "a counterpoint and an alternative template to [Eve's] rape by the rulers."[118] Humans contain the seed of the One, are reflections of the One, and may one day return the One. And we uniquely can act within the plane of the demiurge. As Lillie writes:

> One of the ways in which the Genesis cosmogonies thwart the machinations of the rulers is by positioning Adam and Eve as embodied amalgams of the divine realm and the worldly rulers. While they are subject to the effects of the worldly rulers, they inhabit the trickster position — often through the aid of the divine realm.[119]

---

117 *On the Origin of the World,* 216.
118 Lillie, *Rape of Eve,* 230.
119 Ibid., 235.

When Adam and Eve assert power, it is in accepting their multiplicity and nondualism. They are able to act against the rulers directly because they exist in the rulers' realms, yet they are able to resist the rulers because they contain the power of Sophia. When Adam and Eve act together, they act as a simultaneously male and female, singular and plural, and reflect the harmonious, but nevertheless active, harmony of the pleroma.

However, not all humans act like the Adam and Eve attempt to do in these gnostic texts, otherwise the gnostic mythographer would be unnecessary. The oppression of women, and queer/trans people, in fact all forms of oppression that result from a power presuming his subjecthood against all other bodies, are testament to the control that the demiurge and his archons continue to hold. Patriarchy's ideologies are eerily alike demiurgic cosmology, prioritizing the maker or doer of matter over the material, the creator over the created, the one over the many, the gendered over the nonbinary, the male over the female, the ruler over his subjugated people. But in denaturalizing the creator God by giving him a theogonic myth, the gnostic remythifies Genesis, showing us where and how we might push for a new cosmology.

Challenging the Cosmos

Remythification rescribes multiplicity into a text and serves to denounce specific allegories, including those that support oppressive systems of power. The Priestly narrative, with its omnipotent deity, presents an ordered, symmetrical, authorized, and arguably authoritarian creation: a cosmos designed by the one true subject, God. Yet Yahwist remythification, with its many subjects, it's God who tries and errs and tries again, moves the story into the realm of the multiple. Finally, the gnostic remythifications of both Genesis texts highlight a cosmic tragedy, the transition from the nondualist realm of the pleroma to the rigidly dualist dominion of the demiurge with his obsession of self against the world and worldly creatures, binary gender, and the relegation of eros to reproductive heterosexuality. Each of the three "tragedies" of the demiurgic cosmos affect trans and queer people in unique ways. The static, eternal self either tells us that, in transitioning, we are too malleable, more matter than spirit, and can and should be treated as more temperamental and in need of more control than a body "in stasis," or that forces us to accept reductive narratives where only our "soul" matters and that to be trans is for the soul to discipline the body into a more appropriately binary sexual morphology. This leads to the problem of the gender binary. The gender binary punishes those who do not fit within it, and forces trans and queer people — and, really, all people — to cut off aspects of themselves which do not fit into their assigned gender's ideological form. Finally, the gender binary is held in place by the heterosexual matrix, where authority sanctions marriage and heterosexual reproduction, alternately ignoring or punishing sexuality outside of that matrix, the consequences more and more severe depending on how far the sexuality is from the heterosexual norm. These are only some of the ways that the demiurgic cosmos naturalizes queer/trans oppression as revealed through the gnostic remythification of the Genesis cosmogonic myths.

As such, we need to develop cosmoi that speak to each of these issues, by rethinking how worlds, genders, and sexualities might exist in pluralistic, nondualist, and excitingly queer ways.

3

Theyogony: The Queer Cosmogonies of Erotic Worlding

Perhaps the big project of the nonhuman turn is to find new techniques, in speech and art and mood, to disclose the participation of nonhumans in "our" world.
— Jane Bennett, "Systems and Things"[1]

Everything was sliding into that unreal domain beyond the mirror where my earliest sexual experience had stranded me, a world wherein the most outlandish things were possible, bounded by nothing save the logic of desire. Dreams kissed my quim. I dissolved in tea and luscious nonsense.
— Alan Moore, *Lost Girls*[2]

---

1 Jane Bennett, "Systems and Things: On Vital Materialism and Object-Oriented Philosophy," in *The Nonhuman Turn*, ed. Richard Grusin (Minneapolis: University of Minnesota Press, 2015), 225.
2 Alan Moore, *Lost Girls*, vol. 2: *Neverlands* (Marietta: Top Shelf Productions, 2006), chap. 17, 5.

> *People say in Boston even beans do it [...]*
> *Romantic sponges, they say, do it*
> *Oysters down in oyster bay do it [...]*
> *Let's do it*
> *Let's fall in love*
>
> — Louis Armstrong, "Let's Do It (Let's Fall in Love)"[3]

In the previous chapter, I suggested a reading of several gnostic mythopoetic texts that exposes the (dis)order of presumed singularity over multiplicity, "the one" over "the many." The demiurge presumes his selfhood and agency over and against the complex multiplicity of the pleroma, which, while unified, is described as and sustained through shifting relationships between divine entities. These entities *also* tend to be multi-sexed, act out multiple gender roles, and engage in a multiplicity of erotics.[4] In establishing his singularity, the demiurge acts out a sole sex or gender despite his anatomy and other potentials for gendered behavior. Through his presumption, the demiurge also genders the world as something feminine or female to be acted upon, extending from Eve to all matter and indeed to all matter and all humanity. The demiurge then relegates desire to a singular function: the perpetuation of his dualistic empire. While just as much an object for the demiurge to act upon, Adam is also positioned in the scheme to model his actions on the demiurge's. The dream that the archons put in Adam's mind is one of false authority over and against his surroundings, beginning with dominion over Eve. Adam, and any Adamic descendent, enforces the dualistic cosmology of Yaldabaoth by becoming a demiurge in his own right, denying the syzygy of himself and Eve, which could be, and should be, modeled off the aeonic

---

3   Louis Armstrong, "Let's Do It (Let's Fall in Love)," by Cole Porter, Spotify, recorded August 13, 1957, track 6 on *Ella and Louis Again*, Verve Records, 1957.
4   For the gnostic mythopoets who discuss pleroma, many-ness and unity are not contradictory. How unity and plurality co-exist within the world and particularly in the divine will be the focus of the next chapter.

organization of the pleroma, a community of entities rather than a self-delineated over and against everyone else.

As a queer mythopoet, I refuse a cosmology where a demiurgic model is the only viable one. This chapter presents a redistribution of values, beginning with a multiplicitous and, insofar as it resists being locked into the heterosexual matrix, queer erotics. I offer the cosmogony of erotic worlding, processes of desiring and animated matter that form the cosmos, and, by extension, genders, bodies, worlds, and gods.[5] These processes fall under pantheistic and animistic cosmologies and are informed by ancient Greek (meta)physical erotics, lyric poetry, and feminist and queer pornographic imagination. Erotic worlding locates the sanctifying and animating force of eros in all things, not just a singular eros employed by a ruler. Erotic worlding offers an alternative to the subject One over the object Many.

In both *Worlds without End: The Many Lives of the Multiverse* and *Pantheologies: Gods, Worlds, Monsters,* scholar of religion, science, and society Mary-Jane Rubenstein wrestles with the one and the many, in the first book by exploring many worlds or multiverse models over singular world or universe models and in the later book one-god theistic models over many-god pantheistic models. In both books she examines ethical and ontological problems of "one"-world or -god models and explores how many-world or -god models might address those problems.

Multiverse cosmologies "consistently rearrange the boundaries between and among philosophy, theology, astronomy,

---

5 My work on erotic worlding is aligned heavily with the movement of artists and activists who identify as ecosexual. Indeed, towards the end of writing *The(y)ology* in the summer of 2021, I joined Annie Sprinkle and Beth Stephens with a number of environmentalist friends for an ecosexual tour at the Franconia Sculpture Park in Minnesota. There I took Sprinkle and Stephens's non-monogamous wedding vows to the earth. For more on the emergence of ecosexuality, see Annie Sprinkle, Beth Stephens, and Jennie Klein, *Assuming the Ecosexual Position: The Earth as Lover* (Minneapolis: University of Minnesota Press, 2021); and SerenaGaia Anderlini-D'Onofrio, *Ecosexuality: When Nature Inspires the Art of Love* (Puerto Rico: 3WayKiss, 2015).

and physics."⁶ Our scientific, theological, philosophical, and, I add, mythopoetic, tools can lead us into the depths of pancosmic thinking. The multiverse models refract our disciplinary insights back, and the investigative tools are changed by the models they unveil. Rubenstein shows how one form of theological questioning — for instance, how a creator created the world — has led thinkers from the pre-Socratics through Plato and Aristotle to Giordano Bruno to twentieth and twenty-first century scientists to reimagine processes of pancosmic formation, explore how worlds beget worlds, to see that there may in fact be no creator god. Rubenstein concludes her study:

> Tuned in to the background noise of many-worlds cosmologies — of their failure to disentangle physics from metaphysics from religion from science — one can pick up the faint but unmistakable signals of an ontology that entangles the one and the many; of an "order" constituted, dismantled, and renewed by an ever-roiling chaos; of a "truth" that remains provisional, multiple, and perspectival; and, perhaps, of a theology that asks more interesting and more pressing questions than whether the universe has been "designed" by an anthropomorphic, extracosmic deity.⁷

Her next book, *Pantheologies,* begins where *Worlds without End* ends, although that is not the explicit reason she gives for her project. Rubenstein identifies how, throughout history, "'pantheism' is primarily a polemical term, used most often to dismiss or even ridicule a position one determines to be distasteful."⁸ She then proceeds to ask, why does pantheism "so rarely get the opportunity to be a stance in the first place? Whence the vitriolic, visceral, automatic, and nearly universal denunciation of

---

6 Mary-Jane Rubenstein, *Worlds without End: The Many Lives of the Multiverse* (New York: Columbia University Press, 2014), 18.
7 Ibid., 236.
8 Mary-Jane Rubenstein, *Pantheologies: Gods, Worlds, Monsters* (New York: Columbia University Press, 2018), xx.

pantheism?"⁹ One answer, which she returns to throughout the book, is that pantheism challenges traditional theology's and even traditional scientific models' reliance on dualism. Thus, pantheism

> not only unsettles, and not only entangles, but demolishes the raced and gendered ontic distinctions that Western metaphysics (with some crucial exceptions) insists on drawing between activity and passivity, spirit and matter, and animacy and inanimacy — distinctions that are rooted theologically in the Greco-Roman-Abrahamic distinction between creator and created, or God and world. Insofar as pantheism rejects this fundamental distinction, it threatens all the other privileges that map onto it: male versus female, light versus darkness, good versus evil, and humans over every other organism.¹⁰

Pantheism threatens the demiurgic model. The distinctions between himself and his creation, between his masculinity and others' femininity, between his presumed divinity and others' weak mortality are shattered when everything is divine. It ruptures his singular cosmology, itself an illusion considering the multiplicitous pleroma. When matter is perceived as animated by an alien force of reason, the physical world by a distinctly separate God, the feminine by the masculine, the animal by the human, it is not that these "opposites" are on equal ground. It is rather that "the oppositional logic of classical metaphysics does not [...] give us two; it [...] gives us one, and a falling-short of that one."¹¹ In a dualistic cosmology, only one half of the dyad is empowered, true, and good. While I think it can be quite fruitful to investigate the ideology of a singular model and how different bodies fail at reaching this model, pantheism helps us to see a world or, more appropriately, worlds, that follow not only

---

9   Ibid.
10 Ibid.
11 Ibid., 17.

a different metaphysics, but also the politics modeled from and informing that metaphysics:

> [T]he real concern over pantheism is not the collapse of some abstract notion of "difference"; rather, it is the collapse of one particularly insistent and damaging way of configuring difference — one that gathers each instance of "difference" into a static category, forever held in place by an oppositional overlord.[12]

The demiurgic model exists not only in mythologies, but in the ritualized enactment of these myths in the political, social, psychological, religious, military, you name it, arenas. The regulations of sexes, sexualities, and genders as well as the regulations of races, ethnicities, body shapes, indeed all bodies, are aligned with a myth of a demiurge whose nazi-esque appeal to a cosmic order in his own image is founded on and sustained through complex violations of all other agents and disavowals of their agency. Demiurgic politics harm us all. This is especially true for queer people. We consistently exist outside "the natural" order, whether that's an order defined by physicians, psychologists, legislators, clergy, or marketers, all of whom, in flexing their power, replicate Adam's delusion. While those deemed "unnatural" for their sexuality, their bodies, or their gender status are persecuted by the "natural," those who are "natural" are still "the created" in the eyes of the ultimate creator. In reenacting his violation of other subjects as objects, we serve to perpetuate his reign.

The myth of the demiurge underlies the hegemonic reception of our physical surroundings, our religions, and our politics. Theologians invested in queer liberation cannot accept the demiurgic cosmos as *the* cosmos, which may in fact mean we cannot except *a* cosmos, in its singularity, constituted by something acosmic. Similarly, liberation theologians who envision worlds of multiplicitous sexuality, subjecthood, vibrancy, and

---

12   Ibid.

imagination must address the commitment to monotheism, particularly those monotheisms which assert a God who sets history on its course, entering the fray as the ultimate subject against the chaotic object of his creation, to move us closer toward His acosmic, Platonic kingdom. By settling for the ultimate agent, we begin the process of renouncing our and one another's agency.

In what I take as a call to action, Rubenstein notes, "there has not been a widespread, or even a small-scale, turn toward pantheism among feminist, queer, anti-racist, post- and de-colonial, or ecologically oriented philosophers and theologians."[13] As a queer, nonbinary theopoet, I wonder with her about my communities' commitments to holy narratives and cosmic models that still appeal to the demiurge, even if a more liberal one. I worry that in our liberational pursuits, we simply tack more and more of our characteristics onto the demiurgic skeleton, accepting the same old tenets as long as he uses our idioms. But a demiurge who votes for my candidate, frequents the same gay bar, or lets me love who I want to love, is still a demiurge. The universe is still hers. We are still their subjects.

Whitney Bauman is one scholar working at the crossroads of ecology, queer theory, and theology, who espouses pantheism and animism. In his essay "Queer Values for a Queer Climate: Developing a Versatile Planetary Ethic," Bauman writes how, amidst our current ecological crises, "once seemingly hermetically sealed categories and boundaries between self or other, human or animal, nature or culture, organic or machine, and science or religion, have now been uncovered as leaky and porous."[14] But what were the processes that led to these separations in the first place? I have been using the language of a demiurgic model, but Bauman's, while complementary to my own,

---

13 Ibid., 12.
14 Whitney Bauman, "Queer Values for a Queer Climate: Developing a Versatile Planetary Ethic," in *Meaningful Flesh: Reflections on Religion and Nature for a Queer Planet*, ed. Whitney Bauman (Earth: punctum books, 2018), 103.

highlights some theoretical and theological histories that merit their own discussion.

He identifies the overarching model of our current moment as industrial or global capitalism held up by three pillars: the reduction of causality to efficient causality, the reduction of reason or thought to instrumental reason, and the reduction of the family or social to the nuclear family.[15] The first, the reduction of causality, traces a model of multiple causalities to one model of efficient causality. In an early model of causality in the history of Western thought, Aristotle

> argued that there were four different types of causality: material, efficient, formal, and final. The material is what it sounds like: what the thing is made of. The efficient cause is an external cause that brings about change in motion or form. The formal cause is roughly equivalent to structural forces and shapes that cause change. And, the final cause or telos is the ultimate purpose toward which something moves or changes.[16]

Causality, that is some sort of agency or animacy, exists in all matter and is "not limited to immediacy."[17] For Aristotle, and other ancient thinkers, "just as contemporary emergent theorists and new materialisms claim, agency is distributed throughout all of life and not located in one place or type of thing."[18] However, with the rise of modern Western thought "causality was narrowed to those forces that immediately shape a current situation, so agency was reinforced as power over or control of something."[19] As we have already seen, in line with ancient metaphysics, this active principle is gendered male, the passive female. These categories are also fraught with racial, ethnic, sexual, ability, and class hierarchies:

---

15 Ibid., 109.
16 Ibid., 105.
17 Ibid.
18 Ibid.
19 Ibid., 105–6.

> In a patriarchal society where different races, sexes, and classes of peoples are empowered according to a hierarchy of privilege, it becomes all too easy to mistake one's place of privilege within that hierarchy for one's ability to have causal effect. This is done through a series of 'backgrounding' other's agency and focusing in on one's own actions in a given situation.[20]

This is to say, the system reinforces itself. Humans see their own immediate actions as having causal effect in a way that is less apparent in the behavior of other animals, even less so in vegetable matter, and the least in minerals. Thus, the kind of causality we identify in ourselves against other matter becomes idealized, reduced as the only animacy. Then, through patriarchy, the perfect, white, cisgendered male form becomes the beacon of efficient causality. Those with greater proximity to that form are seen as being more active and agential, while those of further proximity are more passive, that is, more like the animal, vegetable or mineral than the human. The society then rewards the former with more political and social mobility and the latter with less, in a way "proving" the dualisms as fact.

With this reduction of agency comes the reduction of reason as "the instrumental variety," and the question became, "what can we get out of the world or what can the rest of nature do for 'us' (however defined), rather than what our place is in the world in relationship to other entities"?[21] Again, this parallels the demiurge who believes in his right to exploit all other matter, to use us and everything around us for his benefit. And, as an Adam who is beholden to the demiurgic illusion sets up an abusive hierarchy between himself and Eve, so too do efficient causality and instrumental reason have dangerous effects for human relationships through the establishment of the nuclear family. Borrowing from Jack Halberstam, Bauman writes: "The narrowing of family to the nuclear helps to transform 'the com-

---

20 Ibid., 106.
21 Ibid., 107.

mons' into private property (owned by individual families) and social welfare concerns into 'private' family concerns."[22] Bauman continues:

> What was once a communal or state responsibility becomes more and more the responsibility of the individual family unit (with its so-called "head" of the household assuming control over the supposed "body" of the household). Second, these individual units become more manageable, taxable, and accountable to the productionist model of science (medical, political, economic, and otherwise): without social welfare, each family is responsible for its own housing, daily bread, education, etc. Such a narrowing of "family" helps to shift concern from the polis and public good (a very messy and inefficient entity) toward the immediate concern of what is good for "me and my immediate family."[23]

This model narrows who we are supposed to be in relationship with, draws fine lines between private and public, and sets up an image for the perfect (obviously heterosexual) family. Importantly, "this model of family has an efficient way of dealing with the responsibility of raising the next generation, inheritance, and units of consumption, one that models the narrowing of causality to efficient and reasoning to instrumental,"[24] meanwhile, "the abject in this model are the insane, elderly, widowed, orphaned, unmarried, enslaved, disabled, and poor."[25] As far as erotics are concerned, they are employed and sanctioned for use as long as they are efficient in producing another generation of consumers. These same erotics are denied to those abject members of society through their desexualization, this desexualization a key component of denying these abject members' overall agency.

---

22 Ibid., 108. See also Jack Halberstam, *The Queer Art of Failure* (Durham: Duke University Press, 2011), 11.

23 Bauman, "Queer Values for a Queer Climate," 108.

24 Ibid.

25 Ibid.

In response to these ideological pillars, Bauman deploys again Halberstam's queer theory to offer "an ethics of ambiguity and unknowing rather than progress,"[26] and he explains: "Such an ethic does not transform all reality into the human narrative of progress (whether technological or environmental or both), but rather acknowledges the multiplicity of planetary times and values that refuse to be captured by any singular story."[27] Bauman takes a stand, similarly to Rubenstein, of the many over the one, of rejecting the reduction of causality, of reason, of family.

In the face of climate change, we can reject that there is only one outcome or only one path to human salvation:

> We are beginning to understand more deeply our interrelatedness and co-constructedness with the rest of the natural world; and rather than merely responding with scenarios for how to manage climate change, we have an opportunity to do some deep interspecies listening and unknowing and focus on the indeterminacy of the planetary future.[28]

Bauman's project is thus concerned with interspecies listening or more broadly heeding those voices of further proximity from the patriarchal center. This includes a deep dive into queer theories, particularly those theories that challenge the mainstream narratives of time, success, and progress. Temporality, along with studies of affect and materialism, have been a major area of focus for queer theorists in the last decade or so. We have seen this trend already with Muñoz's utopianism in the first chapter. Here again, Bauman looks to Halberstam's understanding of failure in relation to the chronological, forward movement of Western society:

> Halberstam, again, argues for the queer art of failure; failing, in a hetero-patriarchal society, may be just what we need to

---

26 Ibid., 103.
27 Ibid., 103-4.
28 Ibid., 110.

think anew about what it is we are doing [...]. In other words, if our worlds have been structured into narratives of progress that through efficient causality and instrumental reason, turn all of life into fodder for certain human's progress, then haven't our desires, hopes, and dreams been distorted toward creating this reality?[29]

Time is a key component of the cosmos. In the *Secret Book of John,* the demiurge uses it as a final and most powerful shackle to keep humans in check. The Western, Christian understanding of time, with its eschaton, might only see in the events of climate change one possibility, that is, the end of the world. The relationship of human-against-world, spurred by the temporal movement of progress, forces us to act until we or the earth are obsolete. How we conceive of time affects how we move through it, and how we move through time shapes the worlds we inhabit and our relationships with other inhabitants. Queer theorists help us discern what temporal ideologies shape the world that perpetuates our oppression and offer tools to reimagine other times and thus other worlds.

Bauman concludes with a plea for us to listen across the divides of time and species: "Our ancestors really are here with us in this process, as are future generations of life the exact nature of which we cannot even fathom. We need hopes and dreams that are not 'out of this world' but that are of, for, and with this world."[30] He invites us into co-creation with a multiplicity of beings and their numerous causalities, ways of thinking, and relationships. Harkening temporalities outside the dominant temporality of progress, pasts, presents, and futures, and their various generations, can coexist. Together, we can problem solve, imagine, and fight for new life, for justice, for different worlds. And yet, importantly, "different worlds" are still of this matter. They are not outside this world. This is a queer, ecological, and pantheistic vision, where agency is no longer the sole

---

29 Ibid., 118–19.
30 Ibid., 119.

disposal of an alien demiurge and those who model themselves after him. I take Bauman's invitation and turn now, with heed to the ancestors, to my offering of a pantheistic, pananimate, panerotic, and queer cosmology.

Cosmic Erotics: The Pananimism of Aphrodite and Her Kin

In the second chapter of *Pantheologies*, "Hyle" (Greek for "matter"), Rubenstein addresses the problem of matter. We have to think deeply about what it is we mean "when we say that this-or-that 'pantheism' reduces God to, or conflates or identifies God with, the material world."[31] As we have already explored, the dominant strands of Western cosmology require an ontic distinction between the "spiritual" demiurge and his "material" creation, where "matter is the undifferentiated, persistently feminized, often racialized stuff that a rational, male principle brings to order."[32] The distinction is key to both Plato's cosmogony and to that of Genesis 1. In Genesis, "matter is rendered as similarly passive, undifferentiated, and chaotic in the first few verses [...], wherein a silent, primordial 'deep' (*tehom*) awaits the divine breath that calls creation forth from it — or her."[33] Order is strictly separate from chaos. Order, intelligent, agential, and alien, forces its design onto matter. The birth of the world, cosmogony, cannot occur from matter itself.

However, this dominant myth, with its denigration of matter, is not the only explanation for creation. Rubenstein uses her chapter to explore materialist counterontologies. By materialism, both new *and* quite old, she refers to philosophies "that locate creative agency — whether it be called life, spirit, animacy, or emergence — within matter itself."[34] Rubenstein shows the pantheist possibilities of matter by putting into proximity the new materialisms of Karen Barad, Jane Bennett, and Donna

---

31 Rubenstein, *Pantheologies*, 64–65.
32 Ibid., 65.
33 Ibid.
34 Ibid., 69. This will also be the definition of "materialism" I will be working with throughout this book.

THE(Y)OLOGY

Haraway to Lynn Margulis's biological studies of symbioses and Indigenous animist teachings from the Ojibwa in North America and the Aboriginal Yarralin community in Australia, while also charting subordinated materialist traditions from Europe and, in particular, the ancient Mediterranean. Rubenstein discusses at length the Epicurean atomists of the first century BCE, to a lesser extent the earlier Stoics, and most briefly the much earlier pre-Socratic Ionians. As both a classicist — and, as will make sense soon, an avid erotics enthusiast — I am most interested in discussing the Ionian pre-Socratic philosophers.

These philosophers were "*hylozoists* (etymologically, 'matter life-ists'), meaning that, contrary to the post-Socratic philosophers to come, they taught that 'matter as such has the property of life and growth.'"[35] For them, matter is alive, and life derives from matter. All these thinkers posited a single or a group of elements whence all life, worlds, bodies descend:

> for Thales of Miletus, the generative substance was water; for Anaximenes of Miletus and Diogenes of Apollonia, it was air; for Heraclitus of Ephesus, it was fire; and for Empedocles of Acragas, it was all four elements in alternating cycles of "love" and "strife."[36]

It is the latter of these two thinkers, Heraclitus and Empedocles, to whom I turn in beginning to build the model of erotic worlding.

As previously discussed, one of the origins for Greek cosmology can be traced to Hesiod's *Theogony*. About the beginning of the cosmos, Hesiod writes,

> at the first Chaos came to be, but next wide-bosomed Earth, the ever-sure foundations of all the deathless ones who hold

---

35 Ibid., 70–71.
36 Ibid., 71.

the peaks of snowy Olympus, and dim Tartarus in the depth of the wide-pathed Earth, and Eros (Love).[37]

There was chaos, there was Earth and its shadow Tartarus, and there was Love. Eros, Hesiod says, is "fairest among the deathless gods, who unnerves the limbs and overcomes the mind and wise counsels of all gods and all men within them." To Eros is attributed an incredible power over deities and humans alike. And these deities include elements, rivers, celestial bodies, concepts of wrath and death and fear, dreams, monstrous titans, chthonic beasts, as well as the more humanlike Olympians of Zeus, Hera, and their kin. This is to say, Eros can overcome the most personal and the least. Indeed, after invoking Eros, Hesiod describes the emergence of all subsequent divinities, some born through sexual reproduction of others, some asexually, or perhaps autosexually, Chaos birthing from itself new forms. Introducing Eros before the various theogonies implies its causality toward the world and its personalities. From lyric poetry to the poetry of Greek theater to epics and religious hymns, the power of Love is ascribed to numerous deities, in particular Eros and Aphrodite, but also the retinue of Erotes, the plural of Eros.[38] In the Orphic religion of the Orphic hymns, a late collection from some time after the birth of Christ but still composed within a thoroughly non-Christian milieu, this divinity is also called Phanes or Protogonos. Protogonos, literally "first born," is described as "two-natured,"[39] "ether-tossed," "born of the egg," "delighting in his golden wings," and, like in *Theogony*, "the

---

37 Hesiod, *Theogony*, in *Hesiod: Complete Works*, trans. Hugh Evelyn White (East Sussex: Delphi Classics, 2013), ll. 116–17.

38 These include figures like Anteros (god of requited love), Himeros (god of unrequited love), Hymenaios (god of marriage), Hermaphroditus (god of hermaphrodites, effeminate men, and intersex people), and Pothos (a god of yearning).

39 In Orphism, "two-natured" connotes androgyny or neither male nor female. Often attributed to Dionysus as well.

begetter of blessed gods and mortal men."[40] An Eros born of ether and an egg is described in the much earlier (fifth–fourth century BCE) choral ode of Aristophanes' comedy *The Birds*. The birds, who are the chorus, sing that "Black Winged Night produced an egg, an egg from wind created / And from that egg, as time revolved, there grew the lovely Eros."[41] They continue with a theogony "the universe contained no gods, till Eros mingled all,"[42] and its interrelated cosmogony, "once the elements intermixed, then Heaven and Ocean formed / and Earth herself, with all the race of blessed and deathless gods."[43] Lest we write off this witness of Eros for its comical context, we can look to tragedy. The nurse of Euripides' *Hippolytus* tells Phaedra, lovesick for her stepson, "the goddess Cypris[44] has the power of a flood tide; / she's overwhelming,"[45] adding "Cypris wanders through the upper air; / she is in the ocean wave. All things on earth / come from her, the sower of desire."[46] The particular command of the elements of water, sky, and earth are corroborated in the Orphic Hymn to Aphrodite:

> Everything comes from you:
> you have yoked the world,
> you control all three realms,
> you give birth to all,
> to everything in heaven,
> to everything upon the fruitful earth,
> to everything in the depths of the sea.[47]

---

40 "To Protogonos," in *The Orphic Hymns*, trans. Apostolos Athanassakis and Benjamin Wolkow (Baltimore: John Hopkins University Press, 2013), l. 3.
41 Aristophanes, "The Birds," in *Aristophanes: Birds and Other Plays*, trans. Stephen Halliwell (Oxford: Oxford University Press, 1998), ll. 695–96.
42 Ibid., l. 700.
43 Ibid., l. 702.
44 Another name for Aphrodite.
45 Euripides, "Hippolytus," in *Alcestis, Medea, Hippolytus*, trans. Diane Arnson Svarlien (Indianapolis: Hackett Publishing, 2007), ll. 488–89.
46 Ibid., ll. 493–95.
47 "To Aphrodite," in *The Orphic Hymns*, trans. Apostolos Athanassakis and Benjamin Wolkow (Baltimore: John Hopkins University Press, 2013), ll.

The hymnist similarly claims that Eros is "master of all: / of the sky's ether, of the sea and the land."[48] Once again described as "two-natured"[49] and granted the same dominion as Aphrodite, we might even see in the Orphic hymns that Aphrodite and Eros are two aspects of the same multi-sexed, multi-gendered divinity, not unlike the gnostic aeons. Perhaps we might even imagine the mythopoetic Eros, Aphrodite, or Protogonos who are sometimes singular entities, sometimes a community of Erotes, as similar to the shifting personalities and realms of the generative pleroma, an erotic pleroma.

At the same time, we must ask, is Eros, or Aphrodite, of the world or an outsider enforcing her power on the world? Are they another demiurge bending matter to their will, or are erotics part of every atom, every body, every world? The poetic witness not only celebrates the omnipotent Eros but is pained by it, especially in lyric poetry and the poems of Sappho in particular. Sappho calls the god "giver of pain,"[50] and "rattles [her] bittersweet, / irresistible, / a crawling beast."[51] The theological questions these stir up are ones of "this-worldliness" — is love of this world or an alien force acting upon it — and of theodicy — is love good or evil, the cause of both or one?

Empedocles writes of four elements — earth, water, air, fire — and two forces, Love and Strife, which respectively combine and separate matter. The word he uses for Love is not *eros* but *philia* while Strife is *neikos*. Many Christian interpreters have spent significant energy on parsing out the different forms of love described in Greek writing, in order to understand exactly which kinds of Love are God or godlike and which are not, including such works as C.S. Lewis's *The Four Loves*. As such,

---

6–7.
48 "To Eros," in *The Orphic Hymns*, trans. Apostolos Athanassakis and Benjamin Wolkow (Baltimore: John Hopkins University Press, 2013), ll. 4–5.
49 Ibid., l. 4.
50 Sappho, fragment 13, trans. Julia Dubnoff, *Poems of Sappho*, n.d., https://www.uh.edu/~cldue/texts/sappho.html.
51 Sappho, fragment 15, trans. Julia Dubnoff, *Poems of Sappho*, n.d., https://www.uh.edu/~cldue/texts/sappho.html.

terms like *philia* might be interpreted as more like friendship or companionship and very different from erotic love. However, that the Greeks used distinct words does not mean that the distinctions they drew between their words were the same we draw or that the distinctions were universally accepted. Surveying its many ancient uses, classicist James Davidson cautions against a desexualization of *philia*: "There is nothing intrinsically 'pure' or unerotic [...] about '*philia*.' Eros indeed can be called 'hunting for intimates (*philoi*),' and a history of '*philia*' that excludes eros is a waste of time."[52] He continues to parse out the terms: "*Eros* is an ambition, *philia* is a relationship. *Eros* is driving force, *philia* is where you are driving to."[53] Davidson holds that *philia* is not necessarily or typically nonsexual or aromantic, but a state of loving while *eros* is the movement toward that state. But as we will see, Empedocles' *philia* is both a destination *and* the pull, and thus Davidson's distinction is also brought into question.

Empedocles' *On Nature*, which we retain only in fragments, describes his cosmological and religious thoughts. Fittingly, the work is dedicated to his young male lover Pausanias, "presumably the 'you' the fragments frequently address."[54] What we might have then is a cosmogony as love letter — ooh, là, là! For the content of the philosopher's thought is as amorous as his attitude toward his addressee. Empedocles, Richard D. McKirahan writes, seeks to "teach his knowledge to Pausanias to the extent that he will be able to comprehend it, and to that extent Pausanias will be able to transcend the limitations of human experience."[55] Empedocles wants to save his lover from a certain station in life, but to be "saved" from that station, Pausanias must know what "life" truly is: contextually, materially, cosmically.

---

52 James Davidson, *The Greeks and Greek Love: A Bold New Exploration of the Ancient World* (New York: Random House, 2007), 31.
53 Ibid.
54 Richard D. McKirahan, *Philosophy Before Socrates: An Introduction with Texts and Commentary* (Indianapolis: Hackett Publishing, 2010), 255.
55 Ibid.

Empedocles writes: "(But under Love) we come together into one kosmos, whereas under Strife [the ordered whole] grew apart, so as to be many from one, from which all things that were and are and will be in the future."[56] Our cosmos exists between the One mixture of all things together that is Love and the many disparate elements of Strife. This is to say, our world is a combination of movements toward the Many and movements toward the One, and

> these never cease continually interchanging, at one time all coming together into one by Love and at another each being borne apart by the hatred of Strife. Thus in that they have learned to grow to be one out of many and in that they again spring apart as many when the one grows apart.[57]

Love and Strife, like the elements, are immortal. Matter does not come from nothing but exists continually changing. The universe is also a multiverse, in a temporal sense, going through cycles from Strife into Love, where everything is one, and then out of Love into Strife, where the four elements are completely separate. The cycle of the individual person, animal, and plant follows: "Behold her with your mind, and do not sit with your eyes staring in amazement. She is also recognized as innate in mortal limbs. Through her they have kindly thoughts and do peaceful deeds, calling her by the appellation Joy and also Aphrodite."[58] Love is an innate part of anything that exists. Additionally, Empedocles does "not consider psychology separate from physiology, which is a part of physics."[59] *Philia* is not simply an ancient law of attraction. Both the body, how we are constituted physiologically, and the body politic, how we interact socially, are affected by Love and Strife:

---

56 Empedocles, "Fragments," trans. Richard McKirahan, in *Philosophy before Socrates: An Introduction with Texts and Commentary*, ed. and trans. Richard McKirahan (Indianapolis: Hackett Publishing, 2010), 238.

57 Ibid., 237.

58 Ibid., 237.

59 McKirahan, *Philosophy before Socrates*, 283.

> This is very clear in the mass of mortal limbs: sometimes we come together through Love into one, all the limbs that have obtained a body, at the peak of flourishing life, while at other times, split apart through evil Quarrels […], [and] they wander each kind separately on the furthest shore of life.[60]

Knowing the tides of the social body gives us insight into our individual anatomy and psychology. Studying the body, we learn about the world. And when we learn about the formation of the world, we learn about the body. It is combinations of the elements precisely determined by levels of Love and Strife that create uniqueness, that distinguish one thing from the next. Importantly, this means they are not only movement but ingredients, not separate forces enacted on us but crucial parts *of* us:

> Love and Strife are directly responsible not for all motion but specifically for the mixing and separation of the elements. For a compound to form we need both the correct amounts and proportions of its constituent elements and also of Love (and […] Strife) in the right amounts and proportions to unite them in the right way."[61]

Socially and physically, "things under the influence of Love 'love one another,' while those under Strife's power are 'enemies' and 'very mournful.'"[62] *Philia* is thus "responsible for kindly thoughts and peaceful deeds" and is "identical with the familiar force of Love which unites different humans."[63] From this we can discern that we would not know Love if we did not know Strife for Strife on the atomic level accounts for our differences, while Love accounts for those differences relating to one another. This also implies that there is no true, eternal self, but, like the world, processes of matter forming and unforming.

---

60 Empedocles, "Fragments," 239.
61 McKirahan, *Philosophy before Socrates,* 259.
62 Ibid.
63 Ibid.

Empedocles interestingly has sort of a soul in his cosmology, although he specifically uses the term *daimōn* (or here in this volume, "daemon"), which means something like an intermediary between humans and gods. But what are gods for Empedocles? How are they different from any other body? For Empedocles, McKirahan comments, "gods are the sorts of things associated with the local prevalence of Love in a strong degree. We may suppose that their life, founded on Love and unity, is happy, unwearied, and free of distress," and "the bonding force of Love is so strong in these compounds as to give them 'immensely long life.'" The answer then, is that gods are *not* ontically alien to the nature of humans, but are simply closer to love, more mixed than separate, closer to an erotic pleroma. Gods are not immortal while we are mortal. They are simply longer lived. Thus, daemons are the events of our personalities existing as "exceptionally long lasting (yet still 'mortal') compounds."[64] The full description of the daemons in Empedocles' cosmology is as follows:

> They are long-lived divine beings compounded of all four elements, in which Love has great strength. By committing certain sins a daimōn introduces Strife into its composition — not enough to disperse its constituents and so destroy it, but enough to disturb the unity that existed before. In punishment the daimōn is forced to become living creatures of various kinds. Its goal is to be purified of Strife and return to its state before the Fall, though this is a difficult task to accomplish given the increase of Strife in the universe and also given the nature of animate existence Strife-increasing sexual reproduction and the likelihood of committing Strife-promoting actions unwittingly.[65]

Here is a doctrine of reincarnation, but even that which is reincarnated is not eternal. It is constituted by the elements, by Love,

---

64 Ibid., 287.
65 Ibid., 288.

and by Strife. It is not immaterial, and there is no acosmic divinity. But in his description of the daemons, Empedocles is saying that there are ways to make our personalities longer lasting and to affect *more* love in the world, even when the cosmic cycle is moving toward strife, where "some mortal compounds have some power to affect the relative prevalence of Love or Strife within themselves by doing or refraining from certain activities and by thinking friendly or hostile thoughts."[66] We wrestle our daemons, material beings that belong to rocks to plants to all kinds of animals, from a cold passivity of dissipation, of falling apart, toward the embrace of one another, the combining of different elements into unities and communities, and so become more like gods.

In both the processes of disintegration toward Strife and integration toward Love, the self, the individual daemon, even the individual God are not eternal. Neither are they separate from the processes of being created or of co-creating. Divinity becomes a measure of proximity to Love and a matter of relationship. Relating in certain ways to other beings facilitates our own apotheoses. Empedocles writes his love letter to Pausanias that the beloved might know his own body in relation to the principles of the world. He wants his beloved to acknowledge his potential for divinity, that salvation is not about escaping from the world but embracing it, loving it, cultivating divinity until we stop being selves, until we are integrated into complex unity that is community. All things making love made into love.

This is not love determined by genitals. This is not love for a singular relationship. This is love in the self, love in the world, love in all components of existence. It denies the illusory, essential self and any claim toward singularity. Separation and purity are the signs of Strife! Diversity in communion moves us toward divinity. The demiurge traps himself in fear and paranoia from his creation, both revealing his weakness and perpetuating it. A love tied only to sexual reproduction and marriage between one man and one woman is a love concerned with the perpetuation

---

66 Ibid.

of a self or a type — a name, family, a legacy — not recognition of the multiple loving agents that constitute every body and event. This is love radically democratized.

But then the pendulum swings back. Strife pulls apart. Separation commences. Empedocles is clear that Love and Strife exist as two forces of equal power. However, they are not to be *valued* equally. Empedocles has a clear preference for Love, that is, he attributes more goodness to Love. This worries me insofar as dualisms turn into hierarchies. Why are integrations necessarily better than disintegrations? How could we love if we were not in some ways separate? Is attraction necessarily good? Or is *neikos* another form of attraction, the attraction of same to same — earth loving earth, water loving water, fire loving fire, air loving air — so much that the compounds of everything else rupture? Is Strife ontically so separate from the Love that mixes compounds? Socially, are we never attracted to things that would repulse others? Heterosexuality has no lesser stake in eros than homosexuality or pansexuality, but put on a pedestal, it has regulated, punished, even destroyed other loving relationships. A love that is all is more expansive than either good or evil alone. A pantheist cosmic love contains multitudes.

To help articulate this pantheist cosmic love, I turn to the earlier pre-Socratic philosopher, Heraclitus, whose fragmented writings lend a fiery nondualism to our discussion of Empedocles. Lamenting most people's misunderstanding of the cosmos, Heraclitus writes, "they do not understand how, though at variance with itself, it agrees with itself."[67] How can this be! How can there be disagreement in the very cosmos! We have many fragments from Heraclitus. Constantly quoted by later thinkers, his philosophizing covers a very wide range of topics, and a fairly consistent strain of thought concerns the false duality of disagreement versus agreement. He is concerned with dynamism and the truth beyond dualism that variance, especially so

---

67 Heraclitus, "Fragments," trans. Richard McKirahan, in McKirahan, *Philosophy before Socrates: An Introduction with Texts and Commentary* (Indianapolis: Hackett Publishing, 2012), 116.

called opposites, is not essentially unrelated stuff, but the result of a unifying matter shifting characteristics within its everlasting movement, where "cold things grow hot, a hot thing cold, a moist thing withers, a parched thing is wetted."[68] Heraclitus's cosmos is not made by a creator, a "kosmos, the same for all, none of the gods nor of humans has made."[69] Instead, "the most beautiful kosmos is a pile of things poured out at random."[70] There is a sense of chaos in Heraclitus's cosmos, another seeming contradiction since cosmos is the order of the world and that all the mythopoetic cosmogonies we have seen so far include a movement out of chaos into a system.

This chaos is not so different from Empedocles' Strife, but it is reevaluated as something beautiful and good. The most important distinction between his and Empedocles' thought, however, is that stuff that separates is not ontically distinct from stuff that brings together. All things are "an ever-living fire being kindled in measures and being extinguished in measures."[71] This everlivingness is key. Matter is alive, creating identities and destroying them, as Heraclitus describes immortal mortals and mortal immortals "living the death of the others and dying their life."[72] Thus, Heraclitus agrees with Empedocles that "we and everything else have a share in immortality — even if not a personal immortality," which paradoxically means that mortals are immortal and immortal stuff becomes mortal. Death is not the opposite of life, just the conclusion of a particular compounded identity, and there is no lifeless matter. Identities shift in the matrix of fire, the momentary unity we call "self" or "world" or "god" is a result of matter coming together and pulling apart, and "things taken together are whole and not whole, <something that is> being brought together and brought apart, in tune and out of tune; out of all things there comes a unity and out of a

---

68 Ibid., 119.
69 Ibid., 120.
70 Ibid., 117.
71 Ibid., 120.
72 Ibid., 121.

unity all things."⁷³ Again, this unity is not separate from plurality. Each constitutes the other, they stem from the same flame, "the real nature of the world is simultaneously and equally a unity and a plurality."⁷⁴ The "nature of the world" is not that there are four ontically distinct elements. Empedocles' earth, water, fire, and air are those distinct forms, but in another way are *different manifestations* of the same fire, "the one behind the many, the unity in all the diversity of the kosmos."⁷⁵ That stuff that all is made of is change, is movement, is living, animated sparks. In light of Empedocles, it is erotic stuff, loving stuff, but love, considering Heraclitus, is both attracting and separating. The difference between the two is an illusion. Heraclitus is a nondualist.

The "one matter" is a substance of endless change. It is many matters! Perspective determines whether world is worlds, whether one is many, where "the world can be regarded either as composed of many distinct things or as a whole. An individual thing is a part of the world; the world as a whole is made up of parts that have their own identities."⁷⁶ Identity is created amidst change, the result of fire becoming "opposites" like air and earth so each can revel in their temporary uniqueness. We know ourselves through strife, through separation, through distance between ourselves and another. We cannot move toward, act out our animism, our erotics, if there is not at the same time space between and movement from each other. Heraclitus is attempting the difficult task of explaining how all that exists is related (we come from the same substance) and how we are all different (that substance is a multiplicitous, ever-changing substance). The Heraclitan ethic is that "we can better appreciate a thing's individuality when we know how it is related to other things."⁷⁷ There is a moral sophistication in the fragments of Heraclitus, where good and evil, love and chaos are not diametrically opposed. Nothing is not opposed! "Opposition" is necessary for

---

73 Ibid., 116.
74 McKirahan, *Philosophy before Socrates*, 129.
75 Ibid., 136.
76 Ibid., 130.
77 Ibid.

cooperation to manifest. The philosopher, writes McKirahan, "puts equal weight on change and on stability, on plurality, and on unity, on difference and on identity: stability is guaranteed by change; change is stable; diverse individual things form a unity; identity is preserved through difference."[78] A Heraclitan cosmic love is paradoxical and multiplicitous, unifying and disintegrating, where selves and worlds are in one moment born and in the next destroyed.

As relating to, for instance, animality or humanity or divinity, identity resulting from perspective is a key point in Rubenstein's book. It is in this way that Rubenstein draws parallels between Donna Haraway's Chthulucene with Native ontologies. Haraway's Chthulucene involves worlds constituting worlds, that is matter creating the conditions for their worldly perpetuation. To decenter humans from every consideration of cosmic health, Haraway suggests a turn from imagining the Anthropocene towards a Chthulucene, a world shaped by the likes of worms and fungi and insects, that is, the Chthonic agents of decomposition. This is a change of perspective where we go from seeing organisms that take us apart toward seeing the same organisms as "earthly creators, working from the messy middle of things to make the multispecies kinship structures that amount to worlds."[79] Creatures that in the traditional cosmologies of the West are the most earthly, the most dirty, the smallest, and furthest from reason, let alone the sanctity of love, now replace that immaterial demiurge as creators of worlds. Matter, symbolized by such "nonhuman" and "nonrational" beings, disintegrate bodies and reintegrate worlds. We must appreciate the erotics of worms.

Democratized animacy provokes us to rethink where and how we exist in our contexts. Following Haraway, Rubenstein cites Indigenous cosmologies as conceiving a "living world of intra-active persons."[80] Though, culturally, temporally, and geo-

---

78 Ibid., 137.
79 Rubenstein, *Pantheologies,* 135.
80 Ibid., 136.

graphically distant, the Jurana and Campa make an argument that could be drawn from the Heraclitan fragments that there are no "self-constituted entities that precede the relations that locally determine them. Rather, every term is akin to the designation 'mother-in-law': any thing is only what it is from the perspective of the one for whom it is that thing."[81] Therefore, humanity and animality "are not static or essential categories; rather, a being is only human or nonhuman from a particular perspective."[82] Erotics of the demiurgical variety are so heavily tied to marriage and the authority of one sex or gender over the other. Eros is enslaved as a sex drive toward human selves who in turn imagine themselves in the image of their creator. But if we knock eros from the pedestal of subject–object relationality and human exceptionalism, then who "our creators" are, and therefore their images, becomes a much more mysterious, ambiguous, and multiplicitous conundrum. Gods, humans, daemons, and worlds bubble from and dissolve into an erotic soup.

This is the model I call erotic worlding, where Love births the microcosm of an entity like the human and the macrocosm of a solar system. We are what our constituent parts embrace, tug, fill, pull, suck, tickle, lick, jerk, and cum into being. We are the results of matter pulling together and of matter separating so that it can come together again, of matter pleasuring matter. The orgasm in erotic worlding is the "pleasurable release, explosion, or streaming of built up erotic or sexual excitement (energy) in its broadest sense"[83] and extends to all worlds or bodies and body or world parts. Amoebas, crystals, and kitchen tiles are friskier than we presume in our anthropocentrism. Sappho sang of fiery love — "You set me on fire"[84] — for love is blazing, moving, shifting. The Heraclitan flame joined with the Empedoclean *philia* is Eros, Protogonos, Aphrodite, Erotes, male, female and

---

81 Ibid., 137.
82 Ibid.
83 Sprinkle and Stephens, *Assuming the Ecosexual Position*, 190.
84 Sappho, fragment 11, trans. Julia Dubnoff, *Poems of Sappho*, n.d., https://www.uh.edu/~cldue/texts/sappho.html.

nonbinary, animal, vegetable, and mineral, junction and disjunction, the one that fucks off to couple into many, and the many that fuck until they are one.

Challenging a reductive, utilitarian, and procreative erotics with a working cosmology of erotic worlding, we can now return to two of the paradigms exposed by the gnostic myths, static gender roles with man-over-woman and a hierarchy of demiurge-over-world. First, we will look at the possibilities of gendered embodiment when the body is seen as a one constituted by an erotically engaged many. Then, we will explore subject-subject creativity as an alternative to a Platonic demiurge and his object world.

The(y)ogony: Birth of the Many-Gendered Body

In 2014, I cofounded the House of Larva Drag Co-Operative with Guadalupe "Pita" Angeles, and McKay Bram joined in 2017 and has been my primary collaborator since. House of Larva is a queer performance art and experimental drag group that has performed numerous acts in the Midwest and New England. Each show is more or less connected with another through a loose mythology. The world, our bodies, our homes are terrorized by the omnipotent and violently patriarchal demiurge Admiral Benwa Breedwinner, who has tricked mainstream society, "the breeders," into eternal slavery to his alien sex drive. The Bitchfaggots, a diverse group of beings unified only by their refusal of reproductive heterosexuality, are the only humans who resist Breedwinner. At least, they attempt to resist him. By and large the Bitchfaggots end up enlisted in the service of, forced to submit, or destroyed by Breedwinner and his minions. The mythology is only occasionally explicit in our acts, and many acts are parodies of current news events, sci-fi films, public lectures in response to scientific theories, domestic dramas. What is fairly consistent is the alternative to an established order, the Bitchfaggot attempts to exist outside of an imperialist, patriarchal rule, but ends up replicating or being killed by that same rule. Not quite chairing Pride Parade drag, but you get the picture.

"Bitchfaggot" is a hybrid term combining gendered slurs, and that hybridity is key to our drag personae. Pita, a queer Chicanx woman, performs not as a drag king but as Enfanga Sphinx — alternately hypersexual and asexual, monstrous and human, slave and liberator, hunter and prey. She rarely wears much, but various combinations of pasties, rags, dried glue, and plastic insects. There is much coded savagery, non-whiteness, European stereotypes. And most importantly to Angeles, is that Sphynx is a parasite, constantly living in relationship with or off the other characters. My own unshaved, barely wigged, tatter-wearing persona is the drag ogress Çicada L'Amour. Hairy and primordial, she is a being of wrath and carnality, hungering, lusting, and enforcing *her* "radical" world onto others. Whether appearing as a goddess, an experimental fly-woman, or an unhinged housewife, L'Amour is usually deluded by her sense of self and power, often discovering by the end of a show that she is just another cog in the imperialist, violating system of Breedwinner or even a key part of that oppression. She is hybrid of man and woman, god and demon, insect and human, subject and object. Finally, is the peculiar emergence of House of Larva's drag king, Pouchet Pouchet. Bram's Pouchet Pouchet might sometimes seem the most like a traditional drag king, but be forewarned, she is also defined by often disturbing metamorphoses, a sex, gender, or body difficult to pin down. In one show, Pouchet Pouchet starts as a blonde woman but goes through Bitchfaggot conversion therapy to become a hyperviolent masculine soldier in Benwa's army. In other shows, Pouchet bursts from a young woman to reveal she is an ancient serpent, transitions from a star male doctor to a lobotomized androgyne, converts a Judge Brett Kavanagh into a martyred saint, and evolves from a nonsexed innocent to a cum-spurting Übermensch. Pouchet's hybridity is often further symbolized through his use of a special prop, a strap-on dildo made from a giant plastic grasshopper, which has pissed in a water fountain, ejaculated yogurt, or thrusted through the mouth of a Louis

Pasteur cardboard cutout. Hybridity and an unstable self are the markers of bitchfaggotry.

When we created House of Larva, Pita and I were in the middle of confusion, depressive bouts, and dysphorias. We were each learning about our own gendered, classed, religious, linguistic, and ethnic hybridities, and experimented with the exaggerations of drag performance to help understand our selves. Eventually, these became shows in which we invited other people to explore their selves — what is a self, is it static, it is real, what does it serve — similar questions to those being explored throughout this book. Eventually, even against the overall pessimistic arcs of our shows, House of Larva has become a celebration of our constructed hybridities, our unique monstrosities.

Rubenstein cites Michel Foucault's definition of monster as mixture of supposedly disparate parts, going on to write that the pantheist monster "is therefore not just a conflation of binaries, but rather an omni-faceted beast appearing under totally different aspects, depending on your point of view."[85] Throughout her book, Rubenstein turns to the god Pan, in mini discussions that serve a chorus-like function to *Pantheologies*'s overall project. Pan is a useful symbol for the ontic effrontery of a pantheist system. Pan is "half-man, half-goat," "a mixture of delight and terror, seduction and repulsion,"[86] having "the horns, ears, and legs of a goat" with the torso and head of a man, and "being moreover a god," whose "very body recapitulates the Great Chain of Being, his low parts embodying the lowest ranks of the universe and his upper parts embodying the highest."[87] Rubenstein's pantheistic, and queer, cosmos looks to Pan, as Susan Stryker appeals to Frankenstein's monster, the sphynx, and the chimera. Similarly, the bitchfaggots serve as mythopoetic representations of our queer bodies — assemblages of disparate parts that, depending on perspective, shift from attractive to repulsive, empowering to

---

85 Rubenstein, *Pantheologies*, 48.
86 Ibid., 29.
87 Ibid., 30.

demeaning, godlike to demonic to bestial to utterly human, and from tragical to comical.

A demiurgic eros employs heterosexuality to regulate what would otherwise be a monstrous body. Psychotherapist Angie Fee trains future therapists to observe the ways "heterosexuality has become an organizing principle for understanding and experiencing sexual and gendered identities."[88] In her contribution to *Transgender Identities,* Fee sets out to challenge the "presumed naturalness of heterosexuality and the largely unquestioning acceptance of this category" and to illustrate "the limited conceptual space of heterosexual discourse that depends on binary sexed and gender categories for exploring and understanding erotic relationships."[89] In her essay, Fee identifies "the heterosexual matrix — the conflation of sex-gender-desire which leads to the normalisation of heterosexuality — as the source of sex and gender categorisation," setting this up as the backdrop for, among other things, the emergence of trans individuals. A history of the heterosexual matrix maps "the rise of a hegemonic heteronormative regime which has become central to how people experience and understand their sexual and gender identities and to how we form erotic relationships."[90] How we experience gender, that is our gendered body, is contingent on erotic formulations.

Fee cites Freud's Oedipal complex as an ideology "that produces heterosexuality as a symbol of 'normal' and 'mature' adult sexual and gender identity."[91] She explains:

> The Oedipal complex structures the direction of identification and desire, in that identification is what one would like to be, and desire is what one would like to have but one cannot identify and desire the same object. In this way, the

---

[88] Angie Fee, "Who Put the 'Hetero' in Sexuality?," in *Transgender Identities: Towards a Social Analysis of Gender Diversity,* ed. Sally Hines and Tam Sanger (London: Routledge, 2010), 207.
[89] Ibid.
[90] Ibid., 208.
[91] Ibid.

> concepts of identification and desire are gendered and heterosexualised. Homosexual desires are seen as heterosexual desires stemming from the wrong identifications. The Oedipus complex is the story that Freud creates about growing up and taming these initial multiple desires.[92]

It is fitting that Fee uses the word "story" to describe what Freud posits. The story, the narrative, the myth of the Oedipal complex is one of progress, where multiplicitous identifications and desires are streamlined into one gendered identification with one sexual desire. In a Freudian theodicy, sexual and identificatory regression are an omnipresent evil. Fee continues:

> It is worth questioning whether Freud's "normal" negotiation of the Oedipus complex is ever achieved. My own psychotherapeutic work with people is testimony to how fluid desire is and how it flows in many directions breaking up all kinds of imposed moral codes […]. In Freudian terms, we can — at any point in life — still be at the mercy of the pre-Oedipal state of "polymorphous perversities" — a time when neither we, nor the objects of our desire, were defined through sexual difference, a time before our gendered fate was sealed by strongly embedded cultural messages. If Freud's theory that all children are polymorphously perverse is to be believed, it is difficult to understand how these multitudinous, undifferentiated desires get so narrowly channeled into adult procreative heterosexuality.[93]

Freud's myth includes a sexual and gendered *tehom,* and the abyss of multiplicitous, monstrous erotics threatens a world of patriarchal power. Chaos must be wrestled into heterosexual order. This conflict, however, is not only of the past but is a constant struggle tied to every emerging body. Childhood is disor-

---

92 Ibid., 209.
93 Ibid.

dered and dangerous. Maturity is not guaranteed. The heterosexual matrix is required to regulate our bodies:

> The Oedipal trajectory manifests itself in the construction of dualistic and hierarchical gender categories whereby, traditionally, sexual orientation is dictated by gender identity. The Oedipus myth, by relying on a heterosexual psychic structure, accepts the social, political and religious forms of domination in modern Western society which effectively control and define desire. Western heterosexuality defines what is male and female, and gender is thus derived from it. This heterosexual matrix is unconsciously lived out to the extent that it is marked as natural and given.[94]

Erotics include who we desire to be and with whom we desire to be. The heterosexual matrix, like the demiurgical ploy for power, says there is a necessary correlation between who we desire to be and whom to be with, such that to be a man is to be with a woman and vice versa. But this rigid order belies the many-ness within and between bodies. The heterosexual champion diligently slices heads from the shoulders of the pleromic gender or sexual beast, but more heads grow in their places. The heterosexual matrix requires a process of constant mutilation, the hydra always evading total eradication. But this is little relief for each of its amputated parts.

After discussing theorists Foucault, Butler, Wittig, and Rich, all of whom challenge the dominant Freudian scheme, Fee explains that "the destabilisation of sexual and gender identities brought about by these shifts in theorising, opened up new ways of thinking about identities and practices outwith binary sex and gender ideology."[95] The given naturalness of the heterosexual matrix, once revealed as discursive, provides new space for imagining other. Imagining other creates new space for

---

94 Ibid.
95 Ibid., 214–15.

becoming other. "Transgender is a concept that emerged in the 1990s," writes Fee, and it is

> an inclusive term for people who have broken away from society's expectation that sex and gender are essential, binary categories. Transgenderists do not necessarily see themselves as transsexuals or transvestites, or, indeed, claim any clear cut [sic] identities. The category of transgender is itself multiple and contested and incorporates a principle of diversity rather than uniformity, moving from dichotomy to continuity where it is not so easy to categorise people into male-female dualities. The term transgender moves away from a physically-based [sic] definition (sex of the body) [...]. [Transgender people] live their lives in a gender that opposes — according to dominant discourse — their biological sex.[96]

Fee echoes some of what we have seen in Stryker's definition of transgender, a term inclusive of a great variety of gender crossings. As nonbinary author Eris Young writes: "Since ancient times and throughout the world, there have always been people, and sometimes established cultural categories for those people, outside of the strict binary of man and woman."[97] Still, citing Stryker, Fee observes "the emergence of transgender studies parallels the rise of queer studies," although "despite similarities, their relationship with each other is often problematic and contested."[98] Many "queer scholars have used the transgender phenomenon to open up new ways of thinking about identities and practices outwith the heterosexual discourse of 'oppositional' categories such as man and woman," but it is precisely this "use" that has been felt by some transgender people as

---

[96] Ibid., 215.
[97] Eris Young, *They/Them/Their: A Guide to Nonbinary and Genderqueer Identities* (London: Jessica Kingsley Publishers, 2019), 63.
[98] Fee, "Who Put the 'Hetero' in Sexuality?," 216.

objectifying.[99] That is, even those whose theories help us speak out sometimes speak of us in such a way that some of us feel as denying our agential voice. Still, I find invaluable how the incorporation of trans witness in queer theory and queer inquiry into transgender theory "represents a move away from the essentialist/constructionist debate, and focuses on how people's bodies extend into available spaces and form sexed and gendered identities."[100] Surely it moves me into asking how bodies operates from the cosmological vantage of erotic worlding?

From the pre-Socratics, we have seen that unifications and disintegrations of animate matter constitute worlds, bodies, and gods, and that a level of separation creates perspective necessary for the emergence of unique but contingent and non-eternal selves, but we have some insight to gain from a later Greek source concerned with love. For example, Plato's *Symposium* is a dialogue wherein a variety of characters — nobles, philosophers, physicians, tragedians, comedians — give speeches about Love. One of these characters is the physician Eryximachus. Eryximachus aligns himself with the Greek zeitgeist of cosmic eroticism: "The body of every creature on earth is pervaded by Love, as every plant is too; it's hardly going too far to say that Love is present in everything that exists."[101] And again, love and divinity are linked: "Love is a great and awesome god who pervades every aspect of the lives of men and gods."[102] We are bodies pervaded by love. And this love is not an alien agent but a pancosmic electricity.

The role of the physician, then, is first to observe love in the body, where "medicine is the science of the ways of Love as

---

99 See Namaste, Viviane, K., "'Tragic Misreadings': Queer Theory's Erasure of Transgender Subjectivity" in *Invisible lives: The Erasure of Transsexual and Transgendered people* (Chicago: University of Chicago Press, 2000), 9–23. See also Jay Prosser, *Second Skins: The Body Narratives of Transsexuality* (New York: Columbia University Press, 1998).
100 Fee, "Who Put the 'Hetero' in Sexuality?," 216.
101 Plato, *Symposium,* trans. Robin Waterfield (Oxford: Oxford University Press, 1994), 186a.
102 Ibid., 186b.

they affect bodily filling and emptying."¹⁰³ Eryximachus distinguishes between two different forms of love through dissimilarity, "where there is dissimilarity between things, there is also dissimilarity between the things they desire and love. The love experienced by a healthy body, therefore, is different from the love experienced by a sick body."¹⁰⁴ One form of Love is harmonizing, another form of love seeks pleasure. This latter love is not necessarily evil, although only the former is called "good," but it is dangerous. Love of certain things can bring disorder to the harmonizing love. Plato in turn maintains that

> moderate people, whose love helps people develop moderation, should be gratified, and their love should be cherished. It's their love which is the good Love, the Celestial Love who stems from the Muse Celestia. Polymnia's Love, however, is the Common Love; one has to be careful that the recipients of this Love enjoy the pleasure he has to offer without being made self-indulgent.¹⁰⁵

The physician helps the patient cultivate harmonizing love and keep in check the Polyhymnia, that is, the "many-song" love. For Eryximachus, harmonizing love differs from Empedocles' and Heraclitus's model. In fact, he specifically addresses Heraclitus's nondualism of chaos and order, that is, "the idea that there's divergence within harmony, that harmony could still exist if the components were divergent, is quite absurd," pondering that Heraclitus, in the instance of harmony and disharmony in music, tries to say that "it's the job of musical expertise to bring about harmony by changing a state of divergence between high and low pitch into one where they are in agreement."¹⁰⁶ Allegorically, we can ascertain that the role of the physician, in serving harmonizing love, involves changing substances so that they can

---

103 Ibid., 186c.
104 Ibid., 186b.
105 Ibid., 187e.
106 Ibid., 187a–b.

agree. Harmonizing love transforms previously divergent parts into complementary ones that can then work together toward an ideal form or body. The "Common Love" however has no ideal toward which it pulls disparate parts. Take for example the oppositional characteristics of hot, cold, wet, and dry, used both in ancient medicine as well as in the description of climate. When hot, cold, dry, and wet

> are under the influence of the moderate Love, there is harmony between them and they blend into a temperate climate. They bring rich harvests, and health not just for plants, but also for men and all other animals; their effects are innocuous. But when the other Love, the brutal one, gains control over the weather, then they cause widespread destruction and harm.[107]

An extra-cosmic order, consistent with Platonic metaphysics, is the ideal toward which harmonizing love moves. There is a "healthy" model, and this model is homogenous. It softens the differences within our bodies until all our pieces are one unified whole. Sickness, then, is the result of too many and too strong individual pieces of ourselves or our landscapes vying for their own desires, and "these are the conditions which lead to creatures and plants contracting epidemics and a wide variety of other diseases, because the result of these factors immoderately encroaching on one another is frosts, hailstorms, and blight."[108] Eryximachus surmises that

> Love fundamentally is, in all his manifestations; it's not going too far to say that he is omnipotent. But it is the Love whose fulfillment lies in virtuous, restrained, and moral behaviour from both gods and men who has the greatest power, and is the source of all our happiness.[109]

---
107 Ibid., 188e.
108 Ibid., 188b.
109 Ibid., 188d.

Like Empedocles, Plato's Eryximachus sees love in everything. And Eryximachus continues with dualistic thinking, although instead of *philia* and *neikos,* he has good, healthy Eros 1 and dangerous, unhealthy Eros 2. A key difference between these dualisms is the location of the body within them. Even though Empedocles prefers love over strife, no single body or daemon exists without both. Every body is a hybrid of attractive and detractive parts, and something which is fully harmonized lacks any identity, relationship, or perspective. Furthermore, while harmony brings disparate parts together, the elements remain divergent. It is their relationships that change, not their essence. For Eryximachus, disparate elements can be changed, and it is through what I am calling Eros 1 that they change. Here, there is an ideal body, and it is harmonious. Empedocles might have a hierarchy of personalities — human, daemon, deity — but all are similar in that they are amalgamations *and* in that there is mobility for transitioning between these states. When the harmony of *philia* is in complete control, which itself is not really "complete" because eventually there is the pull of *neikos,* there is love but no lover and beloved, that is, no body. For Eryximachus the body, at least the healthy, moral, and beautiful body, *is* harmony rather than something that dissolves into harmony. Meanwhile, Eros 2 threatens that body with the dangers of imbalance and divergency.

Eryximachus's outright attack on Heraclitus's thought is because the pre-Socratic thinker has a nondualist approach. Heraclitus understands harmony and chaos as perspectives on an ever-changing matter. Thus harmony and chaos coexist. Furthermore, he argues for identity as *founded* on the differences between communities of matter. Singularity is conditioned by plurality, identity by the recognition of multiple entities. Eryximachus is overtly moralistic, and his moralism coincides with a bodily and social aesthetic norm. I see in Eryximachus's physician someone who cultivates a moderate and moderating love, like Freud's psychoanalyst who guides the patient from divergent and multiple identifications or desires into the heterosexual, cisgender normative. Both doctors acknowledge the many within a given body but deem that manyness a threat to order and to a coherent self.

I am attracted to Eryximachus's model of a body pervaded by divine Eros and to the idea of physician as tracker and coordinator of love. At the same time, it can be disastrous when we ignore, subordinate, or destroy the many in service of the one. I propose that certain bodies, based on their vantage points in the cosmos, have experiences of and insights into how the many and the one coexist. I am talking, right now, of nonbinary, genderqueer, or genderfucked people and to an extent, acknowledging that I am limiting myself to the English-speaking world, those who use they/them gender pronouns.

Eris Young writes that for "a trans person to use a certain set of pronouns that are divergent from those they were assigned at birth is an uncategorical, public statement of their gender identity."[110] The pronouns we use symbolize something about who we are, and, in their intelligibility, affect how we are seen. In Young's experience "they/them/theirs is the most common pronoun set used by the genderqueer and nonbinary community."[111] Living in the American Midwest, this has also been my own experience.[112] The use of the singular they/them/theirs pronouns has been a point of contestation between hegemonic society and those who use those pronouns. This is because "language is often used as a synecdoche for society as a whole, and therefore any perceived 'breakdown' in language, or change in its conventional use, is often taken to indicate a corresponding breakdown in society."[113] Young explains further:

> Gender, and its binary, is one of the oldest and most entrenched systems in human society. The proportion

---

110 Young, *They/Them/Their*, 51.
111 Ibid., 55.
112 Some people use pronouns *xe/xem/xir, ey, em, eir, ve, ver, vis*, and many others. These tend to be singular gender-neutral pronouns as opposed to "they," which is a sign pointing to both singular and multiple referents. It is this ambiguity that I think is an asset as opposed to a hindrance.
113 Ibid., 53.

of words that are gendered in the English language has remained relatively stable for almost a thousand years. So the incorporation of inclusive pronouns into common use represents a change to a longstanding tradition, a change which is often seen, sometimes unconsciously, as a threat to the very fabric of anglophone society.[114]

A symbol of multiplicity once again threatens the demiurgic order. And it does so by obscuring the line between the many and the one. Of course, not everyone who uses they/them/theirs does so with the explicit intention of it pointing to a multiplicity. Perhaps in most cases, a person using they/them/theirs pictures themselves as a coherent, singularity — a self. A non-male or non-female gender, for sure, but not necessarily a rejection of single taxonomized gender, rather, as transgender theorist Jack Halberstam cautions, "vernacular forms of expression and definition are not necessarily less regulatory or less committed to norms than other modes of classification."[115] Transgender people are people and are constantly struggling between surviving this world and building another. As Fee suggests, "the thought of not having a stable gender identity is a frightening one for many — what would our point of reference be if we were not categorised as a man or a woman?"[116] Fee asks some pointed questions. What would our point of reference be? How could we engage a world if we are not fixed, whole, one? Transgender politics need to account for cosmology.

An insistence on they/them/theirs as singular pronoun, instead of, let us say, a hybrid pronoun, might be an acceptance of a certain cosmology where there is spirit and there is matter, an eternal true self and an ephemeral, material body, of agency for some but not for others. I think we might take seriously that this pronoun can destabilize worlds, not only linguistic worlds,

---

114 Ibid., 53–54.
115 Jack Halberstam, *Trans*: A Quick and Quirky Account of Gender Variability* (Oakland: University of California Press, 2018), 12.
116 Fee, "Who Put the 'Hetero' in Sexuality?," 217.

but also the worlds to which they point. Opting for one's body to be referred to in a way that is both plural and singular is an assault on the ontic distinction between one and many. Maybe they/them/theirs is the glint of pleroma in Eve's and Adam's eyes that terrifies the demiurge.

There are fantastic possibilities held by the symbol of they/them/theirs beyond pronoun usage according to a normative symbolic or linguistic structure. Influenced by poet Eileen Myles, Halberstam writes:

> The use of the plural for the singular, the referencing of the many over the individual, contains within it [...] a small step toward utopia, a conjuring of collectivity in the place of individualism and recognition. We might add that genders only emerge in relation to other bodies and within multiply oriented and complex populations.[117]

This is an imaginative use of they/them/theirs, and it is related to why I use that pronoun. I believe they/them/theirs helps me articulate my own multiplicity, a partial renouncement of self, and a full renouncement of eternal self. However, pronoun use and nonbinary identity are not equivalent. For instance, I also use he/him/his pronouns, honoring the relationships in my emergence that constitute such pronoun usage. Too much emphasis on they/them/theirs as pronoun also presupposes an anglophone context, and there are nonbinary people, who articulate their experiences, throughout all the world with all its languages.

For Young, "the question at the heart of the pronoun debate is fundamentally one of autonymy — the ability of a demographic, especially a marginalised one, to name itself and thus claim agency or control over how it is referred to, and by extension, treated."[118] Halberstam agrees that naming "is a powerful activity and one that has been embedded in modern produc-

---

117 Halberstam, *Trans**, 11–12.
118 Young, *They/Them/Their*, 53.

tions of expertise and knowledge production."[119] He discusses the importance of naming in discussing the title of their book *Trans**. Of "trans*," Halberstam writes,

> the asterisk modifies the meaning of transitivity by refusing to situate transition in relation to a destination, a final form, a specific shape, or an established configuration of desire and identity. [...] [T]rans* can be a name for expansive forms of difference, haptic relations to knowing, uncertain modes of being, and the disaggregation of identity politics predicated upon the separating out of many kinds of experience that actually blend together, intersect, and mix. This terminology, trans*, stands at odds with the history of gender variance, which has been collapsed into concise definitions, sure medical pronouncements, and fierce exclusions.[120]

Halberstam's analysis throughout the book *Trans** "pays attention to the ebb and flow of regulation and innovation, governance, and experimentation"[121] in the lives of transgender people and adds "new visibility for any given community has advantages and disadvantages, liabilities and potentialities."[122] The book rigorously engages transgender politics in light of socio economics, race, ethnicity, and nationalism, and has much to say about ideological colonialism in transgender spaces, but by the end of the book, one identifies a hope tied up with multiplicity, imagination, and the building of bodies, where "[t]rans* bodies, in their fragmented, unfinished, broken-beyond-repair forms, remind all of us that the body is always under construction."[123] As trans* people, we might be avatars of the pancosmos, desiring new forms and combinations, becoming bodies constantly and erotically.

---

119 Halberstam, *Trans**, 4.
120 Ibid., 4–5.
121 Ibid., 18.
122 Ibid.
123 Ibid., 135.

There is an incredible charge in Halberstam's work about what our bodies, our lives, our emergences might symbolize in relation to our cosmos. We might even serve as Eryximachean physicians bearing witness to the attracting and detracting elements in our bodies and in the bodies around us, perhaps even offering wisdom from our purview. How can harmonious love and love of difference coexist? What is it to contain personalities of multiple agencies in one body?

In "Kitchen Sink Gender," novelist and educator Nino Cipri talks about an incredibly heteronormative, cisnormative pole dancing fitness class, with terrible music to boot, that they joined and in the end loved. The story begins with Cipri describing themself on their first day of class: "I showed up in a pink tank top that said, 'SEAHORSES AGAINST GENDER ROLES.' I'd shaved off two-thirds of my hair the week before. I was covered in tattoos and body hair and attitude: my normal public armor when venturing into potentially hostile territories."[124] Cipri describes their body as containing elements that are coded as either masculine, feminine, or another gender. They will stand out against the particular femininity of the cisgender women who are their classmates.

About their youth, Cipri tells of rejecting femininity and hanging out with boys instead of girls, picking up "the art of refusing markers of femininity," and noting how "American masculinity currently seems to center on saying no. It so often looks and feels like gender by process of elimination."[125] This fits with both the Freudian and the Eryximachean schemes where multiple, potentially disharmonious emotions, behaviors, personalities, and desires must be eliminated to keep the peace. Having felt alienated in the extreme of masculinity, Cipri writes,

---

[124] Nino Cipri, "Kitchen Sink Gender," in *Nonbinary: Memoirs of Gender and Identity,* eds. Micah Rajunav and Scott Duane (New York: Columbia University Press, 2019), 201.

[125] Ibid., 203.

> I eventually mapped out my own liminal terrain, a space that overlapped both and neither. It was my body, my gender, and my life, and I could define those things for myself. I didn't have to be a woman, and I didn't have to transition to being a man. I could carve out an identity that fit me, rather than an abstract.[126]

Rejecting the choice of one set of behaviors and interests over another, Cipri describes their kitchen sink approach.

> I've started taking a kitchen sink approach to my gender: it all goes in, except the things that don't. Motorcycles are, in fact, part of my gender. So are boots. Whiskey is still a part of my gender. Eye shadow and blue lipstick have gotten mixed into it, but red lipstick and nail polish feel like drag, and not the fun kind. Turtlenecks might have been part of Steve Jobs's gender, but not mine. Practicing martial arts has been a long and complicated part of my gender. The kind of shirts that your gay uncle wears on his yearly visit to Key West? Definitely part of my gender. Cats are integral to my gender. The necklace my mother gave me. DIY haircuts. Calluses, scars, and tattoos. Gray dresses cut in the same style as a burlap bag. This one pair of high heels I bought last month. Baking, but not cooking, and definitely not reality TV shows about cooking.[127]

Gender, here, reads as a list of culturally contradictory things coming together. It is about things that are desired, no longer about denial of desire. The kitchen sink approach to gender is about homing in on a multiplicity of objects in relationship to one another in ways that are delighting, confusing, frustrating, and especially surprising: "My gender surprises me — it dressed

---

126 Ibid.
127 Ibid., 207.

down for a long time, in gray corduroy and a peacoat. It kept its eyes averted. Now it has all kinds of demands."[128]

Cipri writes in beautiful lists, cataloging their body's experiences from shape, "my long fingers, my facial hair, the bone structure of my face"; to interactions, "holds purring cats, makes silly faces, touches other bodies in all sorts of pleasing and enjoyable ways"; to dysphoria, "binders and compression bras that press[,] I'd take them over creeping anxiety and dissociation that pop up when I gaze down at my chest"; to its misinterpretation by others, "strangers[,] friends, family members, and lovers. They see my breasts and soft belly and hips as something different than I do";[129] and simply, to movement, "everything turning in circles, momentum and centrifugal force, friction, and leverage. Forces meeting in a fluid exchange of power, a conversation between the body and its environment."[130] This last sentence ends the memoir on a cosmological note, exploring its relationship to the world and an exchange of interactive forces.

We have here no regimented, pure, healthy body, but a body of dynamism and relation. Cipri is no longer constituted by elimination. And while there is still pain in acknowledging one's own multiplicity, it is not a question of evil. Each body contains multitudes. Cipri's story is about finding those multitudes and honoring their different needs. Parts of the many are sometimes at odds with one another, but learning from them, naming them, feeling them, and loving them are all alternatives to eliminating them, or at least presuming to eliminate them. Cipri comes to terms with their self when they realize there is no conclusive term, no smooth and final end, that being "healthy" is refusing an either/or mentality and a monogender. To be in relationship with yourself, and therefore glean your wisdom, gnosis, power, love, is to be in relationship with all yourselves and with what all yourselves desire.

---

128 Ibid.
129 Ibid., 205.
130 Ibid., 207.

The selves inside a self, the bodies that constitute a body, bring me to the memoir of féi hernandez, "Coatlicue." After depicting a childhood scene of a mother washing her "boy," hernandez tells the story of the Goddess Coatlicue:

> The Aztec goddess Coatlicue (co-at-lil-cu-eh) was regarded as the Earth's mother, the patron of giving life and taking it: childbirth, and warfare; she is the reason for existence on Earth as we know it. Myth states that she found a bundle of heavenly feathers while she swept atop the legendary mountain: Snake Mountain, Coatepetl. Entranced with the bundle of feathers, like any abuela would after seeing an unattended $100 bill, she tucked them into her snake dress and was instantly impregnated with war. Some call it her son, the god of war: Huitzilopochtli. I call it karma.[131]

hernandez compares this divinity with the woman inside of the presumed boy.

> The woman in me cannot be researched. She does not exist on the Internet or in the Ancient History Encyclopedia. She is the history I'm engraving in the hard minds of the world. Féi is very similar to Coatlicue, but is drastically different, a hybrid form of warrior goddess, shape-shifter, and animal. Anima incarnate. She is very comfortable being referred to as La Malinche, the war-starter, or La Llorona, the howling woman searching for her deceased children; she sees herself as Coatlicue, but has the eyes of the god Quetzalcoatl, the feathered serpent; at times she feels more Nagual, shape-shifter; sometimes she turns into a crow, sometimes the body I was born in.[132]

---

[131] féi hernandez, "Coatlicue," in *Nonbinary: Memoirs of Gender and Identity*, eds. Micah Rajunav and Scott Duane (New York: Columbia University Press, 2019), 16.

[132] Ibid.

Féi is an amalgamation of spirits, historical women, goddesses, gods, and shapeshifters. She is also the small body misinterpreted, by some, as a boy. hernandez describes cultivating this persona or these personae within themself:

> When I first saw Féi, her black wings had fallen feather by feather, her beak had grown long like an ingrown nail that gently pierced the soft of her throat like a knife. She was a woman unattended, ignored, abandoned. She was threatened by her own fray. Naked and hungry, she stood before me as I dressed her. I opened her body rolls like an accordion and let the noise fill the temple. I whistled the snake call and they slithered back to join her thighs and form her skirt. Her childless womb filled her stomach. Her claw held a pistol. I didn't need to hold her in my arms like Mary did Jesus after he was brought down from the cross. She stood valiantly. Papel picado sprouted from the walls and the dust cleared. The gold of the temple shone bright. She whipped her arms and feathers shot out.[133]

Féi and the child-to-become Féi have a relationship with each other. The child nurtures the naked woman, dresses her, calls to her until she responds. Eventually Féi stands on her own. A child without a womb, who we later learn yearns for one, cultivates in a spiritual womb a future self, who is also already herself, who is also someone other than the one who becomes Féi. hernandez writes "my boy body was only a doorframe, a portal for the woman in me to walk through," and that "all she wants me to do is speak her name: Féi. She is validated when I let her take flight from the tip of my teeth. She loves it when I let her slide into my arms like long velvet gloves to control my gestures."[134] hernandez is Féi and is also the place whence Féi emerges. hernandez is the nurturer of Féi. And Féi is superbly hybrid, bird and human, goddess and ghost. Ready to emerge

---

133 Ibid.
134 Ibid., 17.

from the child, hernandez writes a "beautiful goddess harpy stood rejuvenated before me. Before she took flight, I held her claw and said, *Tu eres mi mundo, eres mi vida.*"[135] Repeating hernandez's mother's words to her child,[136] hernandez tells Féi, "you are my world," adding "you are my life." Féi finally adds "*Eres mi otro yo.*"[137] "You are my other me." It is difficult to write about hernandez's piece, because hernandez resists a clear distinction and combination of their interrelated gendered selves. Féi is Féi and the origin of Féi and the container of Féi and the release of Féi, a person who is a "me" and another "me."

Again, we have an example of a nonbinary person appealing to mythopoetic imagery, particularly that of hybrid creatures like the harpy and the snake woman. In accessing the places where the fantastical live inside us, we emerge in fantastical multiplicity. Our bodies can desire and become what they desire, worship, and become what they worship, and what we are is a complexity of characters in relation. Hernandez rejects a subject–object relationship with their own body and so rejects a fully binary and dualistic transgender narrative where one gendered soul is trapped in a wrongly sexed, material body. Rather, both are material — the child that births Féi and Féi born of the child are subject in communication, conflict, and love with one another.

Féi's story speaks to my own conflicted self, particularly the relationship between me and my masculinity. I cannot ignore the subjecthood of the male and assigned male parts of me, the parts of me related to maleness, especially of having been a boy, and the relationships that have been built onto that, the desires that have come from that, and my ties to male-male homosexuality that are erotic and spiritual and constitutive of my very ways of thinking. And yet, I am also other subjectivities, feminine and otherwise. In my Jewish upbringing, the androgynous ideals of the Kabbalistic soul and the aeonic partnerships with

---

135 Ibid., 16.
136 Ibid., 15.
137 Ibid., 16.

the sefirot have given me speech and spurred my imagination as I reflect on my own complexities. And there is the eros, the desire kindled, when I create art with the women and nonbinary artists I so often cocreate with, an eros which far outflames any of my fleeting hookups with men. I desire to be with, and partly in, the images of the community of performers in every show I direct. I speak words of many genders when I speak, and this took me a long time to learn.

In 2016 I wrote a blog post "Call Me a Fairy" in which I first publicly spoke about my hybridity. In it I ask my readers to address me: "Call me a faggot, a fruit. Call me a sissy-bear, he-she, chub of a queer. Call me a pervert, an invert, a subvert… all the verts — I love the verts! And above all, call me a fairy."[138] This is a piece outside of my drag persona, although my drag persona has since influenced my out-of-drag persona quite a lot. But whether in drag or out, hybridity helps me understand what is going on with my feelings, my observations, my erotics. I continue to explain that fairies "are as playful as [their] sprites. As dangerous as [their] queens. A tithe to heaven, a tithe to hell, the fairies have bought the freedom to travel in between. And they are wiser for it."[139] Playful and dangerous, angelic, and demonic, my "fairy" certainly inhabited a world of gendered and spiritual poles, but in that cosmos, it is never statically in one. As I write this book now, I think the fields of mythic entities is far greater than those that are heavenly and those that are demonic, but ultimately, the many mes inside of me continue to resonate with when a younger me wrote: "We have relationships with gender ideologies and with queer ideologies, but we don't need to be fixed in either," and "sometimes my gay is on a continuum with trans."[140] Those sometimes are much more frequent now, and I

---

[138] Max Brumberg-Kraus, "Call Me a Fairy," *Homos in Heimarmene,* August 2, 2016, http://homosinheimarmene.blogspot.com/2016/08/call-me-fairy-full-pleasant-is-fairy.html.

[139] Ibid.

[140] Ibid.

have grown to see ogres and daemons, dryads, hags, and horny fauns cohabiting with the fairies in me.

As he writes to his lover, Empedocles shows "the gods' nature must be understood on the one hand in terms of the cosmic system and the physical theory that underlies it and on the other hand in terms of the relation between the gods and ourselves, since we have been gods and have the potential to be gods again."[141] As discussed, Empedocles' gods are entities most in love, that is with the most varying components most in love with one another until everything is harmonized beyond even divine identity. Gods are mixtures, but so are daemons, the spirits, and so are we! But humans are mixtures plagued with the social regulation of the eternal or singular self, the demiurgic model sowing neikos by asking us to worship our separation from our world and our God from us. We all contain hybridity, but because of the particular mixtures, the relationships we form and that have biologically or socially or psychologically or cosmically led to us, nonbinary people often see, frequently because we are forced to, behind the illusion of an eternal static gender, and thus, the eternal, static self. To acknowledge our multiple parts moves us toward being more in love. We cannot know what capacity to love there is if we deny so many avenues within us even a fantasy, even a thought of their existence. We do not have to act out every personality we contain or act on every impulse. Some denial, separation keeps us unique and therefore allows more distinct bodies to move in and out of one another. However, if we completely ignore the heroes, gods, and monsters in us, imagine they are not there, we will be duped when they rear their heads and speak with fires kindled in the wrath of their mental, physical subjugation. The heterosexual matrix facilitates its monstrous enemies in denying its champions their own stake in monsterhood.

Empedocles hopes his beloved can learn of his erotically constituted, multiplicitous body, his cosmically contingent self. He hopes the beloved will be a better lover to the world when he

---

141 McKirahan, *Philosophy before Socrates*, 289–90.

knows his interdependence with it, not his eternal separation from it. In that same spirit, I write to any reader that we are legion, we are many, and we like it!

Another term for genderqueer or nonbinary is genderfucked, and I think it is a delightful term for what we are! We are multiple gendered personalities in various copulations birthing new selves and new desires through constant reintegration. The body is an orgy, an orgy is worlds begetting worlds. Eros is strong enough to contain multitudes and compose a body at the same time. Listen to the hybrid daemons that are at once inside of you and are you, your intersubjectivity. All of us who inhabit race, ethnicity, citizenship, gender, sex, and religion interstices, we have used and continue to use our perspective to survive this world and to change it so that survival can get easier for all of us, for those we love, for those on whom we are contingent. If somehow this current era is distinct from any other, or is more likely another contingency, we can call it is an era of theyogony: the birth of they, the birth of the many.

Having discussed an erotically constituted and multiplicitous gendered body, we can now address the worlds we are contingent on, asking how to facilitate intersubjectivity in a world so often degraded by demiurgic cosmology.

Pornocosmos: Worlds of Intersubjective Fantasy

After attending the first Radical Faeries meeting in 1979, non-assimilationist, gay spiritual leader, and gay rights activist Harry Hay wrote an essay where he defines the term spiritual as "the accumulation of all experiential consciousness from the division of the first cells in the primeval slime, down through all biological-political-social evolution to your and to my latest insights through Gay Consciousness just a moment ago."[142] Gay spirituality, Hay believes, involves embracing the subor-

---

[142] Harry Hay, "Toward the New Frontiers of Fairy Vision: Subject-Subject Consciousness," in *Radically Gay: Gay Liberation in the Words of Its Founder*, ed. Will Roscoe (Boston: Beacon, 1996), 254–55.

dinated consciousness of a gay cultural collective. "When the Fairies reached out to make reunion with that long-ago cast out shadow-self so long suppressed and denied, the explosive energies released by the jubilations were ecstatic beyond belief."[143] He continues to describe the shadow self as a hybrid, Sissy-boy, a sort of third gender, inside of gay men:

> When we caught up that lonely little Sissy-boy in an ecstatic hug of reuniting, we were recapturing also the suddenly remembered sense of awe and wonder of Marvelous Mother Nature [...]. We were [...] even recapturing the glowing innocence of that Sissy-boy's Dream. And in that Dream, the glowing non-verbal dream of young Gayhood, may lie the key to the enormous and particular contribution that Gay people may have to make to our beloved Humankind — a key known as *subject–SUBJECT Consciousness.*[144]

Subject–subject consciousness is central to Hay's understanding of gay spirituality. For him, part of the gay experience involves being a child who is denied the ability to act out one's attraction toward other children. Without knowing other gay people, the gay child begins to dream of another self who is also him. In comparison to the heterosexual matrix wherein boys and girls were taught to think of the other "as SEX-OBJECTS to be manipulated," Hay writes, "HE whom I would love would be another ME. We wouldn't manipulate each other — *we would share* — and we'd always understand each other completely *and forever!*"[145] Hay describes a process wherein gay people, growing up strangers in heterosexual land, do not have the same image of the sexual object as their peers. Denied the sexual, they only know themselves as selves, and as such when they begin to imagine their beloved, they begin with selves. This moves from a narcissistic love of myself to a love of a self when the dreamed love-subject

---
143 Ibid., 255.
144 Ibid., 255–56.
145 Ibid., 257.

and an actual love-subject are engaged. Of an early relationship, Hay discloses that they were *"in ourselves and, simultaneously, in each other,* we also knew, that is, subject-to-subject."[146]

Hay's spirituality generalizes and essentializes a gay (male, often white) experience, but at the same time, he is laying a critique against a societal norm rather than at individuals. For him,

> the world we inherit, the total Hetero-Male-oriented-and-dominated world of Tradition and daily environment, the *summum bonum* of our history, our philosophy, our psychology, our culture, and very languages of communication — *all* are totally subject-object in concept, in definition, in evolution, in self-serving orientation.[147]

His picture of the world, a cosmos, is in line with much that we have already discussed. The radical difference between a subject and object keeps a particular cosmic system in place. In our conceptions of politics, justice, fairness, "a given person is the *object* of another person's perceptions, to be influenced, persuaded, cajoled, jaw-boned, manipulated, and therefore, in the last analysis, *controlled.*"[148] As for minoritized or subordinated people — sexual, gendered, raced, or disabled — the aim is "to make themselves *objects of approval* instead of objects of disapproval — but *objects* nonetheless."[149] In this last point, we clearly hear the anti-assimilationist note. To fight for approval by the same continuous power structure is to continue to see them as the only viable agents of change. By becoming more like the heterosexual, patriarchal man, queer people are accepting only one subject. Paradoxically, becoming more like the ideal subject is to be an object of that ideal's manipulation. Choice, intention, and autonomy are suppressed until they are destroyed, and the individual is made into their idol.

---

146 Ibid., 258.
147 Ibid.
148 Ibid., 259.
149 Ibid.

An object is denied a say in its formation. An object is denied a say in its emergence and evolution. Through the lens of erotic worlding, the object is denied its ability to desire. Worlds, minerals, plants, and many animals are outright denied subjectivity. But so are many, many people. The dominant love-scheme of heterosexuality, according to Hay, helps facilitate objectification. His experiences with queer spirituality give him hope for the broken cosmos. Perhaps queer people can be teachers of subject–subject relationality. A Marxist, Hay has always been influenced by utopian thought, and his vision of utopia constituted by subject–subject relationality bears some resemblance to both Mary Daly's model and Herbert Richardson's. The emergence of intersubjective consciousness, although not heteronormative, still bely a gay male normativity that, like radical feminism, wavers between a complex subjectivity and an essentialist identity.

The life that Hay writes about is not the same life that many queer people of many genders and races necessarily experience today, although I think his insights shed light on a perhaps greater potential to participate in subject-to-subject relationships. Our capacities to relate to other people are challenged by liminal, secretive, and sublimated characteristics, and one important tactic for us lies in our ability to see another's subjecthood. Furthermore, our sometimes explicit objectification on behalf of others' actions might keep us hyper-vigilant toward someone else being objectified. But this is not always the case. Different privileges we might hold as well as the assimilationist survival tactic lead many queer people to demiurgical subject–object perspectives. Still, the utopian is a desire, and that subject-subject desire existing in queerness is what makes us a threat to the heterosexual matrix and is key to our liberation.

There is a lot in Hay's description of growing up as a gay child that I and perhaps my peers can relate to, and there are some differences. One major difference between the times in which I am writing and in which Hay lived are that there are more and more celebrities who are coming out as trans, bisexual, gay, queer, asexual, and more LGBTQIA+ characters on television, film, the internet, and in written media. There are more out couples and queer social institutions, nonprofits, clubs, scholars, bars, and neighborhoods. Of course, many of these things existed, but the mainstream is taking a greater interest in them. Money flows, and queer figures begin to constellate our network of possible relations. The me who is me inside of me and the me who is me outside me, *you,* is significantly less private, and the subject of desire is impacted by endless flow of multi-gendered and sexual bodies. But are these more public, more highly displayed bodies subjects or objects in our relation to them?

The question of subjecthood and objecthood in relation to the proliferation of queer representation is at its most contested in the genre of pornography. In pornography, objectification is the presumed norm by both the religious right and many feminists alike. And there is good reason behind this! The male gaze continues to dominate, and even where it does not, the market has become so specific, bodies taxonomized to the most particular fetishes, that the relation to pornography is almost always of consumer and consumed. However, there are queer and feminist pornographies, pornographers, and audiences of porn who recognize the overwhelming objectification in pornography not as a call for censorship but as an opportunity for a radical reassertion of erotic subjecthood by those so often denied it. By looking at some queer and feminist pornographic tactics, we can gain insight into a poetics of erotic intersubjectivity not only between people denied subjecthood but with perhaps the most objectified being in Western Cosmology: the world.

Before talking about the production of pornography, I want to talk about its reception, since more people tend to be viewers of porn rather than its makers, and its makers are usually its viewers first. Closest to the picture Hay draws, is one function of pornography that sex therapist Don Shewey discusses in *The Paradox of Porn: Notes on Gay Male Sexual Culture.* For many gay men, looking at porn "is an important doorway into erotic existence."[150] In the US context, even schools that have more than an abstinence-only approach to sex ed classes, tend to exclude LGBTQIA+ relationships from their discussion or heavily focus on information primarily useful to heterosexual youths. Most queer people are also born from heterosexual relationships, and do not often have an example of a loving let alone sexually active queer relationship in their lives. Finally, match this up with the threat of violence many queer kids are subject to for exhibiting behaviors outside those ordained by the heterosexual matrix. While hetero-tweens are fumbling through dates, queer kids rarely get that luxury. Our sexual awakening is often postponed. Porn becomes one of the only arenas for education and representation. Shewey contends that for gay men, "porn provides not only entertainment and excitement but crucial exposure to same-sex attraction, unapologetic desire, uninhibited behavior, and fertile fantasy life — what is possible, what it looks like."[151] Particularly in the face of ignorance, Christian puritanism, and the images of queer sex as death sentence in the AIDS crisis, "porn champions embodiment and erotic vitality in the face of sexual repression, political disenfranchisement, and religious pressure to deny the pleasures of the body."[152] At least for Shewey's primarily gay male clients, how does porn do so very much?

Well, for starters, the book is called *The Paradox of Porn* and paradox is part of every chapter. We could call this a nondualistic approach to pornography, in which it serves a variety of functions that ambiguously affect a given body. Some of these effects are empowering to one agent and disempowering to another. In a later chapter, Shewey lays out the paradox that porn is "liberating because it shows the vast variety of possible sexual activities, it inspires creativity and imagination," and it is "intimidating because it creates pressure to master every pos-

---

150 Don Shewey, *The Paradox of Porn: Notes on Gay Male Sexual Culture* (New York: Joybody Books, 2018), 7.
151 Ibid.
152 Ibid.

sible sexual activity."[153] Porn can put up a sexual ideal against which most of us will never compare and teach us to value certain acts over others. It can also inspire us to imagine community differently and ourselves differently, a necessary influence when we are trapped in static and deadening social contexts.

One of Shewey's clients tells him: "What I like watching is porn about seducing a straight guy," and Shewey ascertains from this preference that, for this client, "gay male porn normalizes the experience of sexual fluidity, in contrast to many cultural and social contexts which rigidly enforce gender-role stereotypes and punish non-conformists."[154] Often for political or other social reasons, categories like gay male, lesbian, straight man, normatively presumed as cisgender, are considered static categories. This status relates to the myth that to be a subject is to avoid the material quality of malleability. Agents change and are not changed. However, in the context of pornography where straight men are turned gay, malleability is the seed of erotic possibility and communion, that is, the symbol of the straight, patriarchal order, such as a cop, doctor, businessman, jock, whatever is depicted as transformable. Perhaps then I, witnessing this transformation, might better imagine my own mutability. I am not static, sexually or otherwise.

Moving through such fluid identities from a psychoanalytic point of view, poet, essayist, and psychotherapist Keiko Lane tells a story from when she was an intern. Lane's client was a young butch lesbian who was questioning whether she was transgender. In a conversation around sexual fantasy, the client revealed "the images that turned her on [...] were from porn she didn't really like or, she corrected herself, didn't want to like."[155] The male-made, straight pornography that the client watched involved domination of women. She would imagine herself in the role of the men but that didn't feel right. Rather, "it had taken her a

---

153 Ibid., 40.
154 Ibid., 42.
155 Keiko Lane, "Imag(in)ing Possibilities: The Psychotherapeutic Potential of Queer Pornography," in *The Feminist Porn Book,* eds. Taormino et al., 165.

long time to realize that she didn't want to be in their bodies; she just wanted to do what they did."[156] After a few years, the client discerned that she was not a transgender man and had found a community where she could express her particular butch gender. However, she did not join any kink communities. Instead, what she had found were "images that did not accurately reflect her or her desires, but she was attempting to project herself into these images because they reflected the kind of power that she was attracted to."[157] There were still apprehensions about fantasy and reality, places in both to explore. Lane's work was to help her client explore these erotic fantasies and interpret them. However, her supervisor — "a heterosexual, white, traditionally psychoanalytic, and conservatively feminist psychotherapist" who "believed that all pornography exploits women" — instructed that all "reenactments are always pathological" and "the desire to feed the perpetually overwhelmed state of the psyche and the nervous system."[158] The next time her client described her fantasies, wondering if they were somehow perverted, Lane followed her supervisor's interpretation, that "maybe that is true."[159] This cut the relationship between therapist and client, for the therapist outlawed sexual fantasy, denying her client's ability to talk freely about the fantasy by implicitly shaming her. This story shows the relationship between questions of desire and questions of gender, of how pornographic images can inspire new ways of becoming that are not necessarily replicating the pornography. It also shows how vulnerable sharing our desires can be and how easily the denial of our sexual fantasy can stifle our spirit, close us off from relationships, become silent.

Ten years later, exploration of pornography and engagement with sexual fantasy is a key part of Lane's practice. She also teaches graduate students, and in one of her classes, tells students to "rent pornography and watch as many videos as it takes

---

156 Ibid., 166.
157 Ibid.
158 Ibid.
159 Ibid., 167.

to learn five new things, and then do it again. Not necessarily sex acts or positions — though certainly those are learned — but more complicated representations and enactments of desire and power."[160] Lane believes "good pornography, like good sex education, is useful as a therapeutic tool [...] because it helps to build somatic and visual vocabularies from which to make empowered choices."[161] Pornography is fictionalized representations in film, photography, and writing that not only spur the imagination, but provide the symbols and the narrativization of those symbols and the myths, whence we construct new subjecthoods. Shewey similarly sees porn as "making space for sexual fantasies whether they get enacted or not. Like science fiction and fantasy literature and films, its power can be measured by how far it stretches the imagination beyond your personal experience or even what's physically possible or realistically desirable."[162] It is in this way that porn helps us articulate our visions and assert our erotic potentiality, and fantasy.

Toward fantasy, the poet, novelist, and classicist Anne Carson comments on Aristotle when she writes, "whenever any creature is moved to reach out for what it desires [...], that movement begins in an act of imagination."[163] This act is called *phantasia*, the etymological root for fantasy, where "[p]*hantasia* stirs minds to movement by its power of representation; in other words, imagination prepares desire by representing the desired object as desirable to the mind of the desirer. *Phantasia* tells the mind a story."[164] Pornography is a fantasy put into a medium that can be shared by and with others. It is also a representer of symbols which we receive, interpret, and act out in different ways. This can be beautifully liberating, facilitating transformations and becomings in our bodies that have been denied us through a campaign of desexualization and objectification.

---

160 Ibid., 169.
161 Ibid., 170.
162 Shewey, *The Paradox of Porn*, 63.
163 Anne Carson, *Eros the Bittersweet* (Champaign: Dalkey Archive Press, 1998), 169.
164 Ibid.

Of course, this can be dangerous because the symbols in porn often replicate the power structures that are oppressive to queer people, to people of color, to women.

Porn can awaken the erotic subjecthood of an individual while simultaneously positioning that individual in a demiurgic relationship with the porn object. Particularly, the people within a given porn are real people doing real things, but their real desires, by extension their real subjecthood can be denied both by the form of the porn they are in and by the relationship a viewer has with them. Thus, feminist porn is an area of considerable contestation with objectifying mainstream porn. Taking elements from lesbian porn, porn for women, performance art, and avant-garde film making,

> feminist porn uses sexually explicit imagery to contest and complicate dominant representations of gender, sexuality, race, ethnicity, class, ability, age, body type, and other identity markers. It explores concepts of desire, agency, power, beauty, and pleasure at their most confounding and difficult, including pleasure within and across inequality, in the face of injustice, and against the limits of gender hierarchy and both heteronormativity and homonormativity. It seeks to unsettle conventional definitions of sex, and expand the language of sex as an erotic activity, an expression of identity, a power exchange, a cultural commodity, and even a new politics. [...] Feminist porn makers emphasize the importance of their labor practices in production and their treatment of performers/sex workers; in contrast to norms in the mainstream sectors of the adult entertainment industry, they strive to create a fair, safe, ethical, consensual work environment and often create imagery through collaboration with their subjects. Ultimately, feminist porn considers sexual representation — and its production — a site for resistance, intervention, and change.[165]

---

[165] Constance Penley, Celine Perreñas Shimizu, Mireille Miller-Young, and Tristan Taormino, "Introduction," in *The Feminist Porn Book,* eds. Taor-

Annie Sprinkle, Candida Royalle, and Tristan Taormino are just some of the names associated with this movement. These directors see sex and its representation as a space for erotic, therefore world-creating, possibility. Networks between people who have been denied representation or, in their representation had their humanity denied, are given opportunities to name what they want, who they want to do it with, and how they would like it.

Porn star Jiz Lee provides a personal dimension to feminist theories of porn in their account of their performance work. They describe the beginning of a particular porn project with photographer and artist Syd: "[I]n 2005, on a bright San Francisco day, [...] I met an erotic photographer named Syd, and I hit on her. My desire was twofold: I wanted her, and I wanted to create sexual art."[166] The two met when the former was curating a queer Asian Pacific Islander dance performance and the latter's "large prints of androgynous Hapa (mixed-heritage) queers in BDSM scenarios"[167] were part of an art exhibit of queer, Asian women in the theater lobby. Lee describes that it is "not often I see artists I could identify with, other queers like me. I felt a magnetic familiarity with Syd and the models in her photographs."[168] The two began dating, and during this period, after Lee expressed interest in being a model for Syd, Syd suggested they act together in a pornographic film directed by a friend starting a queer porn company. Lee writes:

> People often ask me, "What made you decide you wanted to do porn?" and I tell them the truth: I want to share my sexual expression with others. I like it, it feels liberating, and I know that it helps others feel free too. I want to show more representations of people like me. I use words like hegemonic, homonormative, and marginalized. [...] I share stories about

---

mino et al., 9–10.

166 Jiz Lee, "Uncategorized: Genderqueer Identity and Performance in Independent and Mainstream Porn," in *The Feminist Porn Book*, eds. Taormino et al., 273.

167 Ibid.

168 Ibid., 274.

people who have written to me, thanking me for putting my sexuality out there, for helping them become proud and stronger in their own battles. All of this is true and it's a part of why I did it. But what I don't say is: *I did it for love.*

And by that, I mean simply that I wasn't really thinking about it.[169]

The erotic impulse is not a matter of conscious thought, but the impulse of animation of movement toward and with and between. Lee's story begins with seeing, receiving images of people like them, seeing another queer mixed-race, Asian American artist. The phantasia of Syd's art stirs Lee into interaction, and phantasia becomes reality when Lee makes love to Syd. And when Lee begins and then excels at making pornographic films, they create new fantasies which stir up the erotic impulse toward connection, becoming, and transformation.

Lee is openly genderqueer: "I'm queer. And though to the untrained eye I may seem like a lesbian, I'm not. I'm not even a girl."[170] However, many films, particularly those produced by mainstream companies mark Lee as lesbian. Rather than expressing a complete alienation to the term, Lee does not mind "much being read as a woman," if it means that they can bring "dyke visibility or butch visibility to a larger audience,"[171] but such categorization undermines Lee's multiplicity. "If someone wants to really know me, they'll understand that my gender is fluid, androgynous."[172] For Lee, "genderqueer is a conscious queering of gender, or an aware nongendering," where "occupying this fluid, undefined status is the most secure [they've] ever felt."[173] Indeed, in a period of exploring a binary transgender identity, Lee realized, "I didn't want to be a man any more than I wanted to be a woman. […] [M]y body, strong in some ways and soft in others, was already perfectly suited for me. It became my canvas

---

169 Ibid. Emphasis added.
170 Ibid., 275.
171 Ibid.
172 Ibid.
173 Ibid., 276.

for art and sex."[174] A given work in that art might lead a viewer to presume a binary gender role for Lee, but the diversity of scenes and partners becomes a site for the enactment of Lee's gendered multiplicity:

> What a discovery to find that gender could be a tool, even a sex toy! Expression can be playful, erotic. I found it comfortable to explore my femininity in queer porn. I was performing with friends and lovers, for friends and lovers.[175]

Comparing queer and mainstream pornography, Lee identifies "choice, or performers' sexual agency, [as] one of the main differences between queer porn and mainstream genres."[176] Mainstream porn requires that Lee shave their body, perform certain positions, enact a kind of womanhood, all of these being "cisgender pressures based on [Lee's] perceived female presentation for (queer-phobic) straight male consumers."[177] Queer porn allows Lee to be alternately masculine or feminine or something utterly other, to be in copulatory relations that defy clear sexual categories, to choose when they will present themselves in ways that are ascribed to particular normative genders, and to choose when not to. In Lee's experience, queer porn respect's the "performers' choice — the choice to safely fuck how they want and to look how they believe is sexy."[178]

Lee focuses on choice, and choice is important when we talk about agency. But preceding agency is animacy, not only conscious action that leads to an immediate effect, but a liveliness that exists beyond that relationship. Earlier, Lee expresses their entrance into pornography not necessarily having to do with choice: "*I wasn't really thinking about it.*" This is not to say that Lee does not consent to do pornography or choose it, but to focus only or primarily on choice can obscure the particu-

---

174 Ibid.
175 Ibid.
176 Ibid.
177 Ibid.
178 Ibid., 277.

lar series of events in which erotic images inspire Lee toward attraction to a person; that that attraction to a person leads to professional artistic, pornographic creativity; that that creativity leads to enactments of Lee's multiplicity; that those enactments can lead others to recognize Lee as genderqueer; and that seeing Lee's nonbinary gender can inspire viewers to witness their own divergencies, enactments, and contradictory feel-goods.

For the gay pornographer Jean Daniel Cadinot, his actors "do not portray things that are imposed on them by me, but things they like to do themselves."[179] Cadinot's long and highly narrative pornographies take place in boy schools, road-trips, barber shops, scouting expeditions, Italian festivals, Moroccan markets — scenes from his own life. But the films are not his life alone. Cadinot died in 2008, and knowing his time was short, published a poetic goodbye to his audience. In it he wrote that his performers gave "unforgettable moments of their most tender intimacy, moments that only a few really know but which I made into images to allow you to admire them over and over again."[180] Cadinot asked his actors what do you like, what do you remember doing, what do you dream of doing, and then these things were done. Each pornographic film is a world built from the worlds of its inhabitants, and they are inhabitants only from one perspective: from another, the actors and their desire are the fabric of their world. Their sexual imagination and erotic memories are summoned by one another and by their director to weave new worlds. What they have known and delighted in becomes new experiences, new networks, the unknown.

"Eros is always a story in which lover, beloved, and the difference between them interact," writes Carson, and the "interac-

---

[179] Jean-Daniel Cadinot, quoted by George Koschel, "Cadinot, Jean-Daniel," in *The Queer Encyclopedia of Film and Television,* ed. Claude Summers (San Francisco: Cleis Press, 2005), 62.

[180] Cadinot, quoted in Jaap Kooijman, "Pleasures of the Orient: Cadinot's Maghreb as Gay Male Pornotopia," in *Indiscretions: At the Intersection of Queer and Postcolonial Theory,* ed. Murat Aydemir (Leiden: Brill, 2010), 111n3.

tion is a fiction arranged by the mind of the lover."[181] Every event of eros includes desirer and desired and the space between. Like fiction, eros is the intermediary between what is (what the desirer is, what the desirer already has, what the desirer has already experienced) and what could be (what is desired, how the desired might change the desirer, what new experiences the desired might bring). Empedocles' *philia* is eventually a love that is whole, a destination reached, but the world and all the bodies that comprise it are not *philia*. They are elements moved by it. Eros "is a movement that carries yearning hearts from over here to over there."[182] That is to say, eros constitutes what is and what can be, what will be. Jean-Daniel Cadinot wished that "all the efforts and work of a whole life, the quest for the moment of pure truth in the sublime communion of two beings under the spell of the undefinable desire for the other, [could] inspire those who inherit my heart."[183] In other words, may the fruits of his erotic desire communing with his actors' erotic desires inspire the erotic desire in others to create new relationships, new lovers, new worlds. Each pornographic film is a cosmos. Some replicate the demiurgic paradigm, others ask each molecule of its making what do you like? What do you dream of doing?

If every porn is an erotically constituted world, perhaps the world is a pornocosmos. Animacy is not being love but being in love, matter reaching toward matter, reaching away, reaching within, and reaching beyond any given circumstance to another potentiality. It is constituted by desiring agents materializing in one moment and dissolving in the next. Sappho calls Eros the *mythoplokon*,[184] the weaver of myths who brings into the present its unrealized wants, combining what is and what is not yet or

---

181 Carson, *Eros the Bittersweet*, 169.
182 Ibid., 172.
183 Jean-Daniel Cadinot quoted in Jaap Kooijman, "Pleasures of the Orient: Cadinot's Maghreb as Gay Male Pornotopia," in *Indiscretions: At the Intersection of Queer and Postcolonial Theory*, edited by Murat Aydemir (Amsterdam: Brill, 2010), 111n3.
184 Carson, *Eros the Bittersweet*, 170.

necessarily ever to be into an utterance, a story, perhaps a pornographic film. The world is a pornography that, if we watch mindfully and interact with ethically, we can imagine, desire, and fuck new worlds into being with it. But even if we do not act in various partnerships with the world, worlds disinterested in our human plights will still be inspired by the pornocosmos. Humans are far from the only desirers. What is most dangerous for the demiurge and his children is that in a panerotic, pansexual, pananimate universe, the cosmos has sex dreams. In their very fabric, erotic worlds fabricate, whether a presumptuous subject calls himself creator. Fully erotic, matter is what it is and is its potential for what it can be. In a pornocosmos, every world is already a new world.

"Dreams of Sexual Perfection": Panerotic Cosmo-Poem

In this chapter we have talked about the conflict between the many and the one, pantheism, animism, Empedoclean materialism and Heraclitan nondualism, and the cosmology of erotic worlding with its microcosmic theyogonies and macrocosmic pornocosmologies. Before concluding this exercise of cosmopoetic imagination, I want to zoom in on how mythopoets might tell the story of erotic worlding by looking an art object, a song by the band The Fugs.

Formed in the 1960s counterculture, The Fugs were committed to that era's spirit of anti-war, freakiness, protest, and free love, even in the 1980s when the band reformed and produced its album *No More Slavery* from 1985. The album includes songs that blast the Cold War, decry apartheid, and adapt poems such as Matthew Arnold's "Dover Beach." The masterpiece of this album is a twelve-minute-long anthem called "Dreams of Sexual Perfection."

The lyrics are written by The Fugs' poet-in-residence, one of two lead singers, Ed Sanders. Its verses are structured as a series of vignettes connected with the refrain "dreams of sexual perfection." The first vignette describes a host of characters and their various kinks:

> He made love with a sheep in 1969
> She slept with her girl inside a ball of twine
> And Murry liked to make it with kasha covered pears
> And Marcy liked to get it on, sliding down the stairs
> And Kama Sutra Kerry who sucked a sycamore
> And Billy who loved to rub against an ornate moving door.[185]

These persons, engaged in sex acts with animals, plants, and inorganic matter, are a snapshot of an infinite array of "love triangles, love quadrangles," and the singer sings of these "miles and miles of bodies" that "gratified desire was all they did require." This chaos of erotically charged bodies is described as smelling, feeling, and looking like Paradise. These lyrics are sung sometimes wildly, sometimes yelled, sometimes almost spoken, and are accompanied by distorted electric guitar and loud drums. Suddenly the instrumentation quiets, and Sanders's voice sings the refrain "dreams of sexual perfection" and the repetition "dream, dream, dream."

The next vignette, set to much more gentle music, describes Emily Dickinson alone with her secret love songs, her verses of "a wild and locked up love." The singer invites Dickinson to undress and dance in the wild, while bees "buzz around her fingers," open herself to her lover whose gender is unspecified, quoting Dickinson's posthumously published poem "Wild Nights": "Were I with thee / Wild nights should be / Our luxury!"[186] And the singer again sings the refrain: dreams of sexual perfection, followed by the "dream, dream, dream." This quiet gentleness is shattered by a countdown and a voice yelling "Party" over and over again. The singer then describes a libertine philosophy when singing, "even if you're filled with gloom,

---

[185] The Fugs, "Dreams of Sexual Perfection," recorded 1986, track 3 on *No More Slavery*, Big Beat Records, 1995, compact disc.

[186] Emily Dickinsin, "Wild Nights," in *Heart Wisdom from Five Women Poets*, ed. Lisa Locascio (Mineola: Dover, 2018), and The Fugs, "Dreams of Sexual Perfection."

you might as well party until the trouble's gone away."[187] Basically, have it all, embracing a kind of pansexuality, and "your longing and aggression shall faded be in your dreams of sexual perfection."[188]

Next the singer describes an adaptation of John Donne's "The Ecstasy." Two seniors in wheelchairs sit beside one another. Their spirits rise above and intertwine in sexual union: "Soul in soul did slide for a taste of paradise," and then the same Dickinson quote is sung again before the returning of the refrain. Again, the music switches from soft to sharp, hard, rhythmic, with intense electric guitar. This next story in the next verse tells of Lydia who "liked her freedom" and has an affair with a man other than her husband. The perspective then changes from third to second, "you're just about to come, like Lydia. / Your forehead vein pops forward. / Your face is ruddy and splotched. / Your eyes roll back and forth. / Your lips a raspy gasp. / And the green cloud descending. / Hands clenched, coming, coming."[189] This verse is full of transitioning perspectives. First, she becomes you, then you start coming like her. It seems to be that the addressee is orgasming, and the physical description can go with that analysis. At the same time, the vein, the eyes, and lips describe something else, the anger in the man pursuing the lover: Lydia's husband. A new voice enters the song, "you slept with my wife," and then we hear a punching sound, as a chorus of "jealousy" is sung, leading to "and all the things that jealousy brings to the dreams of sexual perfection."[190] But Another gentle section follows. A man is hiking in the mountains. He reflects on his youth, implied sex in gay dance clubs. He is dying but not from HIV, as he once worried, but from cancer. The singer sings "O, dip your healing hands inside the healing river / and may those throbbing fears become a pulse of joy." This is followed by a list of names of people who have died, perhaps people the

---

187 The Fugs, "Dreams of Sexual Perfection."
188 Ibid.
189 Ibid.
190 Ibid.

man knew: "Billy had an O.D., Jonny had AIDS." Then, again, the refrain "dreams of sexual perfection. Dream. Dream. Dream."

So far, we begin with Paradise, an assembly of fluctuating, limbs rising and submerging in a heap, an expanse of humans, animals, objects in sexual fellowship. This is followed by a series of vignettes where one or a couple of people reaches toward a dream of sexual perfection against various obstacles. Dickinson must keep her erotic visioning a secret from nineteenth century mores which regulate her non-heterosexual desires. The aged lovers' bodies are no longer able to move into one another as they used to, and yet their engagement in the dreams of sexual perfection transcends the limits of a given body. Their spirits, new forms of erotic consciousness continue, making love above them. Breaches of trust, born from rigid monogamy and the presumption of ownership over another, encroach on the dreams of sexual perfection in the story of Lydia, her husband, and her lover. This story speaks of the dream being infected by jealousy, that it can possibly be distorted by our actions. The penultimate vignette could be interpreted as following how the dream is further deadened by a brutal world. Erotics and death are tied together in the man's meditation on AIDS, yet his submergence in the river water points to another possibility. Communion with the natural world transforms into an erotic, life-affirming pulse. There is life outside the rise and fall of a given body. All those who have died accessed the dreams of sexual perfection, affecting those dreams and the effect of those dreams on others.

When the hiker's story ends, the tempo picks up, and the final piece of the song is a retelling of Hesiod's creation: "The first three things created, / An ancient poet sang / Were Chaos, Earth, and Eros (Eros).[191] The end of "Dreams of Sexual Perfection" is a return to the beginning, but a different beginning, the primordial trifecta. After this cosmogonic vision, the singer sings of his own lover:

I know how to please her.

---

[191] Ibid.

> She knows how to please me
> She knows my perv patterns
> And I know hers
>
> We're two golden stars
> That sizzle on the sheets
> I'll walk with her through the chaos
> From dark til dawn.[192]

Here we have a vision of intersubjectivity. The lovers know each other's "perv patterns," honoring their erotic and co-creative powers. They see eye to eye that each is a person engaging the erotic dream. The lovers are then described through a cosmic conceit of stars in sheets wandering amidst chaos together through the night. Or is this backwards? Could it be that the Fugs are describing the cosmos through the conceit of human lovers? I suppose the answer is both. The song continues: "She's my best friend. (Chaos and Eros) / She's my true lover. (Chaos and Eros) / She's my mate for life. (Chaos and Eros)"[193] Friend, lover, mate for life. Their relationship is held by their mutual reach toward the erotic dream. But that is only part of the pictures. World and individual are not easily distinguished. A refrain of "chaos and eros" is interjected between each utterance. It begs the listener to ask what if the singer and the she are chaos and eros, having witnessed an array of lovers throughout numerous cosmogonies and theogonies. Is the friend chaos, the lover eros, their mutuality life?

The Fugs sing a mythopoetic song of erotic worlding where time shifts between asynchronous moments of erotic fantasy. The beginning of everything comes at the end of the song, and second, third, and fourth listen, chaos, world and eros intermingle in each vignette. Similarly, perspective changes: characters pop up then out of each vignette, and within each story, even then, the perspective shifts. Some places are described,

---
192 Ibid.
193 Ibid.

others are shapeless, defined only by the movement of bodies and limbs. Nothing is steady. Nothing is single. The dreams of sexual perfection are dreams, plural.

The Fugs recognize in the listeners a stake in these dreams. They see our potential to dream, and as part of every refrain speak in the vocative, address us: "Dream. Dream. Dream." As the song concludes, the singer sings "she's the one with whom I dream those dreams of sexual perfection."[194] The singer is the voice of Ed Sanders to his own lover. The singer is the voice of attraction, harmony, *philia,* Eros to his beloved distinction, disorder, separation, *neikos,* Chaos. It is the voice of the cosmos beckoning us who listen to join in the erotic birthing of worlds: "dream, dream, dream."

---

194 Ibid.

4

Theo-Transvestitism, or, on the Origin of Gods: A Drag Theopoetic

Everybody's in drag. Which is fine, as long as they know it.
— *AJ and the Queen*, "Fort Worth"[1]

Many are the shapes the Gods will take,
Many the surprises they perform.
— Euripides, *Bacchae*[2]

At beginning of this volume, we discussed the transcendent role of *mytho*poetic performance in queer/trans liberation theologies. We then looked at an inter-myth *cosmo*poetic dialogue between the Genesis 1 and Genesis 2–3 narratives as well as the critique of Genesis texts from two gnostic remythifications, the Priestly and the Yahwists accounts. That conversation led to an extensive exercise in imagining a nondualist, queer cosmological model. Now, this final chapter combines the theme of *mytho*-

---

1 *AJ and the Queen*, s1e9, "Fort Worth," dir. Dennie Gordon, written Michael Patrick King and Jhoni Marchinko, feat. RuPaul Charles and Izzy G., aired January 10, 2020, on Netflix.
2 Euripides, *Bacchae*, trans. Paul Woodruff (Indianapolis: Hackett Publishing, 1999), ll. 1388–89

poetic performance with *cosmo*poetic imagination in order to suggest a *theo*poetic praxis. The praxis I am putting forward is drag theopoetics.

I first encountered the term "theopoetics" as meaning an interdisciplinary approach to theology, myth, and art, although I now appreciate that it is a term with quite a few referents. Responding both to atheistic death of God theologies and a more general cultural disengagement with the church, the term was coined by Stanley Hopper in the 1960s while working with a number of likeminded theologians at Drew University's Consultations on Hermeneutics and in his involvement with the Society for the Arts, Religion and Contemporary Culture (SARCC).[3] Hopper argues for a movement beyond the "logos" of theology to an experienced and generative "poesis":

> Theology tends to develop talk about God logically, where the logos is constrained within the model of Aristotelian propositional thinking; whereas theopoetics stresses the poem dimension, the creativity of God, his is-ness, if you wish to theologize it, so that I must move within his own creative nature and must construe him creatively, so that I would become co-creator with God, if you must speak theologically. If I am going to talk about God, I must recognize this mythopoetic, metaphorical nature of the language I use.[4]

The term was further developed when pastor, poet, and theologian Amos Niven Wilder, also member of SARCC, published *Theopoetic* in 1976. In his book, Wilder doubts whether any "theology or piety [can] give any account of faith [...] without a continual rehearsal of visionary representations, dramatic vehicles, and affectional language."[5] This is to say, a turn to poet-

---

3 L. Callid Keefe-Perry, *Way to Water: A Theopoetics Primer* (Eugene: Cascade Books, 2014), 17

4 Stanley Hopper, "Introduction" in *Interpretation: The Poetry of Meaning*, ed. David L. Miller (New York: Harcourt Brace, 1967), 3.

5 Amos Niven Wilder, *Theopoetic: Theology and the Religious Imagination* (Minneapolis: Fortress Press, 1976), 8.

ics, aesthetics, new rituals, and arts are key for the survival of religion *and* are a necessary component for the human expression of God, which in his predominantly white, male, protestant milieu had been pushed to the side for the philosophical, logocentric discipline of theology.

In *Way to Water: A Theopoetic Primer*, Callid Keefe-Perry expounds on leading contributors to the loose discipline of theopoetics through Wilder, Rubem Alves, and Catherine Keller, to name a few. In surveying the history of theopoetics through the twentieth and twenty-first centuries, Keefe-Perry emphasizes *embodiment* in our encounters with divinity as well and the ways we represent those embodied experiences in theological and theopoetic works. Addressing the current state of Christian theology, he argues, "a re-enfleshment of theological discourse is called for and that a turn to the flesh will simultaneously bring with it a turn to the poetic rather than the prosaic, to a surplus of meaning rather than a linguistic mechanicalism, and to the Christian imagination rather than ossified doctrine."[6] Harking themes we have explored already — transcendence, horizons of the possible, and remythification — theopoetics are another tactic for the transformation of reality, particularly as it comes to the reality of God. Keefe-Perry's asserts "there is a transformative power in the creative articulation of embodied experiences of God and faith."[7] Since "how we articulate our experiences of the Divine can alter our experiences of the Divine,"[8] theopoetics leads to alternative articulations, spurring new relationships, new meanings, new worlds, and, dare I say, new gods.

In concluding this volume of mythopoetic performance and cosmopoetic imagination toward a theopoetic praxis, my agenda is to lift up alternative articulations of *theos* (θεός, "god," or "the divine") that pay special heed to questions of gender, sexuality, trans*, queer, identity, self, and performance, and I do this by invoking the language of drag. But what do I mean by

---

6 Keefe-Perry, *Way to Water*, 6.
7 Ibid.
8 Ibid.

drag, let alone drag theopoetics? I will begin to answer that by exploring recent and less recent use of the term "drag" in a variety of explicitly theological statements.

On December 22, 2019, Ram Dass, the New Age psychologist and spiritual leader, died. All over social media and in various news outlets, people shared memories of meeting him at wisdom centers, schools, and temples. Others shared how his books changed their lives. Most, however, expressed their grief by sharing their favorite Ram Dass quotes. To find a fitting Ram Dass quote is not a difficult task. Ram Dass has so many popular sayings that he published a collection of his one-liners in 2007. One nugget from that collection was repeatedly shared around the time of his death: "Treat everyone you meet like God in drag."[9]

I am a queer. And it makes sense that many of my Facebook friends, many of whom are also queer, would share *this* quote. Not only does the phrase exalt the virtue of acceptance many of us so desperately want, but it also uses the queer idiom of "drag." This metaphor of people as God in drag is being used more and more frequently in God talk, especially within New Age thinkers and their circles of influence. On February 25, 2019, controversial alternative medicine advocate Deepak Chopra tweeted "We Are All God in Drag."[10] Meanwhile, rabbi, LGBTQIA+ advocate, scholar, and poet Jay Michaelson refers to "God donning the drag of us"[11] in his book on nondualist Judaism. Another poet, Daniel Ladinsky, in his interpretive translation of Hafiz, also deploys the anachronistic term to get at the meaning of a fourteenth-century composition: "You are the Sun in drag. / [...] Sweetheart, O sweetheart, / You are God in / Drag!"[12]

---

[9] Ram Dass, *One-Liners: A Mini Manual for a Spiritual Life* (New York: Bell Tower, 2002), 13.

[10] @deepakchopra, *Twitter,* February 15, 2019, 5:02 a.m., https://twitter.com/DeepakChopra/status/1099987951633813505.

[11] Jay Michaelson, *Everything Is God: the Radical Path of Nondual Judaism* (Boston: Trumpeter, 2009), 68.

[12] Hafiz, "The Sun in Drag," in *The Gift: Poems by Hafiz, the Great Sufi Master,* trans. Daniel Ladinsky (New York: Penguin, 1999), 252.

Drag queen and self-proclaimed self-help "GuRu," RuPaul Charles has consistently used the language of drag to discuss the incarnation of God or the Universe. Being interviewed at the Creative Arts Emmys, Charles explains that part of what makes drag "dangerous" is that on a deeper level it reveals "this idea that you are not your body. You are an extension of the power that created the whole universe. That's drag. We are all God in drag."[13] You are not the self, plain and simple but something bigger, out of "your" control, something only wearing you. In his book *GuRu*, Charles similarly writes:

> You've heard me say, "you're born naked and the rest is drag." In truth, you are not your clothes, you are not your profession, you are not your religion. You are an extension of the consciousness that guides the universe, for which there is no name because it cannot be defined. That's why all the superficial things you list as your identity are in reality your "drag." Years ago, when I heard someone say[,] "we are all God in drag," I know it to be the truth at my core.[14]

In the most basic sense of theology as "God-talk," a rising number of voices find the term and idea of "drag" to be helpful. Most of the individuals I have seen, from celebrities, poets, and scholars to my seminary classmates and local clergy, use "drag" as a way to talk about God's incarnation or immanence, have primarily engaged drag in the realm of theory and secondarily as participant in the audience of a drag or a fan of shows like *RuPaul's Drag Race* or the Boulet Brothers' *Dragula*. It is less common, in my context, for these invocations of "drag" to hail from someone with much experience performing in drag. For RuPaul, drag is not theoretical. Drag is career, artistic medium, claim to fame, and embodied practice. Performing a drag per-

---

13 RuPaul quoted in Tim Malloy, "RuPaul Explains Why 'We Are All God in Drag,'" *The Wrap*, September 14, 2019, https://www.thewrap.com/rupaul-explains-why-we-are-all-god-in-drag/.
14 RuPaul, *GuRu* (New York: HarperCollins, 2018), xi.

sona is not the same as observing one. Having experienced the "how" of a persona's manifestation — wig, gesture, padding, voice, movement, concept, costume — the drag practitioner will have a different appreciation for God's incarnational process. For RuPaul, and for me, drag is not only theory but practice, and putting the *practice* of drag in conversation with *reflection* on that practice, we engage *praxes* of drag theopoetics.

Drag theopoetics, like the art of drag, might mean a number of things. It means theopoetics created by a professional or amateur crossdresser, and to implicate God as crossdresser. It means someone who uses performance to explore questions of self, gender, identity, divinity, and ethics. It means the phenomenon of experiencing the divine while performing in drag, or being in the audience at a drag performance, or watching drag on television or film. It means cross-identificatory practices with other genders or gender performances in liturgy, scripture, poetry, and song. It means myths of divinity becoming gendered deities, of deities becoming gendered mortals, of mortals donning sacred garments to encounter divine presence, of bodies in metamorphosis. It means theater. It means lip-synching to *Ave Maria*. It means gesture and somatics and camp. It means drag kings, drag queens, all non-binary dragsters, drag ogres, drag gods, drag monsters flitting between the centers and the peripheries of queer community as a class of priests and wonderworkers. It means the conscious performance of another gender or a heightened version of one's own gender as a means to understand divinity, the world, "the self," and other "selves." Of specific importance to the conversation of our placement in the demiurgic cosmos and queer cosmoi, theopoetics will help us differentiate between the performance[15] of a self and the pre-

---

15 My use of performance here is *as* a performer. While this project is in no small part indebted to the work of Judith Butler, I am *not* talking about the performative as she defines it. Rather, I am using the term "performance," itself not the same as "the performative," in a thespian sense, that is, a series of actions in the service of an artistic, ritual, or liturgical work, the conscious enactment of gesture, voice, and language in the service of a heightened or otherwise distinct persona.

sumption of a self and will do so by looking at theogonies and incarnations. For, in examining God's or gods' becoming, we might gain insight into our own becoming.

To begin unpacking the performance of self against a presumption of self, take philosopher Seyyed Hossein Nasr's thoughts on the relationship between humans and the natural world. Nasr writes: "The purpose and aim of creation is in fact for God 'to come to know' Himself through His perfect instrument of knowledge that is the Universal Man."[16] In Nasr's cosmological system, God creates the natural world, itself a complex network of symbols reflecting the heavenly realm, humans, and their bodies, are the intermediaries between the natural symbologies and the heavenly. God is known through human knowledge; humans know themselves through communion with nature; communion with nature is communion with a reflection of heaven; communion with a reflection of heaven occurs when we look into ourselves and when we look outside ourselves, for both directions reveal something of the divine. In nature, we see what we are and penetrate "into the inner meaning of nature only on the condition of being able to delve into the inner depths of [our] own being and to cease to lie merely on the periphery of [our] being."[17] But Nasr warns: "Men who live only on the surface of their being can study nature as something to be manipulated and dominated."[18] In the gnostic myths, the demiurge lives on the surface of his being. He does not know *how* he has emerged, and he is ignorant of his place in the pleromic design. Ignorant of how he became a self, he presumes his self as natural. Thereafter, the demiurge, like Nasr's unenlightened man, only knows to exploit and dominate what is around him. He does not know what the world might have to say about divinity, power, or life. Only one "who has turned toward the inward dimension of [one's] being can see nature as a symbol,

---

16 Seyyed Hossein Nasr, *Man and Nature: The Spiritual Crisis of Modern Man* (Chicago: ABC International Group, Inc., 1997), 96.

17 Ibid.

18 Ibid., 96–97.

as a transparent reality and come to know and understand it in the real sense."[19] Knowledge of one's being, that is, gnosis gained through investigations of who and how and where and what we are, shapes our perspective to see in and through nature the divine reality to which nature points.

Full disclosure: I am interpreting Nasr outside of the initial context of *Man and Nature,* but I think his reflection on "self" knowledge, environmental curiosity, and divine gnosis are helpful when developing a praxis of the performed self. I do not necessarily have to accept Nasr's cosmology to appreciate how his metaphysics — what is exterior to my body or self, and what is interior — symbolize one another. Insight and outsight are yet another binary that dissolves in the mystical pursuit of holy knowledge. Ecosystems form units while comprising entities of incredible variance, and depending on the perspective, one is many or many is one. We see ourselves in those ecosystems, and from different vantages, we lose ourselves. But what are those vantages, and how do *they* change? The more we observe, the more we might rethink who or what we are as observers. Observing the coalescing and dissipating movements of life, I grow to understand my body as realms of interrelating, utterly unhuman lifeforms; my body as a limb in the body of my family, my community, this earth; my body as me, a self, a personality; my body as us, selves, personalities. For the pantheist, does the cosmos have a self? Does the cosmos seek to know? Does the cosmos desire relationships? Nasr, who is not a pantheist, suggests something that might easily fit into a pantheist cosmology when he suggests that humans are the instruments God uses to know God's self, if we think of God as everything and the emergence of humans as entities in the everything called to explore, imagine, and transform within that everything. I might phrase it differently as personae, or performances of selves, are the instruments the divine uses to know its selves, to feel its selves, and to love its selves.

---

19 Ibid., 97.

Drag is a study of the self, analogous to mystical inquiry. Like the naturalist or mystic who studies symbols of the natural to know herself, her cosmos, and God, drag performers study gender, sexuality, and a variety of identity signifiers to create personae, in the process learning about themselves, and sometimes even helping audience members learn a little bit about themselves. Drag disrupts gender presumptions with the potential to disorient all identarian presumptions.

Drag is an art of creating selves. It could be said that acting in general is an art of creating selves, and I would not disagree. Indeed, it will become clear how much of what I refer to as drag is indebted to acting and other theater practices. However, an "I am this person and I am not this person" paradox is at the heart of the art, humor, irony, and radicalism of drag in a way that is not typically the case in acting, especially outside the avant-garde, where the audience rarely is supposed to be conscious, let alone hyperconscious, of the illusion. In drag, artificiality is the point, and in acting, it is typically discouraged. With drag, we might think of Philip Core's definition of camp, which is "a lie which tells the truth."[20] Drag tells the "truth" by presenting "falsehoods," by performing exaggerations, by putting the engendering of gender under the proverbial microscope, prodding it with a sequined glove. In the drag genderlab, what lies reveal God?

The rest of this chapter is a piece of queer mythopoeia that engages the praxis of drag theopoetics as related to myth and ritual. It takes the form of a story, a mytho-fictional narrative about divinity in god drag, about gods in human drag, and about humans in holy drag. It comprises remythifications of Kabbalist writing and ancient theater, of Platonic dialogues, and of encounters between queers and radical feminists across generations. I intersperse the story with short, critical reflections about drag and performances. These permutations include Mary-Jane

---

20 Philip Core, "From *Camp: The Lie that Tells the Truth*," in *Camp: Queer Aesthetics and the Performing Subject*, ed. Fabio Cleto (Ann Arbor: University of Michigan Press, 1999), 81.

Rubenstein and Dorothee Soelle's thoughts on perspectivism, myths representing divine drag including the Kabbalist story of sefirot emerging from Ein-Sof and Dionysus's incarnation in Euripides' *Bacchae,* two distinct theories on drag from José Esteban Muñoz and Jack Halberstam, and a final consideration on how scholars, theologians, liturgists, midrashists, and interpreters of myth not only learn from drag but "do drag" when partaking in God-talk. So, without further ado: a drag theopoetic.

Prologue: Prophetic Encounters

Dr. Diotima had once again finished seminar late. "Next week we'll discuss Aspasia's *In Spite of Homer* — read carefully. It's a lot to discuss, but it is necessary, based on today's discussion; yes, I will *try* to keep it within time." Diotima peeked at the clock. Sixteen minutes over. But who could blame her? Today's topic was *écriture féminine* and theories of the soul, the subject nearest and dearest to her heart, despite a certain pain it sometimes could elicit. For over two decades, she had written on the historical toxification of patriarchy on the soul. Her work brought to light how male thinkers have conceived the metaphysics of the human soul in their own male image, denying feminine insight — and later, she argued, the female *origin* — of the soul.

After an initial attempt to receive ordination in the Eleusinian Mysteries, Diotima exchanged a ministerial pursuit for an academic one, notably, a decision to move from a traditionally feminine career to a masculine. She would spend the rest of her life wondering if she made the right decision. Despite numerous publications and an impeccable CV, Diotima was denied a tenure-track position in Athens as the content of her work was branded anti-male by an all-male committee. *If only I had been born ten years later,* Diotima sometimes thought. Feminism became a little bit less scary later on, although she had some hand in making it "scary." Her life was a constant struggle, every endeavor to find an academic home ruptured in conflict, and she stood by her principles, defended tooth and unpainted nail. An honest observer would note her first works weren't even *anti-men,* just pro-women, therefore egalitarian. They only took a misandrist tone once a network of men dedicated their time to ruining her career. Men would blacklist her, and several professors gave her tainted references with a subtext of "DO NOT HIRE IF YOU WANT SOMEONE REASONABLE," reviewing her books as populist and nonacademic, New Age and frivolous. Athens was the worst — the democratic zeitgeist empowered the men to take an equal share in talking over her — but none of the city-states where she sought work were an egalitarian picnic. In Corinth, while presenting on a panel about the exploitation of flutegirls in the symposia circuit, when, after all the comments in the talk-back came from men, most of whom were critical of the "anti-sex, anti-fun" rigidity of the feminist speakers. One even suggested "too much lesbianism twisted these old hags' view of the world, but that's nothing *we* can't fix." It was then that Diotima decided to disallow male students from attending her upper-level seminars, "Demeter and de Beauvoir: Birth of the Woman" and "Poetics of Feminine Wrath." *Let women have a chance to speak.* Unfortunately, her decision went against most school policies in Athens, and most laws. While she stuck to her guns, few institutions risked sticking to her.

Battle-scarred and tired, she settled, in her old age, for a visiting professorship at Mantinea University, a small school with an unexceptional reputation. It was whispered among the faculty that Diotima was only hired because her controversies put the university in the public eye and would boost enrollment. Diotima heard these rumors, but they did not stop her from teaching with the passion she was renowned for, although who was to say whether her flame was kindled by the liberational dream or by the resentment of her living nightmare. Either way, it was a seminar full of eager students and, with the dean's begrudged blessing, all her students were women. At least Diotima assumed they were women.

Among the pupils was a PhD candidate who, despite silver hair, was young, tan, fairly stocky, and, in their words, not *quite* a woman. Not quite a man either. After adolescence struck, Tiresia "Terry" Everess lived the next seven years as a woman.

When those seven years had finished, Terry lived as a man. Such occurrences were not uncommon back in those days of free love, bacchanalias, and Delphic psychedelia. No one was quite sure, however, of the particulars of Terry's miraculous transformation. Some said the change was caused by the gods, others by a redistribution of various hormones, still others claimed each time was the result of a botched experiment on a rare snake. Snakes have transformative powers, after all. Of course, maybe Terry just needed a change of perspective, fashion, and spirit. Regardless, after studying abroad in Thebes, Tiresia was going by "Terry," had shaved the sides of their head but ceased shaving their mustache, and began to dress in a uniform of converse sneakers, black jeans, and one-size-too-large button-downs, usually in some shade of dark red. *She looks like Dracula,* thought Diotima, spying Terry in the university cafe.

"Can I sit here?" she asked her student. Terry blinked and looked up at the old woman, who was bent slightly, hands pressed on the table, and staring into Terry's eyes. "Huh?"

"Can I have a seat? I want to have a word with you."

"Sure, professor," and Terry reached across the table to clear their book bag from the other seat. "Sorry, I didn't see you there. Not always great at seeing what's right in front of my face, you know."

Diotima was never one for small talk. "Do you hate women?" Terry, startled by the question, smiled.

"What?"

"I mean," Diotima continued, "do you hate being a woman?"

"Well," Terry thought for a moment, "not as much as I hate disco." Diotima was not sure how to take this.

"I..."

She was rarely one to stutter, but it was also rare for someone, a student no less, to be so cool in her presence as to crack a joke. "I am serious. Is it regression? Is it true that you were cursed by the gods, or are you just trying to deal with something that happened in your childhood?"

Still grinning, Terry looked down at their hands. "A little of both, probably. No, I am afraid I don't really know. I liked being a woman. Now, I like being a man. But I'm kinda ready to see what's next." They looked up again. "Besides, professor, is this conversation appropriate?"

"No," said Diotima. "But it is necessary. I will do everything in my power to kill the poison of self-hatred wherever I see it in my students."

"Noble. But not very professional."

"Professionalism is a death knell," she smacked the table. "The deployment of a sterilized male psyche on the living bodies of women."

"I never thought of it that way," said Terry, unmoved. "I don't mind talking though."

"Good," said Diotima, starting to relax. "I am sorry if I came on a bit strong."

Terry laughed. "A bit! You're a bulldog."

Diotima grinned. "Did you just call me a bitch?"

"What's the matter, do you hate bitches? I mean, do you hate being a bitch?" mocked Terry. Diotima couldn't keep herself together. She had a deep, loud, and insufficiently practiced laugh, which startled everyone at the nearby tables.

"That's enough of that," said the professor. "It's a horrible word. Even if—"

"You like it," guessed Terry, "the feel of the word in your mouth."

"Yes," Diotima grew stern again. "I was just concerned. I do not intend to lose a sister in the cause. You must love yourself."

Terry sat straight in their chair. "I think I love myself, thank you very much."

"As a woman?"

"Yes," the student's voice grew louder. "I love my woman bits to pieces! But I am not only a woman."

"Only a woman? Terry, a woman is everything."

"Including a man." Diotima sat silently across from her student. She had never been so mesmerized and furious with a student at the same time. Terry broke the silence. "You see, professor, I've known the pleasures of man, and the pleasures of woman, as both, with both... as neither, with neither. You wanna know how I got this way?"

"Yes," whispered the professor, "I want to help you."

"Awfully generous, truly." Terry stood up, hoisted their bag over the shoulder, and dropped a flyer in front of Diotima. "Come to my show this evening, that's how you can help. In the meantime, before you start trying to fix me, here's something you can think about: How do you live? What are you doing? Who are you? Do you even know?"[21] Terry leapt to their feet and vanished before the professor could respond. Diotima looked at the flyer in her hands and said, "Drag King Dyko-nysus presents Theo-Transvestitism, or, On the Origin of the Gods. Suggested admission five drachmas. Performance contains suggestive themes, nudity, and ekstasis."

Well, sometimes, if you're gonna save a sister, you've got to descend into the underworld, thought Diotima as she rushed off to the faculty cafeteria to grab a bite before attending what would prove to be an unforgettable night.

* * *

In a scene from *Bacchae,* the tyrant Pentheus has unknowingly captured Dionysus who is disguised as a foreign stranger, the leader of the Dionysian cult. Pentheus is interrogating the stranger Dionysus, but the latter keeps confounding the former with his answers. In the most dramatic moment of this interchange the god asks the human: "How do you live? What are you doing? Who are you?"[22] Pentheus answers with some basic identificatory information, but his answer evades the profundity of the god's interpolation. In his search for knowledge, a search *not* originating from curiosity but from a desire for complete control, Pentheus approaches the divine. But the divine is the stranger. And it is the stranger who replies to your question with

---

21 Euripides, *Bacchae,* l. 506.
22 Ibid.

another one, a question that alienates. Suddenly, you doubt who you are. Are you the stranger?

In her work on the erotic and the mystical, Dorothee Soelle asks of lovers: "Do they not always have to love more than what they know of each other and what is knowable?"[23] For Soelle, love comprises what is grasped of the lover *and* what is ungraspable. The pain or pleasure of the grasped or ungraspable lover is at the core of the mystical relationship with God:

> Religious tradition answers this question by referring to the amalgam of mystery, both frightening and fascinating [...]. Only the far-near one can stay near. Only the one never wholly known can be known. Deprivation, separation, and ecstasy's bitterness keep its "sweetness" alive.[24]

We are reminded here of Anne Carson and Sappho's "bittersweet Eros." The experience of integration, for instance the integration of bodies in the act of sexual communion, cannot occur without a state of disintegration. The eroticism of the interaction between Pentheus and his captive surfaces in a confrontation over knowledge. Pentheus seeks knowledge of the Dionysian mysteries. His initial disgust at the Bacchic women and their effeminate leader, the stranger, belies his desire to know what the stranger knows. To know the god, the stranger's questions imply, Pentheus must know himself. Each must know a certain perspective: Where does each stand; what does each see? What does each want? Pentheus proves unable to honor the ground on which he stands, his family, and his foundation by divine ordination. He is unable to see beyond his own designs. He suppresses what he wants as a tactic to remain in charge. In so doing, he does not know Dionysus, even as he tugs on the god's hair and mocks his girlish lips. In presuming his own omnipotence, rather than analyzing how the event of Pentheus

---

23 Dorothee Soelle, *The Silent Cry: Mysticism and Resistance,* trans. Barbara and Martin Rurnscheidt (Minneapolis: Fortress Press, 2001), 126.
24 Ibid.

has manifested and by whom, Pentheus has signed away his fate. By standing his authoritarian ground, his gnosis must match his arrogance. Pentheus will be ripped to pieces, but in that moment, he will experience the ekstasis of knowing god.

If we think of this encounter between Pentheus and Dionysus from a pantheological standpoint, we have two incarnations of the same divinity interrogating one another. What the Pentheus persona does not understand is that "love is not simply complete concord," since "there is also the other's strangeness and one's being frightened" by the stranger.[25] It is the strangeness, that aspect of utter difference, the unintelligibility of the other, that makes attraction possible.

Relationship — erotic, cosmic, mystical, generative — is impossible without difference. But it is a contingent difference. Pantheism argues for contingent differences rather than ontic, categorical, and static distinctions. Differences become a matter of perspective, and perspective is determined by constitutive relationships. The emergence of selves, Rubenstein defines as pancarnation, or "divinity's inability not to express itself in and as the endless, stubbornly un-totalized run of all things."[26] She continues:

> This is not, of course, to say that everything is divine to every perceiving agent. Far less is it to say that everything is the same. Rather, it is to acknowledge that what looks like an inert rock from one perspective is a sacred ancestor from another; that the catfish one person serves for dinner could be kin to her partner and a great creative being to both of them; and that what looks in one light like the image of God is in another a peccary, and in another still the billion-year product of bacterial collaboration.[27]

---

25 Ibid., 130.
26 Mary-Jane Rubenstein, *Pantheologies: Gods, Worlds, Monsters* (New York: Columbia University Press, 2018), 173.
27 Ibid.

If the cosmos is cosmoi, a plurality of interrelated beings and agents of their own stories, then any given self fluctuates between being the center of their story, a supporting character, or the background. It depends on perspective. This perspectival pancarnation is not relativism: if "the latter asserts that there are many ways to interpret the same world, the former would assert that worlds — and therefore divinities — take shape differently depending on the points of view that intraagentially construct them."[28] Agents form communities — the body, the self, the world — but Rubenstein reminds us that the constituent agents are never *only* those formations.

What does it mean then, when we presume to have a self who is impenetrable and unchangeable, whose perspective is singular and objective? For one, we get tyranny and violence. But more specifically, we get a conception of the self which cuts us off from new sight. And new sight cuts us off from new becoming, from change, from reintegration into forms of life.

However, without the emergence of selves, the pleasure of formation, attraction, and erotic animacy cannot exist. The animating power of attraction lives through distinction. What is offensive in *the presumption of the self* is not "the self" but "the presumption," more specifically, the presumption of a naturalized, prediscursive self.

The answer to the presumed self is not self-destruction but the performance of self. Performance is a process. It involves articulations and gestures rehearsed into a body. Performance takes time and the denial of certain other interactions or behaviors until a persona is born, able to act and speak from their unique perspective. That unique perspective allows for new pleasure, new encounters. But a performance is importantly ephemeral. It is not meant to last forever. An actor who can only do one single character, not even allowing for slight variations, is a dull actor indeed.

We must allow for change in ourselves. We must confront Pentheus and interrogate him. But we must also allow for

---

28 Ibid.

change in the divine, for divinity is "omnipersonal, taking shape as every kind of person, depending on the circumstance."[29] Pentheus asks his questions either rhetorically, assuming he knows the answer, or with utility, where the stranger is not a person in their own right but a source of knowledge to exploit. He does not ask the stranger how the stranger has come to be. A fatal mistake, for if Pentheus had asked Dionysus, "how do you live? What are you doing? Who are you?" the god's divinity could have been revealed. Were Pentheus to acknowledge the stranger as divine, he would, to paraphrase Rubenstein, "profess a certain humility and awe in relation to [Dionysus], and thereby [...] mark [the stranger] as worthy of reverence."[30]

Perhaps Pentheus, in acknowledging the stranger's divinity, would have saved his own life. Perhaps not. We are not guaranteed to be loved by every god. But in ignoring the other's divinity by presuming my own superiority, I assure that the current, particular articulation of "my self" is in a strained, contentious, and harmful relationship with the co-creative universe that lives through give and take. Imagining a larger scale embrace of the pantheological, Rubenstein concludes her book:

> Those events we call gods would be discovered, sustained, killed off, resurrected, shared, transmogrified, and multiplied between and among temporary clusters of relation. As it has in those queerly intraspecies assemblages of Arcadia, Nazareth, Uluru, the Amazon, Turtle Island, Gaia, and untold multitudes of symbiotic ecosystems, divinity thus construed would show up in unforeseen crossings and alliances. It would frighten and delight us, save, and ruin us with visions of the worlds and gods we've made, and glimpses of those that might yet emerge from our multispecies midst.[31]

---

29 Ibid., 182.
30 Ibid., 184.
31 Ibid., 190.

Embrace the many, she articulates in her Rubensteinian way. I will. And I do this by seeing who is there to embrace, who already embraces me, by acknowledging how I come to be, that as I write this, I am a community of agents performing, for the moment, a self.

* * *

How Do You Live? When God Became Gods.

To her annoyance, Diotima was in the front row. She had been the last one in the theater, and the only seat left was next to a pair of young women in matching green ensembles. The young women were sucking each other's faces with a refreshing impunity. *I guess I'm in the right place.* The professor noticed not only were her neighbors' outfits identical, but so were their haircuts, body height and general shape. Since she could not see their faces, the thought crossed her mind that they might be twin sisters. *An open-minded crowd indeed!* When the women took half a second to snag some breath before diving back in, Diotima glimpsed that they were in fact unlikely to be related. *Well, that's good. When I say* love your sister, *that isn't quite what I have in mind.*

Despite the young couple, the audience was actually quite diverse. Even though they made up only about half of the audience, it was the most men Diotima had been in a room with for a long time. If they *were* men. It was really hard to tell, which made Diotima nervous. *It's like having a broken compass, surrounded by peacocks and minotaurs. What do I look like in the midst of all this?* She looked like a short woman with a serious face, gray hair in a wild shag. When she was a child, people would call Diotima a tomboy, but in her adulthood, while her personality sharpened, her looks softened into a kind of androgyny. She wore loose utilitarian browns and grays, a body adorned in neutrals. Her face was unmade-up under steel-framed glasses through which dark eyes, profound and restless, shifted from face to face and corner to corner in the theater. In a way, she did stand out, although she was not the oldest person in the room. Something about her good old fashioned lesbian unisexuality clashed with the new fashion of the day's queers: spiky, teased, shaved, and padded. But they were queers nonetheless, and Diotima was happy about that, even if she had to share space with the bedicked.

The room fell quiet except for the nearby smooching — *are they prepared to do this for the whole show?* — and the stage filled with light. Terry sat on a stool, hunched over a table with a petri dish, gazing into a microscope. A thin fog descended from the dish. Terry looked up and addressed the audience: "As long as I can remember, I have seen what's before me, what's behind, and what's beyond me all at once. And it is a pain in my ass."

Terry stood up and crouched behind the table. *What's she getting from there,* misgendered Diotima in her head. Someone "woohooed" as Terry arose, holding a tank of snails, then placed it on the table. They put their hand inside the tank and waited until one of the snails crawled onto their hand. Terry pulled out of the tank, and came closer to the audience, displaying the twisted shell of the mollusk. Terry started up again.

"Tonight, you will see what I see, drop your eyes out of your skull to plant my vision in their place, snails in a shell. My eyes will take root, feed on your mind, and in return divulge the secret of the gods!" A loud twang. Diotima turned her head and saw a musician sitting in an unlit corner, his cithara plugged into an amp, his face hard to discern.

"I used to do prophecies, soft stuff, to pay my way through college. And I got this client, who was really nervous. He didn't want bones in the fire, entrails on the table. He wasn't interested in the future. No. He wanted to know about the gods: How did they get here? How do they live? How did we come to live, he asked. I didn't know. I said something like, the answers are in the stars. See, I had spent the first ten years of my calling, gazing at stars. So, when in doubt, I mean I saw many things, celestial bodies embracing bodies, asteroids bonking, planets dancing, but the truth is, gods are not forthcoming with their secrets. And how gods come to be, is quite a secret.

"I became obsessed with the man's questions. I spent hours observing the sky. Nothing. My dreams were as unhelpful as my stargazing. For every oracle I ascertained of futures strange and wondrous, I drew the shortest straw when it came to knowing anything more about the past, my origin and that of my deities.

"I should have followed Hesiod's word, right? That's what a good Greek would have done. But could I ignore the emptiness I felt when reading his account? Who here, a show of hands, believes Hesiod? Okay. Yeah, I thought so. Except for you — and all the power to you, champ — *Theogony* is fun, but it can't be the only explanation. So, I poured over the works of philosophers, who could speak eloquently about the elements but not the souls. Others on the soul but disparaged the body. Others spouted a lot about nothing, and a whole lot of nothing on a little bit. My hunger for the truth was killing me. I don't know about you, but when I'm hungry, I like to eat out."

Terry made a V with two fingers, the snail stuck right in the middle, and licked its shell. The audience hollered.

"Oh yeah, my girlfriend at the time, she really hit the spot. Kept me going, always up for a late-night interlocution." Terry savored this last word, crossed their legs, and swayed their pelvis forward and back. "We'd stay up all night in back and forth, thorough investigations of our sources, fingers tracing every line. Her wisdom was balm on my skin, kept me from withering in my odyssey to know. And one night, I found in my lover the key to my origin.

"After a long and sweaty bout of research, I swung my body off her and sunk into our mattress. It was already morning, and the sun was poking my face. 'Wake up, wake up,' it seemed to say. Irritated, and quite a bit drained, I turned my gaze to my girl. In that moment, I saw her hand cleaving to her cleft, a shimmering goo seeping through the fingers. 'Hey,' I nudged her with my foot, 'what is that?' 'Hmm?' I was incredulous, 'that's not what you normally — do you need to see a doctor?' Her eyes cracked open, and she stared down. She had this like hoarse, breathy kinda voice. Very, you know, sexy, right. And she's like

'Oh, that? That's ambrosia.' And she closes her eyes and turns her face away.

"Ambrosia my ass! I swab some from her fingers and I run to the lab, and I put it in a dish, and I gaze into it with my microscope. Why is the impulse always to go big, when the best things always start with the smallest jolt? In my home, in between my lover's fingers, from my lover's body, I found what I had been longing to find, and not in the heavens. Through the right lens, I finally saw the origin of life.

"Come, come, come!" With each utterance of "come" followed a pluck on the cithara, another pump of fog. "Line up and gaze into the microscope, see what I discovered, and meanwhile, I will tell you what the gods allowed me to see."

The audience rose, taking Diotima by surprise, and began to line up. *Fuck! She didn't say there would be audience participation.* Diotima flattened herself against the nearest wall, looked right and left, and was about to leave the theater, when she got swept up in the line. Unable to escape, she looked down in front of her. *Those girls are still at it.* Wow. Indeed, the emerald twins were every bit enmeshed, even as they climbed the stairs and got on stage. Only when it was their turn with the microscope were they separated at the mouth, but not at their hands, still clenched. *Quit gawking,* Diotima warned herself. *Don't be a creep. You're only young once, and lucky even to have that one time.* As Diotima made her way closer to the stage, she remembered that Terry was still speaking.

"I saw a substance like the belly of a snail," explained Terry. "In the beginning, all there was a miasma of snail bellies, mucus everflowing, glittering gold and gray. Every now and then it frothed into being an eye, a limb, an orifice, but each indent was filled by its excess, every extension drowned in its body. No distances to breach, there was no space that was not it. Its eyes could not see. Its limbs could not touch. There was no pleasure in its orifices. Its froth frothed from something in its mass, a mystery, something love-like but primordial, an absence. A wanting of love. Desiring desire. The before-thought milk, who, like its extremity, had no quality of touch, or sight, ungraspable. But all the same, this before-thought was in the slime, and the slime was iridescent, sapphire. Its iridescence was wisdom, a wise old butch like me, electrifying the mollusk with energy, youthful like her. The electric heat blew up bubbles in the froth, larger and larger until when the largest bubble popped, it made an orifice. Inside this sphincter was space instead of mass, a restless bottom, *Binah* understanding wisdom's thrust, a vessel nodding, 'now, now, now: create!'

"Curiosity was the borne between wisdom and understanding. Curiosity built itself sturdier than any predecessor, and it met friction, for the first time, when it plunged into the fissure in the body, divining proximity through stimulation of the hole.

"When the sphincter closed around the limb, the limb gesticulated, a buck: it stretched the flesh embracing it. The sphincter bellowed, pockets of skin collected in the reverberation of growth, jowls of wind, and the limb became limit, that furthest piece to reach into a newborn gap, flesh shrinking to make way for what could be. But even the hole was part of the whole, though it felt otherwise to the limb. Presence created absence to know presence. Flesh created pockets to know the pleasure of filling them.

"Do you know, my friends, how many times the limb stretches the sphincter into a gap? Every moment. Pleasure domes and their concaves riddle the fog: swiss cheese cosmology. In the modulation of its heat, it melts inward and melts out. In the beginning was raclette, and it was good! So good, in fact it devours itself, then regurgitates itself, so it can eat itself again. A lover kissing its own mouth, delighting. Each new cycle of a morsel moving in the whole, the morsel, hoisted by the maw, evolves in variance, contorting, in those contortions collecting new stories, new experiences, new forms of life, tastes different each ingestion, sliding down the cosmic gullet."

Diotima stood before the microscope. The fog slithered on the ground and found its way around her ankles, seized her, drew her forward. Resigned to the pull, she bent over the tool and eyed the specimen. She gasped. Inside the dish as a viscous glow, and in the glow, she twisted the knob, a garden. Out of the soil spurt gardeners, fruits and vines and baby trees growing in their dirt skin. Was this a trick, a hidden film under the table? From her aerial view, Diotima watched as the gardeners moved into circles, budding, fruiting, spudding, ripening. Ten circles in all, they formed, and when they finally sat, they reached into their bodies, drew pears and seeds and dates and figs, oranges out of their breasts, almonds of their teeth. Passing their harvest, each to the next, their bodies changed in the reintegration, and farmers and the farmed formed differently of the same stuff, emptying and filling.

"Join the feast of autopoiesis!" called Terry, now standing on top of the stool, arms stretched out. Diotima pulled her eye away from the lens. No longer magnified, the substance in the dish was slime again. She bent over again to see if she would see again what she had seen. No garden. Just goo and the occasional glisten of sapphire veins. Strange matter. Diotima moved so the next person could have a turn and made her way back to her seat. En route, however, her shoulder was grabbed, and she looked behind. It was Terry. And Terry, amidst the fray of bodies moving in the theater, leaned toward Diotima and uttered, "You have a prophet's eye, professor."

"Yes," said Diotima. "I had a vision." Terry put their other hand on Diotima's shoulder. They were face to face, a unique bond forming in the crowd.

"I'd love to know what it is you saw?" And in that moment Diotima wondered if she saw an iridescence in Terry's eye. Terry had no doubt, however, that a blue vein was swirling in the professor's eye, one that had only just revealed itself in the wake of new sight. Diotima broke away, and Terry let go. Diotima sat down beside the ever-horny couple. Terry returned centerstage, as the final participant returned to the audience. Terry plucked the snail, which had made its way to the performer's shoulder, looked at it as if it were something remarkable, then placed it back into the tank.

"The divine veils itself in itself until it's selves. The first to undergo this process, the first selves, we call the gods."

* * *

I was always interested in Kabbalah, and its influences were almost always present in my Jewish upbringing. From melodies sung at Shabbos dinner, to Dvar Torahs at the new age minyan at my conservative synagogue, to the ceremony of the Tu B'Shvat seder (a meal that both celebrates the new year of the trees and retells of the migration of the soul toward reunification with God as symbolized by the fruits we eat and the wine we drink), Jewish mysticism helped connect the abstraction of God as well as the grand mytho-historical records of my people with me on a personal level. Mysticism is in the businesses of linking what is above to that which is below. Unsurprisingly, however, it is in the realm of stories and art where I was most impacted by Kabbalah. I learned about the magic of practical Kabbalah through the Golem of Prague as told through children's books and a very beloved episode of *Johnny Quest,* and later when my mother sat me down to watch Michał Waszyński's adaptation of S. Anki's *Der Dybbuk* (1937) about the possession of a woman by a spirit. I became more familiar with the philosophy and mythology of Kabbalah when I bought a translation of the first volume of the Zohar with my Bar Mitzvah money, and Sefer Yetzirah (Book of Formation) the following year. I also read a lot of comics, including Alan Moore's *Promethea,* where the title's superheroine, in order to find her mentor, travels through the sefirot, the ten emanations of God and reality. Around the same time, I wrote my first decent research paper on the character of Samael in Jewish mythology. Throughout Jewish text, the angel Samael has been the guardian of Esau, a sort of devil, the angel of Rome, and God's tricksterish to downright malevolent adversary. For this paper, I examined several Kabbalistic sources and was fascinated by a religious system where evil was not only employed by God but attributed to a distinct personality of God.

In general, I was attracted to Kabbalah because it has a theogony. And as I became aware, in often very painful ways, to my own construction suffocated under the influence and expectations of masculinity, I found new life in these witnesses to a complex and constantly reconstructing divinity who is morally ambiguous, physically complex, and multi-gendered. If I were to believe in God or gods, and throughout my teenage years this was a very fraught "if," then I was to believe in gods who are revealed in the midst of horror and beauty and mundanity all together. Kabbalah showed me a God who could live in the darkest depths and holiest blossoms of my imagination, a God to be found in my pains and in my pleasures. Perhaps I should blame Kabbalah for my interest in drag.

Kabbalah is a theosophical system. "Theosophy," explains foundational scholar of Jewish mysticism Gershom Scholem, "postulates a kind of divine emanation whereby God, abandoning his self-contained repose, awakens to mysterious life; further, it maintains that the mysteries of creation reflect the pulsation of this divine life."[32] In Kabbalah, God doesn't just create the world, God becomes the world. God does this, in large part, by becoming the ten sefirot: *keter* (crown), *chokhmah* (wisdom), *binah* (understanding), *chesed* (lovingkindness), *gevurah* or *din* (might or justice), *tiferet* (beauty), *netzach* (victory), *hod* (glory), *yesod* (foundation), and *malkuth* (the realm), God who is also the *shekhinah* (the divine presence).

In the beginning, God is the Ein-Sof, the limitless, who, according to parts of the Zohar, "has neither qualities nor attributes."[33] When the limitless acts in the world, "it has also certain attributes which in turn represent certain aspects of the divine nature; they are so many stages of the divine Being, and divine manifestation of His hidden life."[34] The sefirot are the ten "fundamental attributes to God, which are at the same time ten stages through which the divine life pulsates back and forth."[35] They are "various phases in the manifestation of the Divinity which proceed from and succeed each other."[36] The sefirot are

---

[32] Gershom Scholem, *Major Trends in Jewish Mysticism* (New York: Schocken Books, 1995), 203.
[33] Ibid., 204.
[34] Ibid., 205.
[35] Ibid.
[36] Ibid., 206.

assigned to parts of God's body, on the macro level as realms and on the micro level in our own body parts. They also are assigned personalities, indeed they are personalities, and are often characters who manifest behaviors and activities while also existing *within* characters, human or angelic, plant or animal. The sefirot are also gendered. The emanation of these personalities is "as a process which takes place in God [...] which at the same time enables man to perceive God."[37] That is to say, the sefirot are perspectives through which God sees and through which God is seen. According to the Zohar, Scholem explains,

> Divine Being Himself cannot be expressed. All that can be expressed are His symbols. The relation between Ein-Sof and its mystical qualities, the Sefiroth, is comparable to that between the soul and the body, but with the difference that the human body and soul differ in nature, one being material and the other spiritual, while in the organic whole of God all spheres are substantially the same.[38]

The dualism of soul and body imperfectly corresponds to the Ein-Sof and the sefirot. They are not separate substances. Rather, they are containers of God, and they are the contained, depending on perspective, "the garments of the Divinity, but also the beams of light which it sends out."[39] In Kabbalah, "theistic and pantheistic trends have frequently contended for mastery."[40] If God is putting on the drag of ten differently gendered personae, the drag and the performer are the same substance in different shapes. The costume and the costumed are both divine.

In the highly pantheistic Lurianic Kabbalah, we find a powerful account of the Ein-Sof's decision to become the sefirot, that is, the world. According to Hayim Vital, R. Isaac Luria's student, the Ein-Sof is described as a divine light:

---

37 Ibid.
38 Ibid., 211.
39 Ibid., 210.
40 Ibid., 218.

> Before the emanation of any of the emanated entities, the divine light completely suffused all of existence, and there was no free space [...], no empty vacuum [...] whatsoever. Rather, everything was filled with the undifferentiated light of Ein-Sof. There was neither beginning nor end, but everything consisted of this one simple undifferentiated light, called Ein-Sof.[41]

The Ein-Sof is similar to the pleroma. In Lurianic mythology, Ein-Sof is at once one thing and very complex: this apparently simple, undifferentiated light was actually made up of radically diverse elements, being "a mixture of good and evil, light and darkness, and (in which) the powers of strict Judgment (*ha-Dinim*) were bound up with the powers of Compassions (*Rahamim*)."[42] Similarly to creation in the pleroma, creation for the Ein-Sof involves an act of desire. Here the divine does drag to know its fullness. Vital reports:

> When [Ein-Sof] determined to create its world and to issue forth the world of emanated entities to bring to light the fullness of His energies [...], names, and qualities, this being the reason for the creation of the world, [...] Ein-Sof then withdrew itself from its centermost point, at the center of its light, and this light retreated from the center to the sides, and thus there remained a free space, an empty vacuum.[43]

The withdrawal, or *tsimtsum,* is the first step of theogony. The Ein-Sof makes room so that it can become entities. As Lawrence Fine explains,

> that the cosmos was completely permeated by divine light made the creation of the various worlds impossible. There

---

41 Hayyim Vital, *126 ShH, Haqdamah* 4, quoted in Lawrence Fine, *Physician of the Soul, Healer of the Cosmos: Isaac Luria and His Kabbalistic Fellowship* (Stanford: Stanford University Press, 2003), 128.
42 Fine, *Physician of the Soul*, 126–27.
43 Ibid., 128.

simply was no room in which something other than divinity could exist. God wished to benefit something other than itself and thus conceived the idea of creating "worlds" by establishing room in which this could take place.[44]

God desires to benefit, to help, to give, to love, to know. God is curious. But there is no space and with no space no distance and with no distance no perspective to perceive anything. God puts on forms, that is, shines light into the space and the light forms, where "the illumination of *Ein-Sof* clothes itself in garment upon garment."[45] God gets dressed in distinct, sexed, and gendered personalities, all of whom interrelate, loving, hating, fighting, fucking, and perpetuating the world.

If the Kabbalist theogony is a myth of drag, then it challenges a clear distinction between the wearer and what is worn. For theologians and drag performers alike who invoke the language of drag, what might we mean when we talk about people as God in drag? For starters, each performance is as authentic as it is false. The lie is the symbol of the truth. We cannot perceive divinity out of drag.

What Are You Doing: Gesturing

For the duration of scene change, the musician moved into the light. He had curly hair, and the ringlets stretched by the weight of sweat collected under the heat of stage lights. He sat on the stool, while stagehands removed the table, and he played the cithara. His plucking turned strumming was accompanied by the vibrations of his mouth, humming until the lips parted, and he sang or spoke a lyric into the space.

> The gods have hidden themselves in clandestine sparks
> Justice hidden from mercy
> Wisdom hidden from thought

---

44 Ibid., 130.
45 Ibid., 131.

> The broken seed is enveloped by sweltering earth.
> We and our daemons give you the earth, Bacchus,
> wreath of soil, your crown.

Diotima had long ago been to the villages of Thrace, those households built on the border of wilderness where few would tread save Orpheus and his followers, madmen, musicians, prophets. The singer had a bit of Thrace in his accent and more than a bit of its mysteries in his song:

> In the splitting of seeds, was your pre-existent law
> Inscribed with sacred knowledge
> From it the vine comes and then it is concealed by the fruit
> The origin of our wisdom is fear of you, God of drink
> Yet we drink your drink, dryness deadlier still.

He finished the song, stood up, bowed, and returned to the dark where another man was waiting for him, embraced him with one arm, and reached in for a kiss, but the musician gently moved his head away. *Not yet. Not until the show is ended. The rite complete.* The other man lowered his head in recognition and backed off, heading backstage. The theater went black. The musician then began to hum again, a tune like a lullaby.

"Even the gods were infants, once," Terry's voice called out. Light returned, descending on Terry, now kneeling on the floor, their back to the audience. They had on a bathrobe and wore a wreath on their head.

"I have arrived. I am Dyko-Nysus, child of the vine, come to Mantinea. My flesh has journeyed through spiraling chambers, worlds underneath and up above the present. *Materia divina* dons human drag: here I am."

Terry looked over their shoulder. Again, in the gaze, a sapphire spark. But Diotima was so distracted by the performer's heavily made-up face that she didn't give the spark a second thought. Terry had purple diamonds around the eyes, golden lips, a spiral on each cheek, in scarlet representing blush, and a gray spiral on the chin, a youthful beard.

"You have heard about the birth of gods, in general, but what of me, my own birth? Am I a self distinct from the mass? How did I get to be?

"Know, I have traversed cobblestones in heels, washed blood from blisters on my feet, stomped Ionian shores in boots, unlearning elegance each step, the skin on foot extending and folding, the bones dividing and coalescing with the rhythms of the sand. I have been shaped by this world."

Dyko-nysus rose to their feet and dropped their robe. Back to the audience still, they were naked, save the wreath and a thin cord around their hips. A spiral was painted on each buttock, and on each forearm. Like a serpent, the right arm lifted, hand pointing up, and was matched by the left arm, in a diagonal, hand pointing down. The lines in opposition carried to the tilt of the neck and the horizon of the hips. As they spoke, Dyko-nysus would counter the balances in their body, shift the angles, switching up and down and right and left. With such mastery of their body, even their back amazed. Even their back conveyed a story.

"The first ten grapes that grew on the vine swelled so large, you could not have seen they were connected by the same plant. And each fruit had a different color, a different scent, a different flavor. I am the wine of the fifth grape, the counterbalance of Love. My bouquet is brimstone, my nose is thistle. I am Justice and the seed of evil; I scour your pallet with my bitter taste, so you might know it when you suckle sweet. When blended with love, I am beautiful; even in my strongest cask, I am never unblent. Always at least a drop from all the others. But since I am in the infancy of my godhood, I am in close proximity to my fullness and distinction. Therefore, I am a monster. Cower before my might!

"I come to Mantinea through bodies gesturing in burning fields," Terry turned their body in profile. The cord around the hips led to a pouch covering the genitals, ambiguously filled.

"The gardeners must overthrow what's overgrown in one direction, and kneeling by the ruin, their knees becoming gray with ash. I am the ash as I was the smoke and the red of the flame. Now I cling to the knee dug in the carnage as I once shadowed the movements of the igniting match. I am the char of the bones of the beasts who could not flee in time for land's rebirth. I am Dyko-nysus!

"The gardeners mourn the sober task and drink my crimson urine, my bubos crushed under their women's feet. Drinking me, they do not forget what they have done. But wine allows them to remember the joy in destruction, that their fires are noble, that they are complicit in the perpetuation of life. Disintegrate, reintegrate, that's what gods do. Surely, the dance is good enough for humans?

"But far from the fields, in this little college town, this center of Mantinea, the culture is very different. Minds are served on silver plates, bodies thrown in the bin. I have been called by the wailing faeries, bulldaggers, faggots, he-shes and sluts, I the Justice of the many-beast, for a man has risen in the assembly of gay liberation. He is a mattachine, a despiser of my many fruits, graph-paper incarnate, the taxonomizer Pentheus, normalizer of the homosexual agenda. 'We are men who love men, and they are women who love women: that is it, let it be so,' he ordains, then spits at the panty-wearing gorgons, the posey-picking punks, sets his ghouls against their participation in their freedom. He is a tyrant of distinction between the natural and otherwise who investigates his body with a sword that he might gut himself of any fruitishness, the feminine, the monstrous. Anyone who reminds him that he is many not only one, not whole, not proper, and complete, he banishes from the movement."

A large woman with green hair called out from behind Diotima. "Fuck that little bitch!"

"Oh, I will," responded Dyko-nysus, and the performer turned once again, revealing their front to the audience, more spirals: one between the breasts, one on the stomach, a golden thread spiraling the silk-covered crotch. "I will cast a spell on him. He will desire me, and his desire will be his undoing. In my ensnarement, I will plant eyes along his body, in unexpected places, and he will see the world in my image, in your image, from angles all around, new sight the midwife to his ruin.

"That is why I have found the balances in my musculature, contorted bones to fit inside this body of Tiresia. I've practiced the ways of men and women, fauns and sphynxes, dangled my tits in the way of harpies. I sway my swish into a strut, speckle my peacock with male musk, adorn my crown with vines. This body in becoming is lathered in the ambrosial cream of lovers, smoothed with their hands, one moment squishing me another pulling my appendages apart. Pentheus will scrape this nectar with his tongue and imbibe. Be changed. Be me. Be broken!

"Anyone who clings to souls like Pentheus, to an eternal nature, male or female, white or black, good or evil, who scorns the body in its formations, I'll reach into your chest tonight, as well, and we will inspect *your* heart." Diotima was sure that Terry was talking to her. Her chest was inflamed. "We'll prod your heart like a hunk of fish. Make incisions with our fingernails, vivisect. I'm a vivisexual!"

Most in the audience laughed at this, but Diotima felt sick. She could feel premonitions of the sting, the cut to come. She pulled at her neck and looked down her shirt. *What am I doing?* She let it go and looked back at Dyko-nysus, now reclining on a couch with a bowl of grapes. *What is she... uh... he... doing?* Biting on a fruit, juice spilled from the mouth of Dyko-nysus.

"Whoever's built their self by cutting off their body's limbs wins a free ticket to my slab. In the ecstasy of the surgery I offer, your self will be demolished. To know the making of the gods is to know the unmaking of the man. Such is the brutal blessing and loving curse of the infant Dyko-nysus," and with that, Dyko-nysus flung the contents of the bowl, raining grapes over the audience. One even fell into Diotima's blouse, though she didn't notice it, and when she reached to clench her heart, feeling another swell of fire, she crushed the grape. Red seeped out of the fabric over her breast, a stain unlikely ever to come out.

* * *

José Esteban Muñoz analyzes drag performer and nightclub personality Kevin Aviance to articulate how "gesture [...] signals a refusal of a certain kind of finitude," and how "dance is an especially valuable site for ruminations on queerness and gesture."[46] The dance floor "demands, in the openness and closeness of relations to others, an exchange and alteration of kinesthetic experience through which we become, in a sense, less like ourselves and more like each other."[47] Muñoz clarifies, this

> does not mean that queers become one nation under a groove once we hit the dance floor. I am in fact interested in the persistent variables of difference and inequity that follow us from queer communities to the dance floor, but I am nonetheless interested in the ways in which a certain queer communal logic overwhelms practices of individual identity.[48]

In describing the dancefloor, Muñoz sets up a scene fraught with delights and terrors of self-dissolution. Within gestures, repeated and reflected, mirroring, and transforming, the lines between individuality and communalism begin to blur. It is amidst the fray that Muñoz explores the performances of Aviance.

Muñoz focuses on the "specific physical acts that are conventionally understood as gesture, such as the tilt of an ankle in very high heels, the swish of a hand that pats a face with imaginary makeup."[49] For him, "gesture atomizes movement. These atomized and particular movements tell tales of historical becoming. Gestures transmit ephemeral knowledge of lost queer histories and possibilities within a phobic majoritarian public culture."[50] If, when we invoked drag in our theological musings, we were to focus on gesture, we might gain important

---

46 José Esteban Muñoz, *Cruising Utopia: The Then and There of Queer Futurity* (New York: New York University Press, 2009), 65.
47 Ibid., 66.
48 Ibid., 66.
49 Ibid., 67.
50 Ibid.

insight on how drag provokes and evokes memories in us. How I hold my foot to the ground has cultural meaning. Where my nose points, how I shrug. What I choose to showcase through my gestures, builds my drag persona, and in so doing, I present a mosaic of memories and of possibilities.

When it comes to performer Aviance, he is "a mainstay of New York City's club world," and "something of a deity in the cosmology of gay nightlife."[51] When performing Aviance is a queer microcosm of the multiverse. Aviance

> displays and channels worlds of queer pain and pleasure. In his moves we see the suffering of being a gender outlaw, one who lives outside the dictates of heteronormativity. Furthermore, another story about being black in a predominantly white-supremacist gay world ruminates beneath his gestures. Some of his other gestures transmit and amplify the pleasures of queerness, the joys of gender dissidence, of willfully making one's own way against the stream of a crushing heteronormative tide.[52]

How exactly does Aviance convey all this? Through particular bodily movements, Aviance

> stands center stage, and as he screams, he quivers with an emotional force that connotes the stigma of gender ostracism. His gender freakishness speaks to the audiences that surround him. His is an amplified and extreme queer body, a body in motion that rapidly deploys the signs, the gestures, of queer communication, survival, and self-making. Spectators connect his trembling with the ways in which he flips his wrist and regains composure by applying imaginary pancake makeup.[53]

---

51 Ibid., 66.
52 Ibid., 73–74.
53 Ibid., 74–75.

Muñoz zooms in:

> One particular Aviance gesture worth noting is the way in which his ankles fold or crack as he walks, or rather stomps, the runway. This gesture permits him to be quicker and more determined in his steps than most high-heeled walkers. This gesture connotes a tradition of queenly identification with the sadism of female beauty rituals. The move — walking with heels in such an unorthodox fashion — constitutes a disidentification with these traditions of gay male performances of female embodiment.[54]

Through gesture, Aviance signals a wide array of experiences, while also commenting on those embodied experiences and transforming them. Aviance is not "attempting to imitate a woman," but is "instead interested in approximating a notion of femininity."[55] Aviance performs layers of gendered experience "to perform such a hybrid gender is not only to be queer but to defy troubling gender logics within gay spaces."[56] With movements "coded as masculine (strong abrupt motions), feminine (smooth flowing moves), and, above all, robotic (precise mechanical movements),"[57] Aviance uses gestures to "permit the dancers to see and experience the feelings they do not permit themselves to let in. He and the gestures he performs are beacons for all the emotions that the throng is not allowed to feel."[58] In gay male clubs, for instance, a majority of attendants are bound to have complex feelings in regard to the ways they fail to embody masculinity. With gay men growing up as gay boys under the threat of their gestures betraying their sexualities, "these men did not stop at straightening out the swish of their walk," but "worked on their bodies and approximated a

---

54 Ibid., 75.
55 Ibid., 76.
56 Ibid.
57 Ibid., 77.
58 Ibid., 78.

hypermasculine ideal."[59] Aviance's performances confront this stifling gendering experience.

Aviance performs as an emissary of a world beyond the gendered and sexual suppression that rigidifies the body. Muñoz asks the reader to

> [i]magine the relief these gym queens feel as Aviance lets himself be both masculine and feminine, as his fabulous and strange gestures connote the worlds of queer suffering that these huddled men attempt to block out but cannot escape, and the pleasures of being swish and queeny that they cannot admit to in their quotidian lives. Furthermore, imagine that his performance is something that is instructive, that recodifies signs of abjection in mainstream queer spaces — blackness, femininity and effeminacy — and makes them not only desirable but something to be desired. Imagine how some of those men on the dance floor might come around to accepting and embracing the queer gesture through Aviance's exemplary performance. More important, imagine what his performance means to those on the margins of the crowd, those who have not devoted their lives to daily gym visits and this hypermasculine ideal, those whose race or appearance does not conform to rigid schematics of what might be hot. Those on the margins can get extreme pleasure in seeing Aviance rise from the muscled masses, elevated and luminous.[60]

In the fashion of Aviance, paying hyper-attention to the gesture, drag creates movements both prophetic and pastoral. Allowing the articulation of our muscles, bones, and skin to fill the space around us, we cannot only echo what others' bodies wish to speak, we invite their whole incarnation into the conversation. My body can refract the wounds in yours. At the same time, my gestures are mouths speaking of other worlds beside the one that forces you to mutilate so many possible yous.

---

59 Ibid.
60 Ibid., 79.

The ideology of the self has us scour off any budding discordancy. But drag gives us the opportunity to nurture that which grows in us, against the planned selves we think we are. We gesture newly. Through repetition, our bodies grow along the lines the gestures draw.

Gesture-centered drag breaks through a conception of a body adorned in objects, that gender is an object worn upon a neutral subject. Such neutrality is a lie, and only accessible to those whose denial of body is their power over the rest of us. Gesture cannot be captured and reminds us that we should not be captured. To resist rigidity is not to have nothing, and "rather than dematerialize, dance rematerializes. Dance, like energy, never disappears; it is simply transformed."[61] Drag is the dance of Dionysus, who pulls the rug from under the tyrant, who uses illusion to break illusion, who shatters prison walls, who feeds the masses on his magnificent body, feminine, masculine, androgynous, monstrous, animal, and divine.

What Are You Doing: Jestering

"You are a disgrace," said Pentheus. He was dressed in a light blue polo and gray khakis: veritable dictator! So primped, so polished, he could've almost passed as a heterosexual, except he was a little too primped, too polished. To intent on straight lines. Pentheus was played by the same man who earlier had attempted to kiss the musician. Pentheus was addressing Dykonysus.

The god had discarded the wreath and replaced it with a wig of slick, black hair. To what little they had been wearing, the posing strap, was added a ridiculous pair of leopard-print thigh-high boots, a chain necklace off of which hung some rose-tinted glasses, and a leather bomber jacket. On the back of the jacket was stitched a hybrid of mysterio-phallic symbols, a caduceus, the staff traditionally held by the messenger of the gods, with

---

61 Ibid., 82.

two snakes weaving around but topped with a pinecone, like a thyrsus, the special of Dionysus.

"Disgusting," Pentheus barked, eyeing the god's still uncovered ass. "Flaunting your sickness, we'd be lucky to get their scraps at this point."

"Don't you have bigger dreams than a straight boy's scraps," replied Dyko-nysus coolly as they glanced over Pentheus's outfit. "No, I guess not. Not in those pants, anyways."

"What's wrong with my pants?!" shrieked Pentheus, who immediately covered his mouth.

"Gotta stifle your voice, Pentheus, otherwise something might slip out," Dyko-nysus looked amused.

This back and forth had been going on for about five minutes. The actors reflected the embroidered snakes, circling each other, lashing out. But Dyko-nysus remained cool no matter how hot-headed Pentheus would get. Each jab out of the dragking's mouth left the gay-lib tyrant a little more disheveled, exasperated, and foolish. Ironic how the nearly nude Dyko-nysus left Pentheus so exposed.

Diotima was aware of the context in which this strange little play was being performed. Two years ago, there was a series of protests at the university's Institute of Health and Sexuality, where the local Gay Lib organization was housed. The protests occurred after a raid on L. Lothario's, a dirty bar frequented by butches, drag queens, and other queers who had little interest in the respectable members of their collective's liberation movement. They were having a benefit concert to raise money for a local queen who had just been evicted from her apartment. The music was apparently too loud and drew to the neighborhood such an unsavory crowd, that someone found it necessary to call the cops. Only a few arrests were made, and most of the queers escaped. But the revelation of the night was that the person who had called the police was the chair for the Apollonian Society for Homosexuals in Pursuit of Excellence, an arts and science fraternity of usually wealthy homosexual men that held a great influence on the local Gay Lib.

The protestors, made up of L. Lothario's regulars, local performers, and students, called for Gay Lib to withdraw their support for what they perceived as a collective of "homosexuals whose self-hatred is a menace to our collective, sexual liberation." Since withdrawing support of ASHPE would also mean denying ASHPE's money, Gay Lib refused the demands. Soon enough, the protests ended, in no small part because of the threat of campus security becoming involved, but the whole affair brought to attention what many of the diehard activists already knew, that there was a serious cultural gap in movements for gay and lesbian liberation.

Diotima had not been part of these protests. It had seemed to her primarily a conflict between gay men, and she had had enough of gay male politics for a lifetime. Her assessment was of course incorrect, for L. Lothario was tended by a butch lesbian and was a mixed bar not only of lesbians and gays, but of a great swath of genderbenders, freaks, anarchists, and bums. But Diotima had been at the front lines of her own community's schism, back when she was in college, between the academic lesbians arguing for their androgynous utopia on one hand and the butch and femme lesbians, often working class, who, when they dared enter the lesbian political movement, were looked down upon as regressive, self-hating, and conservative by the former. By now, some twenty years later, Diotima had relaxed, to a degree, when it came to "correct" lesbian embodiment. But this had given way to an antagonism toward transvestites and transsexuals, the subjects of her more recent scholarly polemics.

This whole history made the fact of a growing warmth in Diotima's body all the more disorienting as she watched her would-be enemy perform.

> DYKO-NYSUS: Come with me, and we will pray to Dyko-nysus.
> PENTHEUS: Ha, that's cute, stranger. I wouldn't be caught dead in your rat-infested bars. Eternally smelling of piss.
> DYKO-NYSUS: You should hear what the rats say about your establishments.

PENTHEUS: We don't have rats.

DYKO-NYSUS: Agree to disagree.

PENTHEUS: We hold our meetings in only the most respectable institutions.

DYKO-NYSUS: Fine-ass supper clubs?

PENTHEUS: Yes, in fact.

DYKO-NYSUS: Every inch of them bleached white.

PENTHEUS: I suppose you prefer dirt.

DYKO-NYSUS: I don't share your anal preferences.

PENTHEUS: No, you wouldn't, you're like — Hey wait a minute, get your mind out of the gutter.

DYKO-NYSUS: You were the one who brought in the piss-reeking bar.

PENTHEUS: Because I was disgusted by it, by you.

DYKO-NYSUS: Disgusted or fixated?

PENTHEUS: Both. I can only imagine what goes on in your underbelly circuit with this Dyko-nysus who you treat like a god.

DYKO-NYSUS: Only imagine? Why not make the fantasy come true, join the party. And see that the god is as real as I am.

PENTHEUS: You would invite me to your den to spy? Ha, I could get all the evidence I need to shut you down.

DYKO-NYSUS: Unless you open your eyes, you'll never see the truth.

PENTHEUS: What are you on about? The movement is tarnished by you freaks.

DYKO-NYSUS: There would be no movement if we were as rigid as you.

PENTHEUS: Not all homosexuals are faggots!

DYKO-NYSUS: A tragedy.

PENTHEUS: Do you take nothing serious!?

DYKO-NYSUS: If you admitted you were nothing, I'd take you serious.

PENTHEUS: That's it, isn't it. You lot have no self-esteem! No self-worth. That's why you dress like clowns, shove

your performance — because you don't have any real
self — down our throats. Children.
DYKO-NYSUS: I bet you were a sad kid. I'm sorry. But I am
still in my infancy.
PENTHEUS: The only true thing you've admitted. Yes. You
are an infant.
DYKO-NYSUS: But you're the one soiling yourself.
PENTHEUS: Shove it!
DYKO-NYSUS: Is that an invitation?
PENTHEUS: Either take me to this Dyko-nysus, stranger, to
your pathetic little underworld, or get out of my sight.
One way or another, our movement will be purged of
you.

Are they about to fuck? Diotima squirmed to hear each actors' venereal locution. She was unhappily moved by both of them, her fantasy tickled by this Euripidean parody. At first Diotima was not able to articulate it. She had never seen drag before, and from what she had heard, it was very different from what she was seeing now. She came to understand that Terry was not the only one "in drag" but also the actor playing Pentheus. A sort of parody. His movements were articulated through uprightness, as if every cell was erect. It reminded her of a colleague, a closeted man, who aligned his spine to an invisible rod, as if any bend, curve, or inclination would out him to the world. Paradoxically, it was his obsessive rectitude that made his more generous colleague pity and his adversaries snicker. He protested too much.

DYKO-NYSUS: All right but know the world I represent is a
configuration of all sorts of bodies, clothed and — as it
were, underclothed, in the pelt's transformation. Where
I come from, we are in flux. Many work to become one
body, one body melts to join another, and each of us is a
fragment and fragmented, depending on the light.
PENTHEUS: Tell me everything.
DYKO-NYSUS: I can't. You've gotta see it for yourself.

PENTHEUS: Then take me.
DYKO-NYSUS: You'd stand out like a sore thumb. No one would talk to you, allow you entrance. You could not spy on us, so obvious a prude.
PENTHEUS: Then dress me up.
DYKO-NYSUS: Suddenly eager to wear a dress!
PENTHEUS: No!

Diotima was taken aback by how loud Pentheus answered.

PENTHEUS: I mean... not unless it would get me in?
DYKO-NYSUS: Yes, it would.
PENTHEUS: And I'd find you all high on poppers, soliciting your bodies, breaking more than just the natural law... Yes, I could entrap someone.
DYKO-NYSUS: Oh yes, definitely, someone will be entrapped.
PENTHEUS: Then it is settled. Drag me up, stranger, so I might confront this Dyko-nysus.
DYKO-NYSUS: And in so doing, you will confront yourself.
PENTHEUS: Sure. Whatever. Let's go.

The musician began to play, as the half-naked god, incognito, led his enchanted homosexual offstage to his demise. Diotima looked at her notes, scribbled on the back of a returned check. For all the details that go into this queer theatrical excursion, the detail of "the plot" is occasionally overlooked. In her jottings-down, Diotima ascertained that 1) a God of justice, and for some reason wine, had descended into Mantinea and taken the form of a human stranger to confront a leading figure in intra-homosexual politics; 2) Pentheus, that leading figure, wants to discredit the less savory members of his community and close down their institutions, so that his movement for a respectable gay liberation can gain traction; 3) To gain access to the gay, lesbian, and genderbending underground in order to sabotage *their* efforts, Pentheus must dress like them, otherwise they'd know he was a narc; and 4) Pentheus employs the stranger, who is actually Dyko-nysus, to help transform him, but Dyko-nysus seems to be leading Pentheus into a trap. Diotima let out a breath of self-gratulations. *I figured it out!*

What made less sense to her, however, was a triangle of attraction that had appeared when the actors were on stage. In Pentheus's self-denial and put-upon masculinity, traits she would never have considered appealing, she found a kind of animacy, a dynamism in the movement between the actor's gendered embodiment and his character's. She found it... well... she found it sexy. A world-famous lesbian separatist enthralled by one kind of gay man performing as a very different kind of gay man. And if this betrayal of her heart to her ideology wasn't enough, there was Dyko-Nysus/Terry. What an abstraction! What a paradox! If indeed Terry hated that they were a woman, as Diotima believed, how could the fruit of that hatred become so viscerally endearing. *Do I hate myself? I don't think so.* Diotima felt as if she were Pentheus spying on a secret, sacred rite. She shouldn't have been there. But she was. And she had been invited by the performer. She paid the five-drachma fee. She *did* have every right to be there. But it felt like a trap. As the performers struck at one another, circling each other, Diotima saw flashes of her face replacing theirs. A part of her was Dykonysus, and a part of her was Pentheus. Then who was sitting in the audience? Some say the power of the gods is to make you see double. She looked at the nearly identical lovers still beside her, then back at the stage where her partial mirrors had been. The double sight is an omen. It foretells your undoing.

* * *

A mythopoetic depiction of drag is central to *The Bacchae*. Dionysus opens the play: "I have arrived. I am Dionysus, son of Zeus / come to Thebes [...] / I have changed from divine to human form, and here I am."[62] Already, we are faced with a multi-sexed, world-traveling lightning-born entity becoming a person.

---

62 Euripides, *Bacchae*, ll. 1–6.

He explains that he is worshipped prolifically outside of Thebes. All around the world, except in *this* place, he is loved and feared as a god. But in Thebes, where he was born, Dionysus is not recognized as divine, not by his mother's sisters, nor by his cousin, Pentheus, the city's leader. Enraged by this injustice, for Pentheus has also outlawed the Dionysian cult, the god sets his eyes on Pentheus: "Pentheus wages war on the gods through me, / shoves me away from libations, pays no attention / to me in his prayers."[63] If the human wishes to set up a contest of powers, then the god will meet him: "I'll show him / I am truly god."[64] To show Pentheus the error of his ways, that is why the god incarnates as a human: "It's to do this that I have taken human form / and changed myself into a man."[65]

But it is not only that the androgynous god performs through the body of a man that centers drag in this unique tragedy. Later in the play, Dionysus as human stranger agrees to bring Pentheus to the Bacchae, but only if Pentheus dresses as the wild women. So, the hyper-masculine, misogynist Pentheus does, through the charisma and enchantment of the god, agree to dress as a woman. When he comes out in full regalia, it is a ridiculous scene. He is made a buffoon in front of the chorus, he is pranced around the city, in the garments of his supposed antithesis. And yet, it is only in this state, when he perceives something unusual about the stranger: "I think I am seeing two suns, I'm seeing double [...]. And you're a bull, ahead of me in procession; I see new horns sprouted on your head. / Were you ever a wild animal?"[66] Pentheus begins to see pluralities through this double seeing. He sees outside the overbearing monovision of his authoritarianism. And he sees the hybridity of the stranger. The stranger is the bull like Zeus, a wild animal, more than human. To see the god, who he could not see from his day-to-day perspective, Pentheus has to dress in drag. Only through the

---

63 Ibid., ll. 46–47.
64 Ibid., ll. 48–49.
65 Ibid., ll. 54–55.
66 Ibid., ll. 918–22.

destabilization of his gendered, sexual, classed, and theological self can he perceive what was once imperceptible. Drag is his death. Dionysus will see the contest through to the end of Pentheus. But drag gives Pentheus life. A new world has opened up. The rationalist Pentheus now turns his head up to the sky and gazes on a pair of suns. And what does he do beneath this unfamiliar heaven? He dances.

What Are You Doing: Gendering

"Distinguished guests, including the few ladies and the few gentlemen who somehow made it into this crowd," Dyko-nysus was now wearing the rose glass, had replaced the necklace with a bowtie, and was holding a microphone, "put your hands together for... Agave Nectarrrrrrrrrrrr!"

Pentheus stomped on stage, adorned in a sheer peplos, silver heels, and a boa whose fullness of feathers might have explained the extinction of the dodo. One could make out an intermediate skeleton, between the skin and the outer costume, of ties, stirrups, garters, duct tape, braziers, pads, panties, and belts. Clearly, a panoply of moving parts was required to present this miraculous "woman."

"So, we're not going with Panty-us," implored Pentheus, feeling his arms.

"No," said Dyko-Nysus matter-of-factly. "I wanted something sweeter," and they plopped a monstrosity of teased and ombré hair, likely composed of about six or seven smaller wigs, on Pentheus's head. They took a step back to examine their work.

"I am a veritable Pygmalion, and you," Dyko-nysus blew several kisses at Pentheus, "are the work of art and the muse, you are a goddess, you are everything. Ooh, là là! Swoon!"

"Baby's pretty?" Pentheus batted his eye.

"Baby's gorgeous," Dyko-nysus assured the queen, "I could eat you up!"

"They'll buy it? That I am, you know, for real. A genuine," Pentheus gulped, "queer."

"Well, you are a queer," said Dyko-nysus as they adjusted Pentheus's shoulders.

"Not *this* queer." Pentheus reached for the stranger's shoulder.

"Sssh!" Dyko-nysus slapped his hand away. "Enough of that. We've got to work on your routine!"

Dyko-nysus would model a gesture or a step and Pentheus would repeat it. The musician provided a soundtrack. At first, Diotima had been offended by the appearance of Pentheus as Agave Nectar. *This is a woman? This is what they say we are?* She had looked around the audience, hoping to make eye contact and confirm with another that this performance was a form of brutal misogyny, but it seemed no one else in the room thought that Pentheus was making any claim to "true womanhood" or even that such a category existed. *Fucking postmodern bullshit.* Diotima crossed her arms, pouting. *As if you can just wear a woman.* She glared at Pentheus. *My life is not a costume.*

As Dyko-nysus moved their body and Pentheus mirrored, Diotima did not necessarily forgive the drag, but alongside the insult arose a thread of curiosity. It was not only the costume that transformed Pentheus but the gesture. The angle of the finger, arm, hip, thigh, heel, toe. It was as if Pentheus had turned into a magnifying glass, and the most easily forgettable moments in one's day-to-day bodily routine were amplified. When Pentheus cupped the air with a gentle palm, Diotima was reminded of her own hand, back when it used to be calloused and full of little cuts from scraping rocks when digging in the earth, the hands of a child. When Pentheus flipped the hand, to show the topside, Diotima felt the sting of a ruler. *Young ladies don't play in the dirt, Di. They must be clean.*

The actor playing Pentheus playing Agave and Terry playing Dyko-nysus playing the stranger, in portraying this almost mythological origin of transvestic theater, had to reach into their lives and pull on the lessons they had been told on how, and how not, to behave, act, sit, stand, walk, twirl, step, and look their whole lives. Their personae were artifacts of varying and contradictory gendered instructions. Fragments of personalities fusing in various presentations.

In turn, Diotima was punctured over and over again, riddled with windows, gazing at all the lessons she had learned that led to her body and the presumption of her soul. From the vantage of the elbow, the under-boob, the earlobe, and the thumb, she saw her lovers' rhythms, the structures of limbs in motion, the geometry of her family, friends, and foes. What beings, sacred and profane, had congregated this night in order for Diotima to be? Which memories made manifest? Which memories made room? A precise organization of component parts led her to this place and time so that she might see what she was seeing. And what she saw awoke in her pieces of her that often had been put to rest. Eyes sprouted all along the professor's body. Diotima Panoptes: seeing herself, outside herself, the staged selves, all her numerous selves in an ecstasy of sight, and from sight, insight.

Diotima wondered if it was simplistic to assume Pentheus's drag was only a costume, or that any costume is only a costume. Surely, the bacchic queers of Dyko-nysus's world would not accept a Pentheus who was the same-old subject dominating the object of his drag. Agave had agency, at least enough to dislodge Pentheus from the center of his body. And whether the joy in the dance, in the movement of becoming Agave was from Agave, or from Pentheus, or from the actor playing both was impossible to answer. In utter defiance of Pentheus, who sought to mimic a patriarchal man of steel, there was no natural self that could remain amidst the interchange of selves emerging. It was a compound pleasure that Diotima was witnessing. The gods were being born. Dyko-nysus had won. Pentheus was destroyed.

******

A few months ago, I celebrated as drag king Landon Cider won the 2019 season of the Boulet Brothers' *Dragula* drag competition television show. It was a momentous achievement because drag kings are rarely given the media attention or respect for their art that they deserve. As a performer who always performs with a drag king collaborator, I cannot imagine a drag culture neutered by this particular approach to masculine performance.

In *Female Masculinities,* Jack Halberstam looks at a variety of queer women and transmasculine people to show that masculinity "does not belong to men, has not been produced only by men, and does not properly express male heterosexuality."[67] In this study, Halberstam argues that women and nonbinary people not only produce many of the wide range of behaviors that comprise masculinity but also that female masculinities can critique, transform, undermine, and reimagine dominant male and cis masculinities. Naturally, Halberstam's study includes a chapter on drag kings. When looking at both drag queens and drag kings, Halberstam notes:

> The production of gender in the case of both the drag queen and the drag king is theatrical, but the theatrics almost move in opposite directions. Whereas the drag queen expands and becomes flamboyant, the drag king constrains and becomes quietly macho. If the drag queen gesticulates, the drag king learns to convey volumes in a shrug or a raised eyebrow.[68]

Straight, cis, white male masculinities operate, and hold onto power, through perceived invisibility, and "current representations of masculinity in white men unfailingly depend on a relatively stable notion of the realness and the naturalness of both the male body and its signifying effects."[69] When it comes to the act, "the white drag king performing conventional heterosexual maleness, masculinity has first to be made visible and theatrical before it can be performed. Masculinities of color and gay

---

67 Jack Halberstam, *Female Masculinity* (Durham: Duke University Press, 1998), 241.
68 Ibid., 259.
69 Ibid., 234.

masculinities, however, have already been rendered visible and theatrical in their various relations to dominant white masculinities, and the performance of these masculinities presents a somewhat easier theatrical task."[70] Theatricality—illusion, "unnaturalness," and deceit—are categorically aligned with femininity not masculinity. The demiurge is creator not created! He remains a god through the concealment of his construction. For drag kings performing as men who most align with a demiurgic model, they must expose his unnaturalness. Halberstam offers the term "kinging," a counter to the drag queen's "camp" which "depends on several different strategies to render masculinity visible and theatrical."[71]

Kinging includes three specific techniques. The first is understatement: "Kinging can signify assuming a masculine mode in all its understatement, even as the performance exposes the theatricality of understatement. An example of this mode would be the drag king who performs his own reluctance to perform through an 'aw shucks' shy mode that cloaks his entire act."[72] This technique reveals the ways men might downplay their presence. The demiurge is happiest when you don't notice him pulling the strings. Drag kings, in performing this understatement, bring light to it. They reveal its constructedness.

The next technique is hyperbole. Halberstam cites drag king Murray Hill as a hyperbolic performer: "Murray Hill, indeed, is the master of hyperbole. His repertoire includes a range of middle-aged male icons, and Murray satirizes and parodies the forms of masculinity that these men are supposed to represent. [...] The impact of Murray Hill's hyperbolic performance is to expose the vulnerability of male midlife crisis."[73] Hyperbole mocks "the drag" men put on in their own performances.

The third technique is layering. A drag king can "allow her femaleness to peek through, [...] or she can perform the role

---

70 Ibid., 235.
71 Ibid., 238.
72 Ibid., 259.
73 Ibid., 259–60.

almost seamlessly. In these seamless acts, the reason that the performance looks 'real' is because if the audience sees through the role at all, they catch a glimpse not of femaleness or femininity but of a butch masculinity. So, the male role is layered on top of the king's own masculinity."[74] Layering involves an ambiguity between butch masculinity and the male drag persona. What is the audience seeing: the man or the queer? Halberstam notes:

> Layering really describes the theatricality of both drag queen and drag king acts and reveals their multiple ambiguities because in both cases the role playing reveals the permeable boundaries between acting and being; the drag actors are all performing their own queerness and simultaneously exposing the artificiality of conventional gender roles.[75]

Drag at once reveals something of the performer's gender and of gender in general. For me, the bitchfaggot is a parody of hybrid-gendered being, and yet my performance also points to something of my day-to-day gendered. I out myself as queer in performing a hybrid femininity. Similarly, Pouchet Pouchet, when performing as a male icon, reveals the constructedness of the male while giving some insight into his own queer embodiment. As Halberstam writes, "the challenge of the drag king performance is to bring to light the artifice of dominant masculinity," which often is "accomplished by highlighting the tricks and gadgets of the sexism on which male masculinity depends."[76] This surely is the technique used by House of Larva. Pouchet Pouchet abuses me with a grasshopper-shaped strap on, beats girls' dolls with a bat, and is canonized as a saint of frat-boy rapists. But beyond the narrative elements and the very intense blocking, it is in Pouchet Pouchet's gestures, magnified through drag, where the seams of masculinity are exposed. Grimaces

---

74 Ibid., 260.
75 Ibid., 261.
76 Ibid., 266.

and nods, the placement of a hand on the leg, the angles of the spine.

Drag denaturalizes what US, Western, Christian culture holds sacred: that we simply are. Drag says, *we simply are not*. We are the constant flow of presence magnified or underplayed, depending on whatever context calls. Furthermore, what is performed in drag does not only bear weight in the realm of drag, but it says something of what femininity is, what masculinity is in general. Perhaps Mary Daly and similar feminists are right to perceive a threat if a drag queen can influence our collective understanding of femininity. Of course, that would also undermine any essentialist understanding of femininity as tied to female sex, even admit that femininity is dangerously discursive. So too does the drag king reflect, refract, reform masculinity. How would men behave were they to confront drag king performances on the regular? What would men become?

Who Are You? (Trans)Gendered God Talk

As we approach the end of this reflection on drag theopoetics, indeed of the(y)ological mythopoeia, we can find ourselves at the "convergence between artistic production and critical praxis."[77] When it comes to studies on performance and movement, we must pay attention to both their applicability *and* their theological, symbolic relevance. For a concluding thought on drag theopoetics, I consider the work of Eugenio Barba, whose *theater anthropology* "is a study *of* the performer and *for* the performer," that is, "a pragmatic science which becomes useful when it makes the creative process accessible to the scholar and when it increases the performer's freedom during the creative process."[78]

When Barba defines theater anthropology as "the study of the pre-expressive scenic behavior upon which different genres,

---

77 Muñoz, *Cruising Utopia*, 101.
78 Eugenio Barba, *The Paper Canoe: A Guide to Theatre Anthropology*, trans. Richard Fowler (London: Routledge, 1995), 13.

styles, roles and personal or collective traditions are all based,"[79] he is describing not so much a specific technique but the "technique of technique" or "learning to learn."[80] How does a performance technique exist in the performer's body? Barba differentiates between daily and extra-daily efforts: "In the daily context, body technique is conditioned by culture, social status, profession. But in performance there exists a different body technique."[81] He explains that daily techniques "are unconscious, the more functional they are. For this reason," he continues, "we move, sit, we carry things, we kiss, we agree and disagree with gestures which we believe to be natural but which are in fact culturally determined."[82] Such could be said of gender. We use certain gestures to make our cis, queer, and trans, male, female, and intersex masculinities and femininities legible. We do this daily, moment to moment, and, for the most part unconsciously. Hence, for instance, the effeminacy or butchness of a child read as queer or "normal" by their peers, regardless of conscious self-identification. Drag is an extra-daily gender technique.

The principle of drag performance "lies in understanding that the body's daily [gender] techniques can be replaced by extra-daily [gender] techniques which do not respect the habitual conditionings of the use of the body."[83] In the demiurge cosmology, the daily techniques of gender are facilitated, that is "made easy," by the articulation of static differences and social functions in a hierarchical relationship. The extra-daily techniques of drag are based "on the contrary, on the wasting of energy."[84] Gender is supposed to be seamless and invisible. Drag exerts an inordinate amount of energy into the gendering processes that are supposed to go unnoticed. In so doing, it makes gender hyper visible. When considering the demiurgic sleep discussed in chapter 2 which orders and naturalizes sexual

---

79 Ibid., 9.
80 Ibid., 10.
81 Ibid., 15.
82 Ibid.
83 Ibid.
84 Ibid., 16.

dimorphism and gender hierarchy, drag is the waking up. It is the denaturalizer. It is gnosis.

The techniques of hypervisibility that constitute drag are accomplished through extra-daily redistributions in through three core areas: balance in action, the dance of oppositions, and consistent inconsistency/the virtue of omission.

Barba asserts "the performer's life is based on an alteration of balance."[85] When we perform, we change the physical processes that keep us erect or walking or sitting in our daily lives: "All codified performance forms contain this constant principle: a deformation of the daily technique of walking, of moving in space, and of keeping balance," where the "aim is a permanently unstable balance rejecting 'natural' balance."[86] Practically, this unstable balance moves the performer into an active concentration on the weight and gestural formation of a differentiated persona. Symbolically, a body consistently at the edge of toppling over shows the fragility of a balancing system like gender, like the perpetuation of subject self over object world, like singularity. It reveals how the lone, stable, erect body "can never be immobile," that even in stillness "minute movements are displacing our weight," so that "our weight presses now on the front, now on the back, now on the left, now on the right sides of the feet."[87] The drag performer destabilizes the weights of gender in their performance. Drag shows how precarious genderered, self-order is and how complex the processes of its establishment are.

Balance involves the harmonizing of discordant forces. Unbalance is disharmony. In the demiurgic system of gender and sex, oppositions are highly discouraged, the multiplicitous denied. The principle of opposition is that "the performer's body revealed its life to the spectator by means of a myriad of tensions between opposing forces."[88] When the performer emphasizes their own contradictions, they enter a state of physical

---

85 Ibid., 18.
86 Ibid., 19.
87 Ibid.
88 Ibid., 24.

discomfort, and, potentially, evoke physical discomfort in the viewer whose imagination puts themselves in the contortions witnessed. Symbolically, the dance of oppositions symbolizes the interconnectedness of various agents within us. The dance reveals that we are legion, many genders. We are pleromic aeons, emanations of the Ein-Sof.

It also reveals that daily balance is in fact contingent on oppositional movements. When part of me leans forward, another part leans back so I do not fall. The idea of the balanced singular self runs counter to the realities of balance in the body, necessarily engaged through multiplicitous movements. Perhaps too, our identities persist through their multiplicities, as Adam's salvation comes when the divine Eve shows him of his origins in the manyfold godhead. Extra-daily techniques are not fundamentally different from the gestures that sustain our daily selves. But, through different applications of energy and emphasis, they challenge "what we normally *perceive* in our bodies and in the bodies of others," which illuminate for spectators "one aspect which is hidden in daily behaviour: *showing* something engenders interpretation."[89] The performance makes the body legible. Performances of gender and sexuality make our genders and sexualities legible. Legibility makes us interpretable. Something that can be interpreted is something discursive. The drag performance, dancing the dance of oppositions, makes gender, and the power relationships behind it, a matter of contestation. And so the "rulers" quiver.

Consistent inconsistency "is where behaviour is inconsistent or incoherent with everyday behaviour but is coherent or consistent within the realm of the theatrical practice."[90] While the dance of oppositions shows that there are many gestures, genders, embodied memories that are inside us, consistent inconsistency uses omission of *some* of the many to articulate a momentarily consistent perspective. That is, "we need to create conventions that can be understood by the audience that indi-

---

89 Ibid., 25.
90 Jane Turner, *Eugenio Barba* (London: Routledge, 2019), 54.

cate what is, and what is not, a part of the fiction."[91] It is significant that Barba uses "fiction" in describing performance. If we remember, from chapter one, fiction involves the language and symbols of the ordinary (what is) to express what is not. The performer takes the gestures and movements that already exist in day-to-day motion, in memories personal and cultural, and reorganizes them, emphasizing some over others to represent a personality who does not "exist." Drag is fiction, not in the sense that it is not a performance of a "real" gendered self, but as the intermediary between a gender that is and a gender imagined. To perform in drag is to turn the body into fiction. To perform in drag is to incarnate myth.

Too often has the male theologian, in the spirit of a "shy boy" drag king, let himself be invisible as if we would all appreciate a disembodied voice over one that reminds me what I am reading, that *this* experience of God comes from *a* body. Again, the demiurge's power is contingent on our obliviousness to him. And like the perpetuation of the demiurgic rule through a human hierarchy made in his image, in the world of theology, too often have non-white, non-Christian, non-cis-men been forced to replicate disembodied, genderless speech in order to be taken seriously in the discipline of God-talk. But in denying the body, in keeping the sexual, gendered, ethnic, and raced self invisible, the theologian denies us revelation. Revelation is extra-daily.

If I am critical of the ideology of the natural self, that does not mean I think we should ignore the self in our theological writings. Rather, we are tasked to wonder how the selfed body emerges in theology. For queer and trans theologies, indeed for all theologies concerned with revelation, we cannot allow sexuality and gender or the naturalization of the self to be obscured.

As theologians, as mythmakers and scholars, we have our techniques. We wear costumes, construct voices, use gestures and employ tactics — not unlike those of "kinging": hyperbole, understatement, and layering. But so often we do this unintentionally. We do not ask what the techniques of our techniques

---

91 Ibid.

are. But if we were to take drag's lead, we would not only examine but center our production of extra-daily techniques in becoming theologizing personae.

Drag does not guarantee empathy, but it opens up new paths for the body to be gendered and for the body to gesture toward the holy. In those contortions, our vantages shift. What we see and feel ourselves to be and our worlds to be can change. We transform our selves and approach divinity, divinity being those beings who harmonize their many components and many visions through *philia*. We can move from subordinate children of Adam toward cocreative daemons.

To buy into a single demiurgic illusion is fundamentally different from slipping in and out of many illusions. For Dionysian illusions, that is, to be under his spells, you know and even take pleasure in the knowledge that something is not quite right, not quite believable, not steady. The paradox of the Dionysian illusion is its resulting clarity. Pentheus becomes privy to the revelation of a constantly changing order, to the limits of his self and indeed of all selves, and he gets to this knowledge when Dionysus allows him to become a different self. Would his story have ended so tragically if he had been able to move in and out of the dream selves from the beginning? If he had seen such play as holy?

For queer and trans theologians, for feminist and liberation theologians, and for all who dare speak of holy things, what worlds of possibility are we unable to know if we never undertake the Dionysian illusion? Would I never have seen of my own erotics and my gender(s) if I had never worn a garment designed for something other than my arbitrarily designated body, never dared to move my mouth along with the words of a woman singer? How much does it really mean to say "we are God in drag" if so few of us have ever done drag?

To be in drag is to make the self become other, and to see in that other a poetics of our deepest selves, redistributed. Drag is myth acted and enfleshed. If God created specific personae so God could know, reach, love, and make more of God's selves, then our job is not only to study but to bring to light the various personae that are uniquely qualified to perceive those selves. From those new perspectives, new personae emerge. We turn our bodies into new myths, conduits between what is and what might be.

* * *

The lights went up. The audience applauded as Terry, Pentheus, and the musician took their bows.

"What did I just watch?" Diotima asked herself.

"Beats me," called a voice from her right. It was one of the kissers. "I kinda missed a lot of it."

"You don't say," said Diotima, dryly. The girl smirked and took her friend by the hand and made her way out of the theater.

Diotima was shaking slightly and wasn't eager to return home. She found her way backstage to the dressing rooms and knocked on Terry's door. No answer. She knocked again, and it budged just a crack.

"Hello?" No one responded. She pushed the door open and saw the nearly empty room: a metal folding chair, a bag of makeup wipes, a small trash bin, and a large mirror. Diotima walked to the mirror and stared at herself. Everything about her looked wrong. Her hair, her eyes and her glasses, her nose, her lips, the concave in her neck, the bones beginning to peak above her chest. She leaned closer, inspected spots and wrinkles. Worry lines. A small mole.

"How do you live? What are you doing? Who are you?" she said out loud. Then she repeated one time, then another, until she found herself unable to stop asking the questions. Tears dropped to the floor.

"How do you live?"

Her brain swarmed with memories, angry faces, smug faces, a house with broken front steps and a circle window, the frown of an ancient cat. These moments from her life began to leak out of her head into the rest of her body. Cold saltwater licking her shoulders, chanting echoed in ears, a lover's nails dug right above a tender rib.

"What are you doing?"

Blood rushed to her cheeks. A spark of incense burned her leg. Teeth poked through lips scraping the curve of her left breast. Hands threw the first and only fist of life, the sound of boy's blood hitting the stone they were sitting on. Toes elongated, expanding gaps made way for sand. Fingers rubbed in recollection of fine beadwork.

"Who are you?"

"You do not know," Terry was standing in the door. Diotima saw them in the mirror. There was a long pause.

"Actually," Diotima turned to them. "I have some ideas."

The two of them spent the night sitting cross-legged on the concrete floor. And they talked. Even with so many similar childhood memories, it was unsurprising how different each of their lives was from the other. But where once, differences might have produced in either person a sense of loss, tonight, there was only excitement. As Diotima's lifelong armor peeled like birch bark, Terry leaned against the wall, locked eyes with Diotima, and smiled.

Bibliography

Aizura, Aren, Trystan Cotton, Carsten Balzer/Carla LaGata, Marcia Ochoa, and Salvador Vidal Ortiz. "Introduction." TSQ: *Transgender Studies Quarterly* 1, no. 3 (August 2004): 308–19. DOI: 10.1215/23289252-2685606.

AJ and the Queen. Season 1, episode 9, "Fort Worth." Directed by Dennie Gordon, written by Michael Patrick King and Jhoni Marchinko, featuring RuPaul Charles and Izzy G. Aired January 10, 2020, on Netflix.

Althaus-Reid, Marcella. *The Queer God*. London: Routledge, 2003.

Anderlini-D'Onofrio, SerenaGaia. *Ecosexuality: When Nature Inspires the Art of Love*. Cabo Rojo: 3WayKiss, 2015.

Aristophanes. *The Birds*. In *Aristophanes: Birds and Other Plays*, translated by Stephen Halliwell, 1–78. Oxford: Oxford University Press, 1998.

Armstrong, Louis. "Let's Do It (Let's Fall in Love)." By Cole Porter. Spotify. Recorded on August 13, 1957. Track 6 on *Ella and Louis Again*. Verve Records, 1957.

Baer, Stephanie K. "Here Are All The Times Brett Kavanaugh Said He Likes Beer at His Senate Hearing on Sexual Assault Allegations." *Buzzfeed News*, September 27, 2018. https://www.buzzfeednews.com/article/skbaer/brett-kavanaugh-likes-beer.

Barba, Eugenio. *The Paper Canoe: A Guide to Theatre Anthropology.* Translated by Richard Fowler. London: Routledge, 1995.

Barth, Karl. *Church Dogmatics,* Vol. 3, Part 4: *The Doctrine of Creation.* Edited by G.W. Bromiley and T.F. Torrance. Translated by A.T. Mackay, T.H.L. Parker, H. Knight, H.S. Kennedy, and J. Marks. London: T&T Clark International, 1961.

Bauman, Whitney. "Queer Values for a Queer Climate: Developing a Versatile Planetary Ethic." In *Meaningful Flesh: Reflections on Religion and Nature for a Queer Planet,* edited by Whitney Bauman, 103–24. Earth: punctum books, 2018.

Bennett, Jane. "Systems and Things: On Vital Materialism and Object-Oriented Philosophy." In *The Nonhuman Turn,* edited by Richard Grusin, 223–39. Minneapolis: University of Minnesota Press, 2015.

Bernstein, Ellen. *Splendor of Creation: A Biblical Ecology.* Cleveland: Pilgrim Press, 2005.

Bereishit Rabbah 8:1. Translated by Sefaria Community Translation. *Sefaria,* n.d. https://www.sefaria.org/Bereishit_Rabbah.8?lang=bi&with=all&lang2=en.

Brumberg-Kraus, Max. "Call Me a Fairy." *Homos in Heimarmene,* August 2, 2016. http://homosinheimarmene.blogspot.com/2016/08/call-me-fairy-full-pleasant-is-fairy.html.

Cahana-Blum, Jonathan. *Wrestling with Archons: Gnosticism as a Critical Theory of Culture.* Lanham: Lexington Books, 2018.

Carson, Anne. *Eros the Bittersweet.* Champaign: Dalkey Archive Press, 1998.

Cipri, Nino. "Kitchen Sink Gender." In *Nonbinary: Memoirs of Gender and Identity,* edited by Micah Rajunav and Scott Duane, 201–7. New York: Columbia University Press, 2019.

"Controlled Burn: February 2020." *20% Theatre Company,* n.d. http://www.tctwentypercent.org/current-season/controlled-burn-20/.

Core, Philip. "From Camp: *The Lie that Tells the Truth.*" In *Camp: Queer Aesthetics and the Performing Subject,* edited by Fabio Cleto, 80–86. Ann Arbor: University of Michigan Press, 1999.

Daly, Mary. *Beyond God the Father: Toward a Philosophy of Women's Liberation.* Boston: Beacon Press, 1973.

———. *Gyn/Ecology: The Metaethics of Radical Feminism.* Boston: Beacon Press, 1990.

Dass, Ram. *One-Liners: A Mini Manual for a Spiritual Life.* New York, Bell Tower, 2002.

Davidson, James. *The Greeks and Greek Love: A Bold New Exploration of the Ancient World.* New York: Random House, 2007.

Dickinson, Emily. "Wild Nights." In *Heart Wisdom from Five Women Poets,* edited by Lisa Locascio, 36. Mineola: Dover, 2018.

Driskil, Qwo-Li. *Asegi Stories: Cherokee Queer and Two-Spirit Memory.* Tucson: University of Arizona Press, 2016.

Empedocles. "Fragments." In *Philosophy before Socrates: An Introduction with Texts and Commentary,* edited and translated by Richard McKirahan, 230–92. Indianapolis: Hackett Publishing, 2010.

Euripides. *Bacchae.* Translated by Paul Woodruff. Indianapolis: Hackett Publishing, 1999.

———. *Hippolytus.* In *Alcestis, Medea, Hippolytus,* translated by Diane Arnson Svarlien, 121–92. Indianapolis: Hackett Publishing, 2007.

Fee, Angie. "Who Put the 'Hetero' in Sexuality?" In *Transgender Identities: Towards a Social Analysis of Gender Diversity,* edited by Sally Hines and Tam Sanger, 207–23. London: Routledge, 2010.

Feinberg, Leslie. *Transgender Liberation: A Movement Whose Time Has Come.* New York: World View Forum, 1992.

Fine, Lawrence. *Physician of the Soul, Healer of the Cosmos: Isaac Luria and His Kabbalistic Fellowship.* Stanford: Stanford University Press, 2003.

Foucault, Michel. "Of Other Spaces: Utopias and Heterotopias." Translated by Jay Miskowiec. *Diacritics* 16, no. 1 (Spring 1984): 1–9. DOI: 10.2307/464648.

Freeman, Elizabeth. *Time Binds: Queer Temporalities, Queer Histories.* Durham: Duke University Press, 2010.

Gabbatis, Josh. "London Pride: Anti-trans Activists Disrupt Parade by Lying Down in the Street to Protest 'Lesbian Erasure.'" *The Independent,* July 8, 2018. https://www.independent.co.uk/news/uk/home-news/anti-trans-protest-london-pride-parade-lgbt-gay-2018-march-lesbian-gay-rights-a8436506.html.

van Groningen, Gerard. *First Century Gnosticism: Its Origins and Motifs.* Leiden: Brill, 1967.

Gutiérrez, Gustavo. *A Theology of Liberation.* Edited and translated by Sister Caridad Inda and John Eagleson. Maryknoll: Orbis Books, 1973.

Hafiz. *The Gift: Poems by Hafiz, the Great Sufi Master.* Translated by Daniel Ladinsky. New York: Penguin Books, 1999.

Halberstam, Jack. *Female Masculinity.* Durham: Duke University Press, 1998.

———. *The Queer Art of Failure.* Durham: Duke University Press, 2011.

———. *Trans*: A Quick and Quirky Account of Gender Variability.* Oakland: University of California Press, 2018.

Hay, Harry. "Toward the New Frontiers of Fairy Vision: Subject-Subject Consciousness." In *Radically Gay: Gay Liberation in the Words of Its Founder,* edited by Will Roscoe, 253–64. Boston: Beacon, 1996.

hernandez, féi. "Coatlicue." In *Nonbinary: Memoirs of Gender and Identity,* edited by Micah Rajunav and Scott Duane, 14–23. New York: Columbia University Press, 2019.

Hesiod. *Theogony.* In *Hesiod: Complete Works,* translated by Hugh Evelyn White, 9–46. East Sussex: Delphi Classics, 2013.

Iser, Wolfgang. *The Fictive and the Imaginary: Charting Literary Anthropology.* Baltimore: John Hopkins University Press, 1993.
"Jaffa Aharanov | Controlled Burn Featured Artist." *20% Theatre Company,* February 14, 2019. http://www.tctwentypercent.org/jaffa-aharonov/.
Jauss, Hans Robert. *Question and Answer: Forms of Dialogic Understanding.* Edited and translated by Michael Hays. Minneapolis: University of Minnesota Press, 1989.
Jauss, Hans Robert. *Toward an Aesthetic of Reception.* Translated by Timothy Bahti. Minneapolis: University of Minnesota Press, 1982.
Johnson, Elizabeth A. *She Who Is: The Mystery of God in Feminist Theological Discourse.* New York: The Crossroad Publishing Company, 2017.
Keefe-Perry, L. Callid. *Way to Water: A Theopoetics Primer.* Eugene: Cascade Books, 2014.
Keller, Catherine. *Face of the Deep: A Theology of Becoming.* London: Routledge, 2003.
Kooijman, Jaap. "Pleasures of the Orient: Cadinot's Maghreb as Gay Male Pornotopia." In *Indiscretions: At the Intersection of Queer and Postcolonial Theory,* edited by Murat Aydemir, 97–111. Amsterdam: Brill, 2010.
Koschel, George. "Cadinot, Jean-Daniel." In *The Queer Encyclopedia of Film and Television,* edited by Claude J. Summers, 61–62. San Francisco: Cleis Press, 2005.
Lane, Keiko. "Imag(in)ing Possibilities: The Psychotherapeutic Potential of Queer Pornography." In *The Feminist Porn Book: The Politics of Producing Pleasure,* edited by Tristan Taormino, Celine Perreñas Shimizu, Constance Penley, and Mireille Miller-Young, 164–76. New York: The Feminist Press, 2012.
Lee, Jiz. "Uncategorized: Genderqueer Identity and Performance in Independent and Mainstream Porn." In *The Feminist Porn Book: the Politics of Producing Pleasure,* edited by Tristan Taormino, Celine Perreñas Shimizu, Constance

Penley, and Mireille Miller-Young, 273–78. New York: The Feminist Press, 2013.

Lillie, Celene. *The Rape of Eve: The Transformation of Roman Ideology in Three Early Christian Retellings of Genesis*. Minneapolis: Fortress Press, 2017.

Logan, John. "*Alien Covenant:* Screenplay by John Logan." AvP Galaxy, November 20, 2015.

Lorde, Audre. *Sister Outsider: Essays and Speeches*. Berkeley: Crossing Press, 1984.

Loy, Mina. *The Lost Lunar Baedeker: Poems of Mina Loy*. Edited by Roger Conover. New York: Farrar, Straus and Giroux, 1996.

Malloy, Tim. "RuPaul Explains Why 'We Are All God in Drag.'" *The Wrap*, September 14, 2019. https://www.thewrap.com/rupaul-explains-why-we-are-all-god-in-drag/.

McFague, Sallie. *The Body of God: An Ecological Theology*. Minneapolis: Fortress Press, 1993.

McKirahan, Richard D. *Philosophy Before Socrates: An Introduction with Texts and Commentary*. Indianapolis: Hackett Publishing, 2010.

Michaelson, Jay. *Everything Is God: The Radical Path of Nondual Judaism*. Boston: Trumpeter, 2009.

Moore, Alan. *Lost Girls*. Marietta: Top Shelf Productions, 2006.

Muñoz, José Esteban. *Cruising Utopia: The Then and There of Queer Futurity*. New York: New York University Press, 2009.

Murphy, Patrick D. "The High and Low Fantasies of Feminist (Re)Mythopoeia." *Mythlore: A Journal of J.R.R. Tolkien, C.S. Lewis, Charles Williams, and Mythopoetic Literature* 16, no. 2 (1989): 26–31. https://dc.swosu.edu/mythlore/vol16/iss2/18.

Namaste, Viviane, K. "'Tragic Misreadings': Queer Theory's Erasure of Transgender Subjectivity." In *Invisible Lives: The Erasure of Transsexual and Transgendered People*, 9–23. Chicago: University of Chicago Press, 2000.

Nasr, Seyyed Hossein. *Man and Nature: The Spiritual Crisis of Modern Man*. Chicago: ABC International Group, Inc., 1997.

"Oblivia Nukem Jun | Controlled Burn Featured Artist." *20% Theatre Company*, February 13, 2019. http://www.tctwentypercent.org/oblivia-nukem-jun/.

Ovid. *Metamorphoses*. Translated by Allen Mandelbaum. Boston: Houghton Mifflin Harcourt, 2013.

Penley, Constance, Celine Perreñas Shimizu, Mireille Miller-Young, and Tristan Taormino. "Introduction." In *The Feminist Porn Book: the Politics of Producing Pleasure*, edited by Tristan Taormino, Celine Perreñas Shimizu, Constance Penley, and Mireille Miller-Young, 9–19. New York: The Feminist Press, 2012.

Plato. *Phaedrus*. Translated by Benjamin Jowett. Boston: Action Press, 2010.

———. *Symposium*. Translated by Robin Waterfield. Oxford: Oxford University Press, 1994.

———. *Timaeus*. In *Timaeus and Critias*. Translated by Robin Waterfield. Oxford: Oxford University Press, 2008.

Prosser, Jay. *Second Skins: The Body Narratives of Transsexuality*. New York: Columbia University Press, 1998.

Richardson, Herbert W. "Three Myths of Transcendence." In *Transcendence*, edited by Herbert Richardson and Donald Cutler, 98–113. Boston: Beacon Press, 1969.

Rider, Jeff. "Receiving Orpheus in the Middle Ages: Allegorization, Remythification and Sir Orfeo." *Papers on Language and Literature* 24, no. 4 (1983): 343–66.

Rubenstein, Mary-Jane. *Pantheologies: Gods, Worlds, Monsters*. New York: Columbia University Press, 2018.

———. *Worlds without End: The Many Lives of the Multiverse*. New York: Columbia University Press, 2014.

Rukeyser, Muriel. *Out of Silence: Selected Poems*. Edited by Kate Daniels. Evanston: Northwestern University Press, 2000.

RuPaul. *GuRu*. New York: HarperCollins, 2018.

Sappho. *Poems of Sappho*. Translated by Julia Dubnoff. n.d. https://www.uh.edu/~cldue/texts/sappho.html.

Scholem, Gershom. *Major Trends in Jewish Mysticism*. New York: Schocken Books, 1995.

Shewey, Don. *The Paradox of Porn: Notes on Gay Male Sexual Culture*. New York: Joybody Books, 2018.

Soelle, Dorothee. *The Silent Cry: Mysticism and Resistance*. Translated by Barbara and Martin Rurnscheidt. Minneapolis: Fortress Press, 2001.

Sprinkle, Annie, Beth Stephens, and Jennie Klein. *Assuming the Ecosexual Position: The Earth as Lover*. Minneapolis: University of Minnesota Press, 2021.

Stone, Ken. *Reading the Hebrew Bible with Animal Studies*. Stanford: Stanford University Press, 2017.

———. "The Garden of Eden and the Heterosexual Contract." In *Take Back the Word: A Queer Reading of the Bible*, edited by Robert Goss and Mona West, 57–70. Cleveland: Pilgrim Press, 2000.

Stryker, Susan. "(De)Subjugated Knowledges: An Introduction to Transgender Studies." In *The Transgender Studies Reader*, edited by Susan Stryker and Stephen Whittle, 1–17. London: Routledge, 2006.

———. "My Words to Victor Frankenstein above the Village of Chamounix: Performing Transgender Rage." In *The Transgender Studies Reader*, edited by Susan Stryker and Stephen Whittle, 244–56. London: Routledge, 2006.

Stryker, Susan, and Paisley Currah. "Introduction." *TSQ: Transgender Studies Quarterly* 1, nos. 1–2 (May 2014): 1–18. DOI: 10.1215/23289252-2398540.

"Teighlor McGee | Controlled Burn Featured Artist." *20% Theatre Company*, February 13, 2019. http://www.tctwentypercent.org/teighlor-mcgee/.

The Fugs. "Dreams of Sexual Perfection." Track 3 on *No More Slavery*. Big Beat Records, 1995. Compact Disc.

The Nature of the Rulers. Translated by Marvin Meyer. In *The Nag Hammadi Scriptures*, edited by Marvin Meyer, 187–98. New York: HarperOne, 2007.

The Origin of the World. Translated by Marvin Meyer. In *The Nag Hammadi Scriptures*, edited by Marvin Meyer, 199–222. New York: HarperOne, 2007.

The Orphic Hymns. Translated by Apostolos Athanassakis and Benjamin Wolkow. Baltimore: John Hopkins University Press, 2013.

The Secret Book of John. Translated by Marvin Meyer. In *The Nag Hammadi Scriptures,* edited by Marvin Meyer, 103–32. New York: HarperOne, 2007.

Tillich, Paul. *The Dynamics of Faith.* New York: HarperCollins, 1957.

Tolkien, J.R.R. "Mythopoeia." In *Tree and Leaf,* 83–90. London: HarperCollins, 2001.

Trible, Phyllis. *God and the Rhetoric of Sexuality.* Minneapolis: Fortress Press, 1978.

Turner, Jane. *Eugenio Barba.* London: Routledge, 2019.

Turner, John D. "The Sethian School of Gnostic Thought." In *The Nag Hammadi Scriptures,* edited by Marvin Meyer, 784–89. New York: HarperOne, 2007.

Ward, Jane. "Queer Feminist Pigs: A Spectator's Manifesta." In *The Feminist Porn Book: The Politics of Producing Pleasure,* edited by Tristan Taormino, Celene Perreñas Shimizu, Constance Penley, and Mireille Miller-Young, 130–39. New York: The Feminist Press, 2012.

Wilder, Amos Niven. *Theopoetic: Theology and the Religious Imagination.* Minneapolis: Fortress Press, 1976.

Xiang, Zairong. *Queer Ancient Ways: A Decolonial Exploration.* Earth: punctum books, 2018.

Young, Eris. *They/Them/Their: A Guide to Nonbinary and Genderqueer Identities.* London: Jessica Kingsley Publishers, 2019.